transnational policy innovation

the OECD and the diffusion of regulatory impact analysis

Fabrizio De Francesco

ecprPRESS

First published by the ECPR Press in 2013

The ECPR Press is the publishing imprint of the European Consortium for Political Research (ECPR), a scholarly association which supports and encourages the training, research and cross-national cooperation of political scientists in institutions throughout Europe and beyond.

ECPR Press
University of Essex
Wivenhoe Park
Colchester
CO4 3SQ
UK

Typeset by Anvi

Printed and bound by Lightning Source

British Library Cataloguing in Publication Data

A catalogue record for this book is available from the British Library

Paperback ISBN: 978–1–907301–25–4

www.ecpr.eu/ecprpress

ECPR – Monographs
Series Editors:
Dario Castiglione (University of Exeter)
Peter Kennealy (European University Institute)
Alexandra Segerberg (Stockholm University)
Peter Triantafillou (Roskilde University)

Regulation in Practice: The de facto Independence of Regulatory Agencies (ISBN: 9781907301285) Martino Maggetti

Representing Women?: Female Legislators in West European Parliaments (ISBN: 9780954796648) Mercedes Mateo Diaz

The Personalisation of Politics: A Study of Parliamentary Democracies (ISBN: 9781907301032) Lauri Karvonen

The Politics of Income Taxation: A Comparative Analysis (ISBN: 9780954796686) Steffen Ganghof

The Return of the State of War: A Theoretical Analysis of Operation Iraqi Freedom (ISBN: 9780955248856) Dario Battistella

Urban Foreign Policy and Domestic Dilemmas: Insights from Swiss and EU City-regions (ISBN: 9781907301070) Nico van der Heiden

Why Aren't They There? The Political Representation of Women, Ethnic Groups and Issue Positions In Legislatures (ISBN: 9780955820397) Didier Ruedin

Widen the Market, Narrow the Competition: Banker Interests and the Making of a European Capital Market (ISBN: 9781907301087) Daniel Mügge

Please visit www.ecpr.eu/ecprpress for information about new publications.

To all my friends

| contents

| list of figures and tables

Figures

Tables

| list of abbreviations

ACTAL	The Dutch Advisory Board on Administrative Burdens
APA	Administrative Procedure Act
ASA	Agence pour la Simplification Administrative
BRE	Better Regulation Executive
BRTF	Better Regulation Task Force
CBA	Cost-Benefit Analysis
CEA	Cost-Effectiveness Analysis
CCA	Compliance Cost Assessment
CEECs	Central and East European Countries
DEBR	Directors and Experts on Better Regulation
EHA	Event History Analysis
EIA	Environmental Impact Assessment
ENBR	European Network for Better Regulation
EO	Executive Order
EPA	Environmental Protection Agency
EVIA	Evaluating Integrated Impact Assessment
EU	European Union
FOI	Freedom of Information
GAO	Government Accountability Office
IA	Impact Assessment
IO	International Organisation
IPMR	Indicators of Product Market Regulation
IRMS	Indicators of Regulatory Management Systems
NAO	National Audit Office
NNR	Board of Swedish Industry and Commerce for Better Regulation
NPM	New Public Management
NRCC	National Regulatory Control Council
OBPR	Office of Best Practice Regulation
OECD	Organisation for Economic Co-operation and Development
OIRA	Office for Information and Regulatory Affairs

OMB	Office for Management and Budget
OSHA	Occupational Safety and the Health Administration
P-A	Principal-Agent
PART	Program Assessment Rating Tool
PUMA	Public Management Committee
RPC	Regulatory Policy Committee
RIA	Regulatory Impact Analysis
RIAS	Regulatory Impact Analysis Statement
RIS	Regulatory Impact Statement
SCM	Standard Cost Model
SIGMA	Support for Improvement in Governance and Management
TBS	Treasury Board of Canada Secretariat
UNDP	United Nation Development Programme

| acknowledgements

This book is a revision of my PhD thesis, *A Comprehensive Analysis of Policy Diffusion: Regulatory Impact Analysis in EU and OECD member states*, submitted in 2010 at the University of Exeter. In order to shed light on the role of the OECD in promoting transnational policy innovations, I added a new chapter, rewrote several other chapters and changed the overall narrative and structure of my PhD thesis. The book summarises extensive research activities conducted in England, the US and Switzerland. I spent most of the time necessary to accomplish my doctoral study in England. Between January 2004 and December 2008, I participated in several research projects led by Prof. Claudio M Radaelli. I will always be grateful to Claudio for the great opportunity of working with and learning from him, as well as for being an excellent supervisor and a good friend with great taste in music and food. Claudio taught me how to be a professional researcher. I am indebted to Dr Claire Dunlop, who also supervised me, for providing excellent recommendations on how to improve this thesis and practical suggestions for my career.

In 2004, DG Enterprise funded a research project on indicators of regulatory quality. The outcome of this research project was a technical report, later extended in a book written by Claudio and myself, *Regulatory Quality in Europe*, (Radaelli and De Francesco 2007). Most of the empirical evidence reported in Chapter Seven of that publication has been extracted to form the basis for Chapter Five of this book. During a ten-month period at the Centre for European Studies, University of Bradford, I met great friends - Fabio Garcia Lupato and Ulrike Kraemer - with whom I shared my first experiences of entering the (at that time, unknown) academic world.

In November 2004, I started my doctoral studies at the Department of Politics, University of Exeter. I wish to thank Prof. Tim Dunne for the financial support which enabled me to become familiar with the American literature on the political control of bureaucracy and public administration. The Department of Politics was a superb place in which to work; all staff members deserve great thanks. Special mentions go to Milja Kurki, Bill Tupman, Karl O'Connor and Giorgios Xezonakis. At Exeter, I was involved in three projects funded by the European Commission's Sixth Framework Programme, as well as the ESRC project on regulatory impact assessment (RIA) in comparative perspective. The latter provided an excellent opportunity for Claudio and I to write a literature review on RIA. This literature review paper, published as a chapter in *The Oxford Handbook on Regulation* (Baldwin *et al.* 2010), has been summarised in Chapter Two. I travelled and presented papers at several conferences and appreciated the feedback from Alberto Alemanno, Lorenzo Allio, Peter Biegelbauer, Andrea Lenschow and Wim Woermans on earlier versions of chapters. Through the ESRC, I was awarded a dedicated grant for visiting the Library of Congress, Washington, DC. This was an excellent study period which enabled me to shape my thesis. I wish to thank Mary

Lou Recker and Kersi B Shroff for their assistance and support.

Since beautiful things do not last too long but I was lucky enough to get a Marie Curie Fellowship[1], in March 2009 I moved again. My destination: Continental Europe, the Department of Political Science, University of Zurich. I am grateful to Prof. Fabrizio Gilardi for his guidance and support during my scholarship which was fundamental in allowing me to conduct the quantitative analysis of policy diffusion discussed in Chapter Five (and previously published in *Comparative Political Studies* (De Francesco 2012)).

Thanks to Thomas Schaeubli, Fabio Servalli and Fabio Wasserfallen for the long discussions on public policy, policy diffusion, academic life, Latex, R, Stata and, more importantly, football and the Swiss lifestyle.

The revision and redrafting of this book took place mainly at the University of Lausanne. I am indebted to the members of the *Laboratoire d'analyse de la gouvernance et de l'action publique en Europe* for financially supporting my postdoctoral research. Martino Maggetti, Philipp Trein and Eleftheria Vayonaki provided me with the necessary diversions whilst I redrafted the book.

I thank the Series Editors of the ECPR Press: Dario Castiglione for encouraging me to revise my PhD thesis, and Peter Triantafillou, who supported me throughout the editing process.

Fabrizio De Francesco
August 2013

1.   FP7-PEOPLE-IEF-2008 No 236107 POLISINNOVATIONS.

| preface

This book analyses the role of the OECD in diffusing policy innovations. Through a case study of regulatory impact analysis (RIA), it shows how transnational networks impact on national policy processes. The analytical framework encompasses institutional features as well as the national and international determinants of a policy innovation such as RIA. Drawing on original datasets, three empirical analyses assess to what extent government decisions to adopt, implement and evaluate RIA were driven by the OECD.

Among the tools available to increase the rationality of policy formulation, RIA has captured the attention of many scholars because of its potential to enhance the accountability and transparency of regulatory governance. Although almost all EU and OECD member states have adopted RIA, only a few small-n case comparative studies on its institutional, political and administrative impact have been conducted. By filling this gap in the literature and proposing the rigorous operationalisation of concepts such as adoption, extent of implementation, and learning, this book ascertains the extent of the interdependence between governments in their choices concerning an innovation in regulatory governance. Methodologically, the research draws on a multi-method approach consisting of qualitative analysis to track the process of institutionalisation, as well as event history analysis of RIA adoption based on a dataset covering thirty-eight countries from 1968 to 2006.

The book also argues that concepts of policy innovation diffusion provide a useful framework for understanding the dynamics of transnational governance. It shows that the OECD has been successful in framing and diffusing a template of evidence-based decision making. However, downplaying RIA as an instrument of political control has limited the influence of the OECD's peer review as well as comparative indicators on the administrative and institutional setting. Such empirical findings show that diffusion is a multi-faceted process. In the decision to adopt RIA, the role of the OECD in translating, packaging and promoting such administrative innovation coexists with previous innovations and other administrative variables. Yet the impact of interdependence and the role of the OECD are marginal in the successive phases of implementation and evaluation. Earliness of adoption and common law legal tradition are consistent with an extensive level of implementation. There is little evidence of interaction and communication among adopters on the subject of their learning experience.

chapter one | introduction

The following are only a representative sample of recent titles edited and published by the Organisation for Economic Co-operation and Development (OECD) concerning regulatory reform, governance and tools:

> Measuring Regulatory Performance: A practitioner's guide to perception surveys; Regulatory Policy and Governance: Supporting economic growth and serving the public interest; Risk and Regulatory Policy: Improving the governance of risk; Regulatory Reform for Recovery: Lessons from implementation during crises; Successful Practices and Policies to Promote Regulatory Reform and Entrepreneurship at the Sub-national Level.

As the result of intensive research conducted through networks of policy makers, high-level civil servants, practitioners and academics, publications generate a common knowledge of, and language for, policy reform. Knowledge and epistemic communities legitimate the establishment of transnational governance norms and standards. Through best practices, peer review and policy benchmarking, the OECD is acknowledged as a transnational institution for policy evaluation. Accordingly, the definitions attributed to this international organisation (IO) are disparate: 'teacher of norms' (Finnemore 1993), 'transnational evaluator' (Mahon and McBride 2009), 'editor' of policy ideas and contents (Sahlin-Andersson 2001) and 'orchestrator of global knowledge networks' (Porter and Webb 2008; Carroll and Kellow 2011). Notwithstanding the many definitional terms attributed to it, scholars tend to agree on how the OECD operates. It shares information and knowledge and then, in accordance with its member states' desiderata, establishes norms and standards on policy domains.

Since the beginning of the 1990s, the OECD has been constantly engaged in the establishment and then promotion of international standards and policy recommendations on regulatory reform (OECD 1995; OECD 2005; APEC-OECD Co-operative Initiative on Regulatory Reform 2005; OECD 2012). The rise of economic globalisation and the affirmation of neo-liberal policy ideas endorsed by the Reagan and Thatcher administrations shifted the OECD's focus toward market-based and microeconomic reforms (Carroll and Kellow 2011). Based on previous research reported in *Structural Adjustments* (OECD 1987), a publication which emphasised the increasingly negative impact of regulatory costs on productivity and economic performance, a policy agenda and a network of high-level government officials on regulatory management and reform were set up under the aegis of the Public Management Committee (PUMA) (Carroll and Kellow 2011). Concomitantly, and earlier than the other IOs engaged in good governance and regulatory reform, the OECD began to gather evidence on tools for regulatory governance.[1] According to the OECD, the latter concept embraces wider issues that are integral to democratic governance, such as transparency, accountability, efficiency, adaptability and coherence (OECD 2002a).

Among regulatory governance tools, such as consultation, simplification and access to legislation, this book analyses the diffusion of regulatory impact analysis (RIA). The latter is a tool for analysing and communicating regulatory outcomes (Jacobs 1997) through a standard and structured report on the predicted advantages and disadvantages of a regulatory proposal.[2] All OECD member countries have adopted an analysis to assess the likely future impacts on the economy of a regulatory proposal and, among them, roughly 70 per cent have a requirement to always identify the costs and benefits of new regulation (OECD Regulatory Policy Committee 2009). Furthermore, the 2008 dataset for the Indicators of Product Market Regulation (IPMR) attests that the assessment of alternative regulatory approaches has been widely adopted by OECD member states.[3] At the European Union (EU) level, not only has RIA been introduced by all member states, it has now become the cornerstone of 'better regulation' initiatives. Since 2005, the European political discourse on RIA has reached the highest level of attention. Within the EU mechanisms of facilitated coordination, RIA and better regulation are an integral part of the Lisbon Agenda for growth and jobs (European Commission 2005; Radaelli and De Francesco 2007; Radaelli 2007).

RIA has always been endorsed and recommended by the OECD in order to increase governments' capacities to achieve higher regulatory quality. This book explores the role of the OECD in promoting and framing RIA as the pivotal transnational policy innovation, a new technology of regulatory governance. This study assesses to what extent the OECD has influenced national policy makers' decisions regarding this innovation. Concepts and elements of policy innovation diffusion provide a useful framework for answering this question and for disentangling the dynamics and the effects of transnational governance mechanisms set by the OECD. The main argument is that only through a comprehensive analysis of the stages necessary for institutionalising this policy innovation is it possible to disentangle the question of the influence of the OECD on national politics. Indeed, analyses of implementation and evaluation enable us

---

1. After the last year of observation of the policy adoption analysis (see Chapter Five), other IOs, such as the World Bank, through the 'better regulation for growth' programme (a set of projects for enhancing the regulatory process through the adoption of consultation, standard cost model, e-registry, access to regulation, doing business indicators, and RIA) and the United Nations Development Programme (UNDP) (through the 'ex ante policy impact assessment' project) began funding a set of projects for enhancing the regulatory process of African, Central and Eastern European, and former Soviet Union countries.

2. The label 'regulatory impact analysis' encompasses different terms coined by governments around the world: regulatory impact assessment in the UK, regulatory impact statement (RIS) in Australia and impact assessment (IA) within the European Union institutions. The term 'analysis' is preferred here because it has been used by the OECD.

3. Only Belgium, Chile, France, Hungary, Israel and Turkey are reported not to have such a requirement.

to better delineate the extent of interdependence among governments in relation to regulatory reform and governance.

Although extensive research has been conducted on RIA in the Anglo-Saxon world and in Europe, this is the first systematic analysis of the impact of the OECD on national decision making to have relied mostly on the data produced by the OECD itself. Empirical findings on global administrative reform trends are also sparse. Although the spread of RIA goes well beyond OECD and EU member states,[4] this book focuses on the twenty-seven European Union member states, as well as another eleven OECD member countries (Australia, Canada, Iceland, Japan, Korea, Mexico, New Zealand, Norway, Turkey, Switzerland and the US).[5] This selection of countries was made because of the lack of data on the other adopting countries and because the object of the study was to investigate the impact of the OECD's networks and activities.

1.1 RIA: a 'normal' innovation

The term RIA encompasses 'a range of methods aimed at systematically assessing the negative and positive impacts of proposed and existing regulation' (OECD 1997a). The methodology varies depending on the policy objectives, the maturation of the regulatory state, and even the traditions and cultures of the public administration in different countries. RIA can be used to assess the impact of a new regulation on: business and social welfare; administrative and paperwork burdens; regulatory burdens on small businesses; and the consequences for international trade and employment (Jacobs 1997). Put differently, 'it is a flexible tool. Its objectives, design and role in administrative processes differ among countries and even among regulatory policy areas' (Jacobs 1997). Yet, the following two elements are common to any RIA system:

- an explanation of the specific need for regulation
- a systematic and consistent economic appraisal of foreseeable impacts arising from that regulation

Accordingly, RIA assumes the form of 'a short, structured document which is published with regulatory proposals and new legislation' (Better Regulation Unit 1998). It has also emerged as an instrument at the disposal of the independent regulatory agencies of several countries, including Italy, the UK and the US. Despite the policy relevance of and recent scholars' attention to economic analyses conducted by independent agencies (Schrefler 2010), this book focuses on the

---

4. Several developing countries have also adopted administrative requirements to assess the future impact of regulation: Albania, Algeria, Bangladesh, Bosnia, Botswana, Ghana, Kenya, Jamaica, Moldova, the Philippines, Serbia, Sri Lanka, South Africa, Tanzania, Uganda, Ukraine and Vietnam (Kirkpatrick and Parker 2004; Kirkpatrick, Parker and Zhang 2004; Ladegaard 2005; Jacobs 2006; Jacobs and Renda 2007).

5. The accession of Chile and Israel occurred in 2010, after the data collection for this study.

regulatory appraisal required of executive departments/agencies as this has been subject to a longer and more extensive process of institutionalisation.

Bartlett (1989) expounds impact assessment as a 'strategy of influencing decision and action by prior analysis of predictable impacts'. This strategy is 'one of the major innovations in policy making and administration of the twentieth century'. This definition encompasses two very different perspectives on a conception of RIA. On the one hand, RIA is an information device which influences regulators' behaviour. The American literature has maintained that RIA emerged as an administrative procedure capable of unifying the three different themes of regulatory reform (McGarity 1991; Pildes and Sunstein 1995): the enhancement of the economic empirical basis of decision making; the centralisation of the Presidential oversight on his executive agencies; and an increase in the external accountability and legitimacy of regulators. On the other hand, RIA is a *technological innovation*. Public policy has a technological component aimed at reducing the decisional uncertainty in achieving a desired outcome (Power 1997; Sahlin-Andersson 2001). Strategies, techniques and procedures render programmes operable and establish a multitude of interactions among policy actors (Rose and Miller 1992). The last two decades of public administration reforms have been characterised by the constant introduction of new ideas – based on economic theories as well as the managerial techniques and practices of the private sector – into public administration (Kelly 1996; Power 1997). These managerial techniques have their roots in real-world business but have been formalised and applied to public administration by business schools, consultancies and international organisations (Sahlin-Andersson 2001; Sahlin-Andersson and Engwall 2002).

The latter perspective situates this study within the classical research tradition which defines diffusion as 'the process in which an innovation is communicated through certain channels over time among the members of a social system' (Rogers 2003). The general feature of a 'successful innovation' is an S-shaped trend of adoption (Rogers 2003), implying that the cumulative distribution of adoptions is similar to the cumulative normal curve (Gray 1973). This pattern is an expectation and the element of generalisation of innovation research studies (Mahajan *et al.* 1995; Rogers 2003). Examining the cumulative frequency of adoption (Figure 1.1), one can observe that RIA has spread according to a normally distributed pattern.

Following Gray (1973), a formal assessment of the normality of the cumulative proportion of adopters confirms the S-shaped trend.

$$A_t = A_{t-1} + bA_{t-1}(O_t - A_{t-1})$$ (1.1)

In Equation 1.1, A_t is the cumulative proportion of states that adopted RIA in year t; A_{t-1} is the cumulative proportion of states that adopted RIA in year $t-1$; and b is the coefficient of diffusion from social interaction. The coefficient of the first term A_{t-1} is set equal to 1, given that innovations are usually maintained. This assumption also holds in this specific case since none of the OECD and EU member

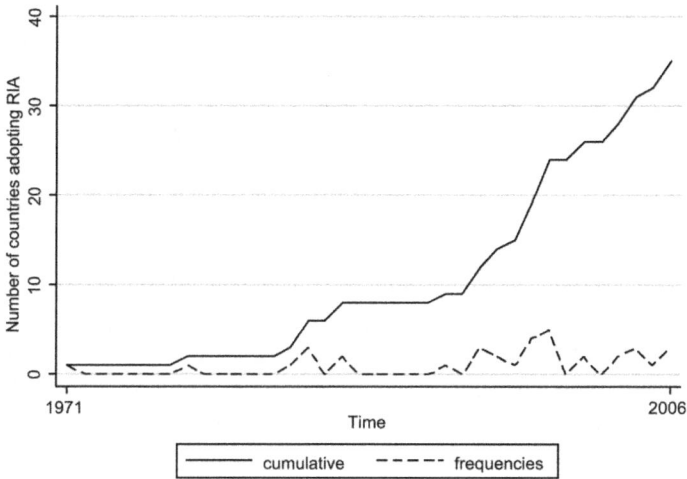

Figure 1.1: Cumulative and annual frequencies of adoption

states have abandoned their RIA programmes. On the basis of the assumption that only members of the OECD are able to interact, sharing information about administrative reforms and, consequently, to adopt RIA,[6] the pool of eligible adopters, O_p, varies according to the proportion of countries that are involved in OECD activities.

By adjusting and regressing such an equation, it is possible to assess the fit of the model: $R^2 = 0.9886$ and the intercept very near to zero ($c = 0.00007$) denote that the model performs well, explaining more than 98 percent of the variance. The impact of interaction is also relevant ($b = 0.24$) and statistically significant (the standard error is 0.1167, $p = 0.049$), denoting that the OECD seems to have played a relevant role in facilitating the interaction among its own member states and those of the EU.

As expected in the normal diffusion of innovations, the spread had a slow start. After the US, Canada was the only country to adopt RIA in the 1970s (Appendix A lists the year of adoption for each of the thirty-eight countries sampled in this study). During the 1980s, six countries adopted RIA: Germany in 1984; Australia, the Netherlands and the UK in 1985; and Hungary and Sweden in 1987. Among this group of pioneer countries, there are several Anglo-Saxon countries. Their similar administrative style, socioeconomic conditions, as well as political ideology and cultural proximity played an important role in the transfer of the American experience with RIA. For instance, the Canadian RIA was adopted

---

6.   This is a plausible assumption since only Hungary adopted RIA before the ratification of the convention on the OECD or participation in the SIGMA project (established in 1992). For Central and East European countries (CEECs), their participation with the SIGMA project is considered a sufficient condition for interaction.

explicitly by reference to the American rulemaking process. This is reflected in the Federal Government's regulatory policy, which imported most of the features of the American Administrative Procedure Act (APA), such as the notice and comment procedure (Stanbury and Thompson 1982). Further, a similarity in political ideology was essential in the transfer of the American experience to the UK (Froud *et al.*1998). However, the mixed group of European countries suggests that their regulatory appraisal systems were developed independently from the American experience.

To assess whether and how a policy has been transferred from one country to another, it is necessary to carry out a process tracing analysis (Weyland 2006) and this goes well beyond the goal of this book, which is based on large-n comparisons. For the European pioneers it is more difficult to grasp if and how the innovation was transferred. Hungary is without doubt an exceptional case among the pioneers. At the time of adoption, Hungary was still a socialist country with a low income per capita. Looking at the similarity in the methodology and the process (i.e. checklists for the drafters of legislation, without any compulsory use of cost–benefit analysis (CBA) – see Chapter Three) used in Denmark, Germany and the Netherlands to assess the future economic impacts of regulatory proposals, one can conjecture that some interactions between these countries occurred. Sweden, with its long tradition of regulatory agencies, may be another exceptional case where no policy transfer occurred. It is also worth noting that among this group of pioneers there are six or seven of the 'core reformers' group identified by James and Manning (1996) in their global review of experience with 'new public management' (NPM). Thus, there is (almost) nothing surprising in the emergence pattern of RIA.

The most rapid increases in the frequency of adoption occurred during two time intervals: 1995–1999 and 2003–2006, respectively. In the first period, fifteen countries (France, New Zealand, Norway, Estonia, Mexico, Korea, Belgium, Czech Republic, Finland, Latvia, Austria, Iceland, Ireland, Italy and Switzerland), the majority of followers, enacted administrative requirements for appraising the economic impact of regulatory proposals. In particular, 1999 saw the highest frequency of adoption: five countries adopted RIA in that year alone. The second interval saw the adoption of RIA by nine laggard countries (Bulgaria, Lithuania, Japan, Slovenia, Spain, Romania, Greece, Portugal and Turkey). Both rises were preceded by a long period with no or low frequencies of adoption. Few countries adopted RIA just before these periods: Denmark in 1993 and Poland and the Slovak Republic in 2001. This may be due to a variation in the diffusion pattern, a variation derived from the IOs' pressure on their member states. First the OECD and then the EU formally endorsed a policy to enhance the quality of regulation. And the vertical hypothesis of diffusion refers to the process of facilitated interaction through a hierarchical level of governance (Gray 1973). As a consequence, it is essential to distinguish between the vertical and horizontal (country-to-country cue-taking) dimensions of diffusion (Menzel and Feller 1977).

Accordingly, 1995 was a crucial year for the diffusion of RIA. In March, the Council of the OECD adopted the 'Recommendation on improving the quality of government regulation' (OECD 1995). The OECD member countries committed themselves to the pursuit of regulatory reform via a set of principles spelled out in the *Reference Checklist for Regulatory Decision-Making* (OECD 1995). This checklist is the baseline for OECD peer review of progress on regulatory reform achieved by each member country and summarised in specific reports. Question no. six, 'Do the benefits of regulation justify the costs?', of the 1995 recommendation referred clearly to RIA: 'Regulators should routinely estimate the expected costs and benefits of each regulatory proposal and of feasible alternatives, and should make those estimates available in an accessible format to administrative and political decision-makers' (OECD 1995). As suggested in the OECD checklist, the OECD member countries have taken 'a pragmatic and realistic approach' in the adoption of RIA (OECD 1995). The variance of the methodology in assessing the future impact of regulation has gone well beyond the methodologies reported by the OECD in its first book on the RIA experiences in the pioneering member countries (Viscusi 1997). Such a variety in the methodology occurs also in the majority of followers and laggards (Radaelli 2005a; Jacob *et al.* 2008; OECD Regulatory Policy Committee 2009), notwithstanding that they could benefit from the information and knowledge exchange among better regulation transnational networks established at the OECD and EU levels.

Following Weyland (2006), the evidence indicates that governments did not follow a detailed blueprint and simply import a policy innovation. On the contrary, they had processed the available information and then adjusted and, indeed, sometimes reinvented an *ex ante* policy appraisal procedure to improve the quality of regulation. Thus, what spread was not a specific economic methodology or technique such as CBA or cost-effectiveness analysis (CEA), which are grounded on notions of welfare economics, public interest and collective welfare maximisation.

2001 saw another important event for the spread of RIA, especially among the EU member states. A group of national experts on regulatory reform gathered together and drafted the cornerstone document of European 'better regulation', the so-called Mandelkern Group Report.[7] The report strongly promoted better regulation and RIA within the European political agenda (see, for instance, the Hellenic Presidency of 2003). Meanwhile, the European Commission (2001) published a White Paper on governance in which the adoption of an *ex ante* appraisal system was reckoned crucial for enhancing European regulatory governance. In March 2002, the European Commission reformed its scattered *fiche d'impact* system – composed of thematic impact assessments, such as environmental, gender, social, business and health impact assessments, conducted by each directorate general

---

7. This advisory group took its name from the chairman, Mr Dieudonn Mandelkern, a French *Conseiller d'Etat*. It was made up of representatives of the then fifteen member states of the EU. Officials from the European Commission's Secretariat-General also attended. An interim report was finalised at the end of February 2001 and considered by the heads of state and government at the spring European Council in Stockholm. The group's final report was released in November 2001 and was tabled at the Internal Market Council on 26 November. It was considered by heads of state and government at the European Council in Laeken in December 2001.

(DG) in isolation – and proposed a system of 'integrated impact assessment', a document for presentation at the inter-service consultation. With the support of DG Enterprise, the Secretariat General of the European Commission drafted the guidelines for impact assessment.[8]

The group of countries that adopted RIA between 1995 and 2002 have very different socioeconomic and political conditions. New Zealand and Ireland can be considered as the laggards among the cluster of the Anglo-Saxon countries. Mexico and Korea may be paired by the influence exerted by the US.[9] Vertical influences from the OECD may explain RIA adoption in the EU and OECD member states such France, Iceland, Italy and Switzerland, whereas geographical proximity to pioneers may be more relevant in the case of countries such as Austria, Belgium and Norway. Furthermore, all the Central and East European countries started participating in network activities set up by the OECD through the OECD–EU SIGMA programme, which provides financial aid for modernising public administrations. Six out of eight of the countries identified by James and Manning (1996) that have adopted significant administrative reforms are also present in this middle group of RIA adopters.

Finally, among the laggards there are essentially two clusters of countries: the Central and Eastern European (Bulgaria, Lithuania, Romania and Slovenia) and the Southern European member states (Greece, Portugal, Spain and Turkey, all listed among James and Manning's group of less significant reformers). In this latter stage of diffusion, several networks of national experts on regulatory reform and better regulation were set up by the European Commission and the Council of the European Union (Radaelli and De Francesco 2007). Modelled on the OECD governance mechanisms, these networks facilitated further interaction among EU member states. However, the EU has not adopted any recommendations from peer reviews on regulatory reform and RIA. It is important to note that two of the three countries that did so had not adopted RIA by 2006, the last year of observation, and also that Cyprus and Malta are not OECD members and that they joined the SIGMA project only in 2005 (Luxembourg was the third non-adopting country).

8.   2002 was also the year in which the 'European Administrative State' emerged. Another six European Commission Communications were issued on policy formulation, ranging from consultation and the use of scientific advice to comitology and regulatory agencies (Allio 2008). Specifically, the Communications were on: general principles and minimum standards for consultation (COM (2002) 704 final); the collection and use of expertise (COM (2002) 713 final); simplifying and improving the regulatory environment (COM (2002) 278 final); a proposal for a new comitology decision (COM (2002) 719 final); the operating framework for the European regulatory agencies (COM (2002) 718 final); and, finally, a framework for target-based tripartite contracts (COM (2002) 709 final).

9.   See Ginsburg (2002) on the influence of the US in the adoption of APA in Korea and Japan, although the latter is a laggard in adopting RIA.

1.2 Concepts, elements and features of policy diffusion

Entangled by numerous elements and dynamics, it is difficult to encapsulate in a unitary framework the many definitional, analytical and methodological dimensions of the policy diffusion process. However, granted that RIA is a technological innovation of regulatory governance, diffusion of innovations denotes, according to Strang and Soule (1998), 'flow or movement from a source to an adopter, paradigmatically via communication and influence'. The same authors have also argued that it is a general and abstract term, 'embracing contagion, mimicry, social learning, organized dissemination, and other family members'.

Before showing how the variance in the definitional aspects has become interlocked with epistemological and methodological issues, it is worth marking the perimeters of the policy diffusion literature. Unlike those found in the convergence literature, research questions on diffusion analyse 'the nature, not the outcome, of the process (Gilardi 2008). Although it has the same focus on the process of policy adoption, the policy transfer literature is instead interested in both the conscious acquisition of knowledge and policy outcomes (Newmark 2002), making the transfer process an 'intermediary variable' (Gilardi 2008). In other words, '[t]he analytical focus of the diffusion literature is on policy change, the main hypothesis being that interdependence matters' (Gilardi 2008).

In political science, studies of diffusion have passed from a narrow analysis of its elements to a much broader and embedded definition. Richard M. Walker's primordial work analysed a series of legislative innovations in order to grade American states' innovativeness. Through the random interaction model, Virginia Gray (1973) focused instead on whether American states' policy innovations diffused normally. It is, however, not yet clear whether the S-shaped cumulative curve of adoption is an essential condition of diffusion. Indeed, the formalisation of the different explanations through models of informational and spatial interconnectedness is rare. Few studies have tested the cumulative adoption curve or the speed of adoption in relation to a series factors that likely affect them (Graham *et al.* 2013), whereas many researchers have simply plotted it graphically.

Collier and Messick (1975) were the first political scientists to refer to Galton's problem which is related to the fact that 'the findings based on the analysis of causal relations within nations (or other units of analysis) may be distorted by the effect of diffusion'. In order to discern such different modes of adoption, they contrasted the prerequisites and diffusion effects of social security systems. Taking advantage of a statistical method, Berry and Berry (1990) unified the internal characteristics of an adoption unit and used some external determinants that would allow an appreciation of whether the domestic political system is affected by prior decisions taken by other governments. Other studies bound diffusion of innovation exclusively with models of communication and interaction (Gray 1973; Menzel and Feller 1977; Glick and Hays 1991). Focusing on causal mechanisms, i.e. competition, learning and socialisation among countries, more recent analyses of democracy and market reform diffusion have disregarded innovation transfer as the founding element of policy interdependence (Simmons *et al.*2008).

In order to define what diffusion is, several scholars have clarified what it is *not*. Granted that there are two drivers of policy change, i.e. the prior choices of other actors and the reactions of independent actors to similar functional pressures, the latter functional explanation has been defined as 'spurious diffusion' (Gilardi 2004), 'the null hypothesis of diffusion' (Simmons *et al.* 2003), 'in-state impetus to action' (Eyestone 1977), 'internal determinants of diffusion'[10] (Berry and Berry 2007), 'prerequisites' (Collier and Messick 1975) and 'common contextual effects' (Van den Bulte and Lilien 2001), respectively. Accordingly, whereas the definition of policy innovation diffusion tended to be vague and confused with 'any pattern of successive adoption of policy innovation' (Eyestone 1977), it now refers unequivocally and exclusively to external influences (Graham *et al.* 2013).

The concomitant causal effects of both policy change explanations generate Galton's problem. To solve it, a policy diffusion analysis would not only determine the amount and strength of information but also take into account any other environmental and institutional factors which shape the individual state or unit of analysis' compatibility with a specific innovation. But only the last generation of policy diffusion studies have taken the role and impact of external structures seriously by attempting to answer the 'why' and the 'how' of policy diffusion (Graham *et al.* 2013; Meseguer and Gilardi 2009). According to sociological institutionalism, the environment of an adopting country is not only a facilitator or a channel of communication among countries but also an institutionalising component. This theoretical shift is grounded in the consideration that 'an analysis of the cultural (in some usage, institutional) bases of diffusion speaks more directly to what spreads, replacing a theory of connections with a theory of connecting' (Strang and Soule 1998). Granted that '[i]ndividual adopters are not acting within a vacuum or on an isotropic plane' (Meir 1982), the degree of environmental influences and the extent of rationality in the use of information about an innovation are two crucial and alternative theoretical standpoints of policy diffusion.

An analysis of the diffusion of regulatory governance innovation has to be set within the broader phenomena of administrative reforms and NPM, a term that captures the emergence of an international discourse on administrative change and reform (Lynn 2001). Since NPM does not represent a 'global paradigm' (Hood 1995; Hood 1996; James and Manning 1996; Gow and Dufour 2000), functionalist explanations may be strengthened or weakened by diffusion explanations (Knoke 1982), or alternatively lose their explanatory power across time (Tolbert and Zucker 1983). In other words, the diffusion of RIA provides an opportunity to test a set of different determinants of policy change (Radaelli and Meuwese 2009). Policy makers' communication and interdependence are set against the traditional theories of administration, transforming how governments conceive rationality, accountability and legitimacy.

---

10. 'Internal determinants' is the term used in this book.

Surprisingly, time is a dimension often neglected by political scientists, who tend to overlook when diffusion became causally relevant and for how long. Is the explanatory power of a variable constant throughout the diffusion process? In this specific case, is the influence of the OECD on domestic politics effective throughout the stages of policy innovation institutionalisation? Rephrasing Dobbins *et al.* (2007), policy diffusion now also concerns a dynamic and 'informed decision making' (Mossberger 2000) process – encompassing not only the decision to adopt but also policy formulation, implementation and evaluation – whereby decisions in country A have been systematically conditioned by prior choices in country B and international institution C. In other words, policy diffusion in this study is essentially about the modes and roles of information related to an innovation. As Mossberger (2000) put it, '[t]he policy information that diffuses includes models (such as legislation or program concepts), criticisms, evaluation research, and the experience of other adopters'. Political science studies rarely analyse the impact of communication and, more generally, interdependence on decision making, through an overarching framework that embeds not only the adoption decision but also the implementation and evaluation phases in order to capture the extent of learning. In this study, another way to take into account the time dimension is to distinguish the diffusion process according to the categories of adopters, namely, pioneers, the early and late majority and laggards.

A further methodological issue concerns the different dependent variables used in cross-sectional analyses of diffusion. Dependent variables vary from the earliness of adoption (Collier and Messick 1975) to the probability of adoption in a specific year (Berry and Berry 1990), from the rate or speed of diffusion (Gray 1973) to the degree of innovativeness of a state (Walker 1969) and to the extent of implementation and reinvention (Glick and Hays 1991). Qualitative process tracing has analysed the diffusion of policy discourse throughout agenda setting and adoption (Mossberger 2000; Weyland 2006; Orenstein 2008). These alternative research strategies have formed the overall framework of diffusion studies in political science. It is, however, a source of instability in the generalisation of empirical evidence (Downs and Mohr 1976). While classical scholars of other disciplines (Mahajan and Peterson 1985; Geroski 2000; Rogers 2003) have conceived diffusion as a normally distributed event, political scientists are generally more interested in the probability of adoption in order to test alternative hypotheses. The latter, however, tend to overlook the extent of reinvention and institutionalisation of a policy innovation. This study relies on three different empirical studies in order to overcome the instability in cumulative empirical knowledge associated with the analysis of a single policy innovation.

Taking for granted the two forces behind the spread of policy change, the ultimate challenge is to have a coherent analytical framework which encompasses the characteristics of innovations, the characteristics of countries and the broader environmental context (Wejnert 2002). In this book, I argue that an analytical perspective centred on the concept of transnational policy innovation is capable of holding together the several elements of RIA diffusion, as well as the cognitive and normative activities of the OECD.

1.3 The OECD and policy diffusion

In 2011 the OECD celebrated its fiftieth anniversary, but there is still a lot to learn about its role in global governance. Article 1 of its Convention states that its mission is to promote among its members economic and trade expansion policies ('Convention on the Organisation for Economic Co-operation and Development' 1960). The OECD's challenge is to enhance global governance through the advancement of 'good governance' principles. In order to accomplish its mission and challenges, the OECD is empowered to act as a transnational hub of information and knowledge exchange. It leads cooperation and consultation among its members on agreed projects and coordinated actions (Article 3 of the 'Convention on the Organisation for Economic Co-operation and Development' 1960). Due to these provisions and the lack of legal and financial resources to push for the promotion of 'good' policies among its members, the OECD relies mainly on cognitive and normative resources (Mahon and McBride 2009; Martens and Jakobi 2010). Essentially, its activities concern data collection, generation, discussion and decision on policy ideas, as well as peer review of the adoption and implementation of recommended policy design (Woodward 2009; Martens and Jakobi 2010). Accordingly, the OECD's organisational structure and its way of working are centred on the production, standardisation and dissemination of knowledge on policy innovations and best practice.

Scholars have proposed different conceptualisations and analytical frameworks in order to capture the modes of influence of the OECD within the global policy arena. Woodward (2009) provides a holistic framework, comprehending governments' identities and shared knowledge, the global legal order and other transnational organisations. Assessing its influence on national governments, Martens and Jakobi (2010) focus on the final 'products', namely publications, policy evaluations and datasets. In a similar vein, Marcussen (2004a) framed the OECD's capacity to play three different ideational roles – as artist, arbitrator and authority – on its system of multilateral surveillance. Mahon and McBride (2009) argued that mediative activities and inquisitive processes are two modes for governing transnational networks.[11] Through a historical analysis of organisational adaptation, Carroll and Kellow (2011) argued that the OECD's value is in its ability to orchestrate a series of transnational knowledge networks from which member states can identify and learn from best practice.

If these conclusions are sound in emphasising the element of learning in a context of shared knowledge, policy and epistemic networks, it is surprising that the literature dedicated to the OECD has not yet provided a theoretical framework for gauging its role in global policy interdependence. Furthermore, notwithstanding the lively debate in the literature that conceptualises its prominent

---

11. Accordingly, reference is made in the present work to the OECD's inquisitive and mediative functions. Inquisitive refers to data collection, peer review, benchmarking and ranking, for instance, whereas mediative refers to the OECD's role in helping its member states to share information and a common agenda (in a process of socialisation).

activities and functions, there are few empirical studies of the OECD and domestic policy change (Armingeon and Beyeler 2004; Mahon and McBride 2008; Martens and Jakobi 2010) or of the OECD and policy diffusion (Sahlin-Andersson 2001; Grigorescu 2003; Lodge 2005).

Policy diffusion scholars have linked IOs with causal mechanisms of diffusion. Specifically, the promotion of new policy ideas can be forcefully imposed by IOs on their member states via aid conditionality and capability setting. Furthermore, moral suasion and the quest for international legitimacy can induce national policy makers to adopt IOs' policy recommendations. The role of IOs is also relevant in providing and enhancing the available information and knowledge on policy innovations that hitherto escaped policy makers' attention; assessments of international experience can also affect policy makers' cognitive processes, given their propensity to generalise on the basis of a few successful cases. Overall, in the real world of limited cognitive processes and capacity, IOs trigger and shape policy diffusion by enhancing and selecting the available information on policy innovations (Weyland 2006). In a similar vein, the OECD provides analyses, classifications and meanings of new worthy ideas (Mahon and McBride 2009). Further, it is clear from the literature that the mediative and inquisitive functions of the OECD have an impact on the adoption of policy innovations that goes beyond national decision makers. The policy interdependence occasioned by IOs' collective knowledge and international norms or standards (based on a specific policy design) can also tend to prescribe or proscribe a specific behavioural change, and so affect policy implementation among member states (Gehring and Oberthür 2009); this actually extends to the means of policy evaluation and the reinvention of policy innovations.

The influence of IOs is even more relevant to the general principles of policy reform than to a single neat policy model. As in the case of regulatory reform and RIA, principles are spelled out in the frequently used legal instrument of Recommendations, through which the OECD can exercise political pressures on its member states via economic incentives and the provision of information and technical advice. Thanks to their normative and symbolic appeal, IOs may opt for the promotion of general principles in order to avoid the political and reputational costs of forcing governments to enact contested policy reforms. Governments are generally more willing to adopt a principle and to retain a degree of freedom in implementing transnational policy recommendations. But vague policy objectives and the consequent large variance of governments' implementation limit the cognitive capacity of national decision makers. As a result, they tend to experiment with a new principle through a piecemeal process of trial and error (Weyland 2006).

In a globalised environment in which governments are influenced by similar environmental pressures and uncertainties, the rationales for adopting an administrative reform are transformed and reconstructed. The OECD provides organisational and socialising platforms for policy makers to exchange and interpret information on prior decisions made by other governments (Finnemore and Sikkink 1998). In order to facilitate the transfer of public reform, the account and narrative of ideas, experiences and models can be reframed, changing the form, content and meaning. Developed by the OECD through publications, analyses and maps of international experiences, this editing process concerns context, logic and formulation of policy innovation. Recommended policy reforms are 'generalised and packaged' through a common functionalist logic, as all OECD countries face a common set of problems (Sahlin-Andersson 2001).

1.4 The main argument

More than thirty years ago, Downs and Mohr (1976) challenged policy analysts to operationalise diffusion as a process, taking into account adoption on a non-exclusive basis. Granted that different but complementary and contingent innovations affect the adoptability of an innovation, other scholars suggested the analysis of the 'innovations relationship' (Mahajan and Peterson 1985; Berry and Berry 2007) within the overall prerequisites (Collier and Messick 1975). Another limitation of adoption studies is the neglect of the extent of change caused by a policy innovation.

The 'stage' heuristic has been criticised by a prominent scholar (Sabatier 1999; Sabatier 2007) who is sceptical about its theoretical application to the policy process.[12] His argument is that different stages, which are often descriptively inaccurate, interact and feed back to each other. And, more importantly, 'the policy cycle lacks conceptual elements of a theoretical model. In particular, the stages model does not offer causal mechanisms for the transitions between different stages' (Jann and Wegrich 2007). Empirically, it is hard to test (in a single coherent framework) hypotheses derived from a different set of theoretical concepts established for the analysis of each stage. Consequently, the public policy literature continues to focus on narrow and specific phases of the policy cycle, each developing its own unique literature, theory and body of research.

Nevertheless, there is an evident conceptual drawback to cross-sectional public policy comparisons which revolve around adoption events. By setting 'a definition of policy that ignores the prospect that policymakers' intentions may be undermined or even undone in implementation', large-n comparative analyses 'do not shed much light on the policy *process* conceived either in terms of stages or in terms of policy change over time' (Blomquist 2007). Given the embedding of political rhetoric (March and Olson 1983), this flaw is even more substantial for administrative reform. Thus, rather than focusing exclusively on whether and how diffusion takes place, an analysis of what has been communicated, diffused and actually implemented is necessary.

In other words, the fragmentation of the policy process is an evident methodological bias in favour of adoption against other governments' decisions

---

12. A prominent diffusion theorist similarly argued that stages are a social construction, a mental framework for simplifying complex realities, and that clear distinctions among stages do not exist, impeding empirical evidence of their discreteness (Rogers 2003).

and forms of change (Pollitt 2001; Pollitt 2002; Blomquist 2007). The 'innovation-decision process' is formed by a series of interconnected decisions and actions that need to be carried out and confirmed over time. Information gathering, conceptualisation, planning for the adoption of an innovation, and implementation are all events, actions and decisions involved in putting the innovation into use (Rogers 2003). Furthermore, the relative importance of policy change determinants, i.e. social and economic conditions, political activities, policy ideas and knowledge promoted by the OECD, may vary across the decision-making process. As Downs and Mohr (1976) warned us,

> the determinants of the time of adoption are not the same as the determinants of the depth of adoption. Thus, an exclusive analysis of the adoption event causes an over-representation of socioeconomic and geographical conditions to be superimposed upon the variables of political actors and systems, distorting our understanding of the nature and extent of policy change. (Blomquist 2007)

To overcome such bias, several political scientists have conceived of policy diffusion as a process of information exchange within policy networks that may influence domestic policy discourses, decisions and practices (Mossberger 2000; Pollitt 2001; Pollitt 2002). Framing a theory that embeds discourses, decisions and practices remains, however, a complex undertaking. With its own purposes and payoffs, each decision and practice refers to different actors and behaviour (Moynihan 2005) and, consequently, is analysed through a somewhat different research strategy. Although further empirical findings on discourses and practices can overcome the policy adoption bias, they stem from different research strategies and operationalisations, typical of each policy stage. Accordingly, in order to formulate their research questions and organise their inquiries, researchers who aim to have a comprehensive analysis of policy diffusion have to rely on an analytical framework composed of the elements that any theory relevant to the same kind of phenomena would need to include (Ostrom 2007). In order to achieve a coherent research strategy, this study relies on the 'integrating concept' (Ripley 1985) of policy innovation and the related exchanges of information prompted and steered by the OECD over time and across governments. Examining the impact of the OECD's diffused information, discourse and knowledge about RIA on domestic regulatory reform, this study has three aims:

(i) to show how the OECD has promoted and presented the discourse on regulatory reform and RIA

(ii) to test the OECD's activities as a relevant determinant of governments' decisions to adopt RIA

(iii) to assess whether and how governments are interdependent across the innovation decision process and the resulting overall extent of policy change

1.5 Methods and plan of the book

This research is not based on the mechanisms of policy diffusion but is about the impact of different modes of communication and interdependence among governments within the EU and OECD. There are several reasons for arguing that empirical findings of an innovation cannot reveal too much about the path(s) connecting a causal factor to policy diffusion. Firstly, mechanisms often consist of vague and abstract factors that are difficult to operationalise; and the conceptual definitions of learning and emulation often overlap and are contested, as evidenced by their as yet unconsolidated operationalisation. Secondly, more often than not the plausible mechanisms are multiple and difficult to tease apart. Thirdly, these multiple causal pathways may operate in an additive fashion, as substitutes, or in interaction with one another (Gerring 2010). Finally, even the most recent theoretical contributions and sophisticated analyses based on causal mechanisms of policy diffusion cannot apprehend comprehensively the dynamics of the policy process.

Given such complexity, a mixed methodology would allow a better understanding of policy interdependence. Soft quantitative and qualitative analyses of the implementation and evaluation practices can confirm the evidence produced by an analysis of policy adoption. For instance, if emulation were the most plausible causal mechanism, one would expect little variance in the implementation score of pioneers, the majority of followers, and laggards. Further, in the evaluation stage there would be interdependence and imitation of others' evaluation practices. On the other hand, bounded learning would allow more variation in implementation and evaluation. Governments would adjust the innovation according to their capacity and internal conditions and would scan other governments' experiences in order to find the most suitable form for their own purposes. In an economically competitive environment, there would be an approximation toward the most economically advanced countries.

Based on Downs and Mohr's (1976) insight regarding the impossibility of finding a unitary and valid theory of the adoption for every innovation, Chapter Two presents the analytical framework, which is founded on three different modalities in which global trends of policy innovation can be formed (Sahlin-Andersson 2001): (i) internal determinants and attributes of innovations capable of solving common problems; (ii) policy transfer among countries which are interdependent and emulate one other; and (iii) the role of the OECD in framing policy innovations (Finnemore 1993; Sahlin-Andersson and Engwall 2002; Bearce and Bondanella 2007).

Part I of the book presents the analytical framework and clarifies the concept and purpose of RIA. It also illustrates the OECD's activities in relation to this innovation. Drawing on an original dataset as well as OECD data, Part II analyses the patterns of RIA across a wide scope of time and space.

The analytical framework is complemented by two conceptual analyses. At the micro-level, the functional attributes of RIA are specified. Based on comparative administrative law treatises, Chapter Three sets RIA in relation to different administrative tradition settings and draws different typologies of regulatory process. In particular, the principal-agent (P-A) model and political control theory reveal the interaction between the attribute of RIA as a control mechanism and modes of regulatory review in a property space composed of typologies, expressed in dichotomous fashion (present/not present) (Elman 2005). Furthermore, this chapter sets out to assess the adoptability of RIA according to a country's administrative tradition, as well as the capacity of governments to reshape and reinvent RIA, from the time of emergence up to the most recent changes. To do so, a longitudinal analysis in a sample of pioneering countries traces the process of institutionalisation of RIA.

At the macro-level, Chapter Four provides an accurate description of the role of the OECD in communicating, framing, promoting and editing the transnational policy discourse on RIA. A longitudinal content analysis of the OECD's major publications on regulatory reform and governance gauges the capacity of this IO to frame a policy discourse around an innovation such as RIA.

In order to develop the empirical analyses throughout the outlined decisional sequence of adoption, implementation and evaluation, different datasets and a mix of methodology strategies are necessary. Chapter Five tests the analytical framework of the three explanatory layers, through a discrete event history analysis (EHA). This method assumes that the dependent variable is the probability of a given country adopting RIA within a specific year. This econometric analysis relies on a year-of-adoption database, covering thirty-eight countries between 1968 and 2006. It is a collection of primary and secondary data sources. When this dataset differs from that of the OECD, a brief description of the methodological choices in selecting the year of adoption is provided in Appendix A.

Chapter Six measures the extent of implementation through an aggregated indicator. Appendix C takes into account the problem concerning the coherence and comparability of data contained in the different datasets of the implementation stages, used for constructing this implementation score. Drawing on categories of adopters, it is possible to test through soft quantitative analysis of an aggregated index the hypothesis that leaders generally have greater resources to invest in policy formulation, and consequently, given the incrementalism effect, they tend to have the most extensive policy at any point in time (Clark 1985). On the other hand, under the theoretical framework of emulation and homogenisation, the assumption to test is the existence of a marginal variance across and within categories of adopters and groups of countries with a common legal tradition and what is here termed legal origin.[13] Following Hays (1996b), further correlations are performed in order to assess the relationship between index of implementation and year of adoption.

---

13. Legal origin is adopted here as a term often used in US economics literature and elsewhere. It is a broad classification of a country's legal system and tradition. Thus, for example, a country with a common-law system is here said to be of English legal origin.

Chapter Seven accounts for governments' experiences in evaluating their RIA programmes. The aim of this chapter is to gauge whether there is interdependence and a learning process among governments in the evaluation phase, facilitated by the OECD. This qualitative review of international and transnational evaluation practices has two purposes. Firstly, it identifies which types of adopters have engaged in evaluation. Secondly, by assessing the similarity of practices used in countries where the evaluation of RIA programmes is well established, this chapter shows whether and to what extent countries learn from each other about how to evaluate a diffused policy tool.

While references to the conceptual framework are made throughout, Chapter Eight draws together the empirical findings of this comprehensive analysis of the adoption, implementation and evaluation of RIA, summarising whether the three different empirical tests of the OECD's influence held up coherently as well as providing a more convincing explanation of policy diffusion. It revisits the aims of this research: to understand the patterns, the extent and the impact of transnationally framed policy innovation on domestic regulatory governance. In doing so, this chapter considers the implications for wider debates on policy diffusion, proposes implications for further research and makes recommendations for policy makers and stakeholders.

chapter two | the analytical framework

The previous chapter remarked on the conceptually and methodologically distinct perspectives on policy diffusion. Notwithstanding the now abundant empirical evidence, scholars are still lamenting the lack of cumulated knowledge and the generalisation on policy innovation (Graham *et al.* 2013). Given the extreme variance in the empirical findings, Downs and Mohr (1976) postulated the existence of distinct types of innovations whose adoption can best be explained by a number of correspondingly distinct theories, with different explanatory variables, different interrelationships among them and different effects upon the dependent variable. Indeed, it is only on the basis of an accurate knowledge of the distinctiveness of the policy innovation under analysis that a researcher can make cogent choices. This perspective sets an analytical framework which revolves around the functional attributes of RIA as the internal determinants of policy change and places this policy innovation within the adoption environment of the transnational NPM movement. The latter 'institutional environment' may directly affect governments that have to conform to what is defined as appropriate and efficient, largely disregarding the actual impact on their performance (Tolbert and Zucker 1983).

Accordingly, this book has two standpoints. Firstly, RIA is a technological innovation – a substantial change of the regulatory process that is broadly defined as the procedure that executive agencies and departments must comply with when proposing bills and delegated legislation. Indeed, administrative reforms are adopted and implemented for their technological and operational elements (Power 1997; Sahlin-Andersson 2001). As an innovation, RIA represents a type of policy change which occurs irregularly and 'represents a break from the past' (Mintrom 2000). The puzzle of the source of change associated with an innovation can be addressed by relying on the general question of structure *vs* agency, as shown by scholars interested in the causality of policy interdependence. Based on collective rationality and applied at the population level of organisations, institutional theory, on the one hand, has explained how innovations are adopted through non-choice behaviours which provide legitimacy rather than efficacy and efficiency (Meyer and Rowan 1977; Tolbert and Zucker 1983; Tolbert 1985; Zucker 1987). On the other hand, the rational-choice perspective assumes organisations can select one course of action from various alternatives, deciding whether to adopt innovations and how to implement and institutionalise them (Goodman and Steckler 1989).

Although policy diffusion analyses have an analytical emphasis on the interconnectedness of adopting units, there is overall agreement in the literature on organisations' capacity to have different responses and adjustments to environmental pressures (Oliver 1991). Accordingly, the present analysis relies on a theoretical foundation of decision making and policy makers' capacity for problem solving and for pursuing their interest. The degree of actors' capacity to pursue their interest – notwithstanding the environmental uncertainty and external actors and institutions – is a key element in distinguishing the different theoretical approaches of diffusion and in understanding the explanations behind the emergence of an innovation (Tolbert and Zucker 1983; Abrahamson 1991). In addition, the absence of a global paradigm of NPM has rendered unavailable a neat and precise policy model of administrative reform and RIA (Hood 1995; Gow and Dufour 2000).

Given this limited theorisation, it still remains to ascertain the intensity of external pressures on an adopting unit. The second standpoint of this research is the relevance of the OECD in setting institutional conditions for the diffusion of RIA. The OECD coordinates transnational networks of reforms and is able to mediate information and experience on regulatory reform. Without the OECD, countries would be less interconnected and less able to screen all policy innovations or to associate them with a specific governance issue. The OECD governance mechanisms include peer review and ranking datasets. The latter establish the perceived authority of this IO and can influence how RIA is implemented and evaluated at the national level. This transnational level of analysis is complemented with another explanatory layer of policy interdependence. Countries can communicate and learn directly from one other. Policy experience is transferred from one country to another because of competition, emulation or bounded learning.

By focusing on administrative reforms, the next section sets the overall analytical framework of this study. Section 2.2 illustrates the internal determinants and functional logic of RIA as a policy innovation. Then, models and mechanisms of policy interdependence are described, paying attention to regional and spatial models. Section 2.4 shows the different roles played by the OECD in the diffusion of administrative innovations. Finally, Section 2.5 concludes.

2.1 An integrated analytical framework

The explanatory power of internal determinants and diffusion variables may vary across innovations (Downs and Mohr 1976), space (Franzese and Hays 2007) and time (Tolbert and Zucker 1983). Although it is still not clear from the literature 'when and where diffusion becomes causally relevant in domestic policy change' (Brooks 2007), a middle-range analytical framework can evidence governments' conscious decisions about innovations. Table 2.1 summarises the framework which accommodates the complexity and heterogeneity of RIA diffusion by taking into account three *layers* of explanations: internal determinants and independent national initiatives; a process of international interdependence; and the OECD transnational construction and circulation of prototypes and templates (Sahlin-Andersson 2001). It also sets scenarios for the adoption, implementation and evaluation of RIA. Although this book pays particular attention to the description of the internal and transnational layers (*see* Chapters Three and Four), models of international interdependence are tested throughout the empirical analyses.

Table 2.1: Layers of explanations and expectations of policy diffusion

Explanatory layers	Internal determinants and independent national initiatives	International interaction and emulation	OECD transnational templates and networks
Main elements and features	Adoptability and administrative traditions	Pioneer countries form an international political discourse	The OECD reframes the characteristics of innovation
Adoption	Similar reaction to common problems based on the functional logic of innovation	Interconnectedness of countries assessed through spatial and regional models or diffusion casual mechanisms	The OECD's mediative and inquisitive functions innovation
Implementation of practices	Marginal convergence according to governments' functional choice and incrementalism	Clustered convergence towards regional or global leaders	High level of convergence based on the OECD's recommendations and policy templates
Evaluation of RIA programme	Independent development of evaluation practices and no evaluation practices in laggard countries	Based on appraisal templates developed by leader countries	Based on the OECD's methods and data. Consistency in policy recommendations and modes of policy evaluation and benchmarking
Type of learning	Learning only through own experience	Learning through socialisation	The OECD facilitates learning through knowledge sharing and standardisation of norm

The choice to focus on the OECD is justified by the fact that 'what is spreading is not practice as such, but accounts of this practice' (Sahlin-Andersson 2001 *see also* March and Olsen 1983). As a consequence, rhetoric, symbols and interpretations of administrative reform matter. The distance between the sources of change and potential adopters provides scope for a communication process in which ideas, experiences and templates are presented, represented and finally transformed through an editing process (Sahlin-Andersson 2001; Sahlin and Wedlin 2010). Indeed, the OECD's editing process understates the contextual (in term of political ideology, administrative connotations, economic and cultural aspects) and time dimensions with the intention of promoting and disseminating the proposed templates of administrative reform.

If diffusion models explain policy adoption through the intensity of spatial or hierarchical flows of information about an innovation (Meir 1982), the emphasis here is on how this information is interpreted and transformed. Within the global discourse of NPM (Pollitt 2001; Pollitt 2002), an administrative reform is promoted for its beneficial features and, consequently, its related concepts of accountability and rationality may vary when transposed. Accordingly, the political rhetorical use of RIA is possibly even stronger at international and transnational levels. For instance, what was created for controlling the regulators may be advertised as a tool for evidence-based decision making (OECD 1997a; OECD 1997b; OECD 2002a). As the OECD is a platform for global policy dialogue (Finnemore and Sikkink 1998; OECD 2010a), it is reasonable to expect that, through different channels of influence, such a transnational agency can marshal and steer national policy making. The OECD involves itself in domestic politics and engages national policy makers through expert meetings and conferences, publications, best practice, peer review and ranking data (Martens and Jakobi 2010). Further, '[t]ransnational actors can provide the legitimate, well-elaborated policy proposals that domestic actors often lack, along with the resources to win domestic support for reform' (Orenstein 2008).

Alternatively, regulatory reform may be either triggered by pioneer countries or developed independently at the domestic level. Whereas the notion of independent choice presumes that governments – facing the same problem of managing an extensive regulatory state – reached the same policy solution of adopting RIA, internationally formed diffusion refers to the interconnectedness of governments. The latter concept is straightforward: governments and their elites communicate and interact, exchanging ideas, solutions and experiences as well as learning from and imitating one other. Environmental uncertainty is faced by organisations and governments through a process of imitation and cognitive shortcuts.

The literature on the diffusion of administrative innovations shows that it is crucial to take into account the overall process of institutionalisation. Rarely does a single moment or event encapsulate the full range of international and transnational influences on domestic policy (Orenstein 2008). In Europe, the formal adoption of regulatory appraisal systems has not been followed by the same pattern of implementation (Radaelli 2005a). The process of putting an innovation into an organisational and institutional context is prolonged and has several phases (De Francesco et al. 2012). Hence, it is essential to allow for broader and longer-term consequences, analysing the extent and the variance of implementation and the modalities of evaluation.

Literature on the diffusion of policy innovations is now abundant. Relying on concepts developed in the fields of communication, organisation and sociology, the study of diffusion has covered the adoption of quite a wide array of public policies and institutions, from lottery games (Berry and Berry 1990) to telephone regulation reform (Kim and Gerber 2005); and from the creation of independent regulatory agencies (Gilardi 2005; Jordana and Levi-Faur 2005) to pension privatisation and health reform (Weyland 2006). However, while adoption is an important aspect of the policy diffusion process, this narrow focus ignores the stages prior to and after the decisional point of adoption. Indeed, classical diffusion theory, applied in disciplines other than political science, developed the concept of the innovation process, in which adoption is a punctuated event anticipated and preceded by interconnected decisions and actions that need to be carried out and confirmed over time: information gathering, conceptualisation, planning for the adoption, actions and decisions to put the innovation into use, evaluation and reinvention (Rogers 2003). In other words, time is a dimension often neglected by political scientists, who tend to overlook when and for how long diffusion became causally relevant and to assume that the explanatory power of a variable is constant throughout the diffusion process. The latter can be distinguished according to either the types of adopters, i.e. pioneers, early majority and laggard, or the phases of the innovation decision, i.e. adoption, implementation, evaluation, institutionalisation and, eventually, obsolescence.

Taking into account the temporal dimension through distinct stages of the domestic policy process is not a novel research strategy in the literature on transnational public policy and IOs. Policy development and the creation of problem definition, metrics and programmes, policy transfer and policy implementation are the components of a model of transnational actors and the World Bank's influence on pension system reform (Orenstein 2008). In a similar vein, the process of the OECD's ideational influence on domestic labour market policy has been broken down into three parts: idea transfer, idea acceptance and idea impact (Grinvalds 2008; Grinvalds 2011). Specific OECD governance tools have been associated with different stages of agenda setting, compliance with recognised international standards and policy evaluation and ranking (Martens and Jakobi 2010).

The cross-sectional research on policy innovation diffusion tends to focus on policy adoption, implementation and evaluation. However, it does this by developing distinct research questions, elements and designs for each phase of the domestic policy process. Furthermore, the role of the OECD and the modes of promoting transnational policy innovation vary according to the different phases of institutionalisation. Adoption of policy innovations is pursued by seeking to win governmental commitment to reforms and to secure parliamentary approval for them. In implementation, IOs attempt to influence domestic actors in order to build administrative capacity for reform (Orenstein 2008). Finally, the OECD proposes its own method and data for establishing its normative templates for evaluating RIA programmes and regulatory reform. While these three phases are not always clearly delineated, they tend to be arrayed in a sequence of the OECD's actions across time (see Chapter Four) and are usually associated with different tools for influencing member states.

The different implementation patterns can be linked to each explanatory layer. Under the micro-level incrementalist framework, one would expect that countries would diverge enormously in the extent of implementation. Indeed, the pioneers would generally be at the cutting edge due to their resource slack and their familiarity with the innovation, whereas laggards would show up as the weaker implementers. By contrast, structuralist explanations would expect more similar and converged patterns of innovation design and implementation. Specifically, international emulation would lead to convergence towards global or regional leaders. The transnational level of explanation would be consistent with a higher level of convergence around the OECD's recommendations and policy templates.

Similar expectations can be formulated within the evaluation or reconfirmation of innovation. By ascertaining which countries have the resources and capacity to perform evaluative practices, it is possible to gain evidence of the extent and modalities of learning. The non-existence of evaluation indicates minimal learning and symbolic adoption. By contrast, there are different extents of instrumental learning, whether RIA is constantly evaluated and reinvented on the basis of the direct experience of a given government or through the recognition and appreciation of multiple experiences of other governments. The OECD can function as a learning platform where policy evaluation occurs at the transnational level and is facilitated through peer review and benchmarking, entailing the auditing, comparison and ranking of state practices (Mahon and McBride 2009).

Studies on the globalisation of administrative reform have become considerable. Combining soft statistical analyses and qualitative evidence, Bennett (1997) argued that prerequisites and diffusion explanations of freedom of information (FOI) laws, ombudsmen and data protection legislation were related to the particular element of each administrative innovation. However, in order to explain the pattern of adoption, one needs to discern how innovation is communicated and to assess the motivations for learning and emulating (Bennett 1997). In explaining the diffusion of FOI laws, Grigorescu (2003) argued that the OECD, through its governance and peer review mechanisms, provides an alternative (to governmental) sources of information aimed at the general public. The hypotheses tested by Grigorescu assumed that a surge of information from the OECD increases the probability of a national government adopting institutions for transparency. IOs have also influenced the adoption of environment appraisal systems through international agreement and financial support. Also, Hironaka (2002) evidenced the role of scientific communities in legitimating the use of rational decision-making tools (i.e. environmental impact assessment (EIA), and promoting environmental awareness.

Compared with such cross-sectional analyses of policy adoption, the main added value of this book is that the cumulative knowledge about policy attributes, discourse, adoption, implementation and evaluation provides a more accurate assessment of the extent of interdependence and governmental modes of learning. It enhances our understanding of the diffusion process. For instance, an analysis of evaluation can reinforce or contradict the empirical evidence on the influence of the OECD on governments' decisions to adopt a policy innovation.

To clarify, the contribution of this research is not to offer a meta-theory of the policy process or the diffusion of policy innovation in which coherent and overarching causal mechanisms are tested along different stages. The advance here is on the design of research into the extent of governments' interdependence in the field of administrative and regulatory reform. Comparative analyses of the interrelated phases of adoption, implementation and evaluation provide a stronger analytical lens for appreciating how and why an administrative innovation such as RIA spreads and the impact of the OECD on domestic policy. Within a large-n comparative analysis, the methodological challenge is to operationalise the different modes of policy interdependence by relying also on qualitative evidence for reconstructing the process of communication and interaction among international and transnational networks. These aspects are the focus of the next two chapters.

2.2 Internal determinants and the functional logic of RIA

Analyses of the extent of policy innovativeness have shifted the focus from institutional characteristics towards the adoptability of an innovation. Downs and Mohr (1976) suggested taking into account the interaction between the attributes of an innovation and the attributes of the organisation adopting it. Accordingly, the unit of analysis is not exclusively either the innovation or the adopting country, but the innovation in respect of a specific country, given that the attributes of the innovation are defined by policy makers' perceptions. Meir (1982) embedded such an interaction in the adoption environment, composed of all identifiable internal conditions, such as the adoption unit's level of experience, norms, values, intentions and socio-economic status, and environmental factors determining the extent and quality of communication on policy innovation.

Internal determinants of, and prerequisites for, diffusion are associated with functionalist explanations within countries and general theories such as the modernisation and rationalisation of government interventions (Collier and Messick 1975). However, internal determinants not only give rise to the null hypothesis of diffusion, they also determine policy makers' capacity to receive and process information about the prior choices of other governments. Public administrations, however, are stable organisations that, due to their considerable size and hierarchical structure, are not easily permeated by environmental pressures. 'Public administrations change less quickly than the political, economic, and social framework in which they have to operate' (Cassese 2003). The term 'reform' is exclusively associated with public organisations and refers to planned policy interventions (Cassese 2003) - self-conscious actions (Lynn 2001) that adjust the dimensional, structural and hierarchical constraints according to environmental changes. Financial crisis and dissatisfaction with the public sector's performance are the main and common drivers of administrative reform (Cassese 2003), and also promote an agenda for direct participation or at least the representation of citizens in decision making (Ansell and Gingrich 2003). Thus, since the 1970s administrative reforms among Western governments have become a constant and autonomous policy that have a prominent position on the political agenda (Cassese and Savino 2005 *see also* March and Olson 1983 on the evolution of administrative reorganisations in the US) and are institutionalised in a specific department or ministry.

Administrative lawyers and scholars of public policy and public management tend to agree that the internal characteristics of public administrations explain the persistence of the different modalities of adoption and implementation of administrative reform (Cassese 2003; Pollitt and Bouckaert 2004; Peters 1997):

[U]nder the pressure of the same problems, similar solutions are chosen. But once adopted these solutions fit into different administrative frameworks. They are selected and elaborated by different political actors and are implemented at different times, which means that differences arise at a later date and are juxtaposed with the uniformity of policies. (Cassese 2003)

And, more importantly, the initial conditions of reformers are different in terms of efficiency, legal and constitutional frameworks (Cassese 2003), and administrative culture – identified by families of nations or state traditions (Peters 1997). Thus, path dependence matters (Page 2003). Administrative change is more common in those countries that have already developed patterns of administrative reforms (Drori et al. 2006a). Also, the extent of implementation varies enormously among countries according to who the promoter (politicians or bureaucrats) is and which community elaborates the reform plans (bureaucratic experts, private consultants or administrative lawyers) (Cassese 2003).

Technological innovation is the main factor behind administrative reform, essentially in the form of a new set of management tools and techniques imported from the private sector. Different disciplines have different perceptions of rationale and attributes of regulatory appraisal systems. Economists argue that analytical techniques imported from economic theories would help regulators to avoid casual and rough decisions not buttressed by empirical analysis (Arrow et al. 1996a; Arrow et al. 1996b). But this conception is much too apolitical and neutral. Lawyers and administrative scholars perceive RIA as an administrative requirement inserted into the terrain of public law. Political scientists would consider it as an incentive mechanism in the relationships between regulators, political agents and their constituencies. Furthermore, organisational scholars would be interested in its compatibility with existing institutions.

Scant attention has, however, been dedicated to the linkages between regulation theories and the regulatory process, wherein RIA is supposed to work (Croley 1998; West 2005). A joint consideration of regulation theories and theories of the administrative process allows us to recognise the institutional compatibility and broader governance implications of RIA. Another limitation is the tendency to reflect on RIA with the US political system in mind. The latter is characterised by key features such as delegation to regulatory agencies, presidential oversight of regulatory process, the presence of administrative rulemaking processes (the reference is to the APA which is subject to judicial review. In Europe, where administrative requirements are still less specific on rulemaking, there is more direct ministerial or parliamentary control over delegated legislation (see Chapter Three).

With these caveats in mind in relation to the functionalist logic of RIA, the first reason a state might want to adopt and institutionalise the innovation is based on delegation. An administrative procedure such as RIA is effective in several ways in achieving the political control of bureaucracy. Firstly, it allows interest groups to monitor the agency's decision-making process. Secondly, by imposing procedural delay, RIA allows politicians to intervene before an agency finalises its regulatory proposals (McCubbins et al. 1989). Finally, by 'stacking the deck', RIA benefits the political interests represented in the coalition supporting the principal in question (McCubbins et al. 1987). CBA plays a specific role: it minimises error costs under conditions of information asymmetry (Posner 2001).

Assuming that administrative procedure can change the opportunity structure in which actors (executive agencies and pressure groups, including civil society associations) interact, the second reason comes from two models of administrative governance that are potentially more open to diffuse interests and more accountable to citizens.[1] Indeed, in a neo-pluralistic framework, appraisal systems are adopted to produce equal opportunities for pressure groups so that they can compete on a level playing field and help optimal decisions to be reached (Arnold 1987). Alternatively, where weaker interest groups participate in decision making, the civic republican model posits that, in the pursuit of the broader community interest, administrative procedures such as RIA provide an opportunity for public-spirited dialogue and deliberation about regulatory priorities (Croley 1998).

The third functional logic relates to rational policy making. The requirement to use economic analysis systematically in rule formulation (restated in all US Executive Orders, but defined in much milder forms in European guidelines) fosters regulations that increase the net welfare of the community (Arrow *et al.* 1996a; Arrow *et al.* 1996b). The notion of 'legal rationality' is more encompassing and refers to process as well as economic outcomes (Heydebrand 2003).[2] In other words, rationality plays an important role in the achievement of regulatory legitimacy. Regulators are credible if they provide reasons for their choices, support decisions with transparent economic analysis and objective risk analysis, and enable courts to review their decisions (Freedman 1978; Majone 1989; Majone 1996). Ultimately, rational policy making is associated with new forms of accountability and legitimacy (Vibert 2007).

Finally, administrative requirements can also lead to symbolic politics via rituals of verification (Power 1997). Given the increasing relational distance between principals and agents (a distance generated by decentralisation, contracting out and the creation of independent agencies), formal procedures replace trust and administrative procedure replaces informal coordination. If political organisations produce knowledge about the expected impact of policy in order to increase their legitimacy rather than efficiency (Brunsson 1989), we would expect tools like RIA to play a role in the symbolic dimension of the regulatory state.

Although the determination of preferences of special groups can be problematic (Waterman and Meier 1998; Kerwin 2003) and the theory of delegation neglects the bureaucratic agency's reaction (West 1988; McGarity 1991; Ayers and Braithwaite 1992; Hammond and Knott 1999; Kerwin 2003), it is uncontested that RIA as an administrative procedure solves the principal's problem of controlling bureaucracies (Froud *et al.*1998; Shapiro 2005). Although embedded in political rhetoric and notions of rationality, accountability and legitimacy, as well as

---

1. In fact, the American Congress and the European Commission have increased participation in the rulemaking process. Further, American and EU courts have also imposed requirements on regulatory agencies to release data, disclose the basis of discussions with pressure groups and carry out public hearings (Stewart 1975; Stewart 1981; Bignami 2001; Shapiro 2001; Stewart 2005).

2. The use of 'rationality' is also synonymous with 'independence from the political sphere', as shown by the long tradition of technocratic political and legal theory in the US, from James Landis (1938) to Stephen Breyer (1993) and Bruce Ackerman (1981).

the intervening variables in the explanation, there are indeed strong theoretical arguments for political control being the most likely reason for a country to adopt and institutionalise RIA. The next chapter will show that its position within the family of control systems is perhaps unique. Whereas some instruments operate either *ex ante* (e.g. statutes and appointments) or *ex post* (e.g. judicial review of an agency's regulatory process), RIA provides *ongoing* control, functioning whilst rules are being formulated and regulatory options are assessed. Overall, although the internally generated political discourse revolves around economic rationality and legitimacy, the practices on RIA are based on political control (March and Olson 1983; *see also* Chapter Four).

Overall, the internal layer of explanation identifies the functionalist logic of a policy innovation. It postulates that organisations with specific characteristics, such as greater size and greater level of slack resources, are more compatible with an innovation. Rather than the strength of information flows, it is the inner environment of a given country and its characteristics – such as the extent of modernisation (Collier and Messick 1975) and the size and complexity of the public sector (Tolbert 1985; Dobbin *et al.* 1988) – that matter.

2.3 International policy interdependence

In a globalised and competitive economic system, public administration is a production factor that is exposed to the judgement of the market. To increase efficacy and efficiency, neo-liberal political agendas have imposed market discipline on administrative agencies (Ansell and Gingrich 2003). In particular, the NPM is composed of several elements or techniques for introducing market logic into public organisations, e.g. agencification, process re-engineering, value for money, result-oriented budgeting, privatisation, public–private partnerships, contracting out, customer orientation (Cassese 2003; Gow and Dufour 2000, citing Osborne and Gaebler 1993). This new mode of public management has now become a 'global innovation' (Karmack 2004), a 'global trend' (Sahlin-Andersson 2001)[3] and 'the gold standard' for administrative reforms (Peters 1997). These global trends are embedded in management ideologies such as standardisation and accountability, and facilitated by various global players, such as professional groups, businesses, civil society organisations and world powers, over time and across countries (Sahlin-Andersson and Engwall 2002). Furthermore, globalisation forces national governments to coordinate, collaborate and harmonise their policies in order to solve transboundary externalities (Cassese 2003).

---

3.   *See also* Ansell and Gingrich 2003 on the diffusion of administrative reform among OECD member states.

Institutional and external influences may lead to a homogenisation of public organisations. Forcing 'one unit in a population to resemble other units that face the same set of environmental conditions' (DiMaggio and Powell 1983), structural determinants of collective rationality are institutional conditions for diffusion (Strang and Meyer 1993). Institutional scholars explain change through national linkages to the 'world society' (Meyer *et al.* 1997). Besides transnational institutional linkages (*see* Section 2.4), economic and trade openness and the extent of scientification have explained the increasing similarity of public administrations around the world (Drori *et al.* 2006b). The combination of these homogeneity factors originated with the NPM movement, which encompasses pre-existing management activities but which is also in itself a new, established discipline, constructed against traditional Weberian public administration (Gow and Dufour 2000). Accordingly, government agencies may be even more vulnerable to the pressures of isomorphism than private profit and non-profit organisations (Wejnert 2002).

Policy diffusion, on the other hand, is often described as a rational process (Strang and Meyer 1993). Through the systematic collection and treatment of all relevant information, policy makers scan and monitor all policy innovations present in the external environment. Successively, they rationally update their beliefs about policies through the ascertainment of options' payoffs through CBA (Meseguer 2006). This mode of comprehensive rational learning is, however, an ideal type. Bounded rationality, instead, emphasises the clustered component of information gathering and the relevance of inferential shortcuts that allow administrative personnel to identify satisfactory solutions (through successive assessments of single options), rather than optimal solutions, using utility maximisation (through a systematic and simultaneous assessment of all the possible options) (Guseh 2003; Weyland 2006).

Based on the central assumption that 'information diffusion drives technology diffusion' (Geroski 2000), several 'relational models' frame the extent of rationality and learning (Meir 1982). The random learning model presumes that 'officials from states that have already adopted a programme interact freely and mix thoroughly with officials from states that have not yet adopted it, and that each contact by a not-yet-adopting state with a previous adopter provides an additional stimulus for the former to adopt' (Berry and Berry 2007). Relying on the distance of potential adopters from the origin of the innovation, the spatial model delineates, instead, patterns of interaction within networks. It posits the existence of 'sets of small separate groups, with full communication between some but no communication between others' (Tolbert and Zucker 1983). Similarly, the regional diffusion model assumes a given country's remoteness and lower hierarchical position within a spatial system causes smaller volumes of information flow and weaker awareness of the innovation (Meir 1982; Berry and Berry 2007).

Rather than making use of a spatial model to explain the extent of information exchange and learning, imitation relies on information cues such as the prestige and hierarchical status of a country and similarities in identity (Berry and Berry 2007). Cognitive shortcuts and information cues are given by 'the most important foreign economic competitors' (Simmons and Elkins 2004) in order to achieve an economic advantage over other states or avoid being disadvantaged (Berry and Berry 2007).[4] '[G]iven that one country's international standing is conditioned perforce by that of other nations, reputation and status gains are inherently competitive' (Brooks 2007). Competition overlaps with the hierarchical model which assumes that the higher-status social units are the pioneers and, as a result, communication about an innovation follows a precise top-down pattern (Knoke 1982; Berry and Berry 2007). In this model, countries can be perceived to be of a higher rank with respect to economic growth (Collier and Messick 1975), reputational status (Brooks 2007), legislative experience, technical expertise or administrative personnel (Leichter 1983).

Similarly to the spatial model, there may be predictable patterns of emulation: 'we can expect that as one country has imitated another country earlier, it may continue to imitate the same country' (Sahlin-Andersson 2001). In other words, countries tend not to change their role as a 'borrower' or a 'lender' (Dolowitz and Marsh 2000, citing Robertson 1991, and Rose 1993). For instance, Anglo-Saxon countries are regarded as the first to adopt administrative innovations as more adaptable to new policy ideas, whilst civil law and Mediterranean countries are usually the laggards.

This clustered pattern of communicative influences and policy transfers among countries is expected throughout the policy stages. Families of countries can explain the timing of adoption, the extent of implementation and the modes of evaluation of RIA. Pioneer countries are expected to have greater resources and institutional preconditions – such as their administrative and legal origin – for implementing the RIA system. Accordingly, in these countries the scope of implementation is broader than that of the other adopter categories, derived according to the timing of adoption (pioneer, majority of followers, or laggards) and legal origin (see Chapter Six). Policy interdependence and transfer within clusters of countries also concerns evaluative practices. Indeed, countries could exchange information and knowledge about policy innovations, including institutional models, methods and measures to conduct evaluation studies on RIA programmes. There are essentially four scenarios for interdependence of policy evaluation: (i) no policy evaluation; (ii) policy evaluation relies exclusively on a given country's own experience; (iii) exchange and transfer of evaluation practices among countries with similar RIA models; and (iv) the use of transnational policy benchmarks (see Chapter Seven).

Overall, a diffusion model based on communication flows among policy networks has to encompass the professionalisation and socialisation of policy makers (Knoke 1982). Rather than focusing exclusively on spatial influences, an analytical framework of administrative innovation should take account of policy

---

4. Competition and countries' competitiveness are not meant here as a condition of the institutional environment but as a country's strategic choice to identify and select its 'competitive networks' (Simmons and Elkins 2004).

makers' attributes and attitudes by discerning the types of international interaction and communication and the motivations for learning from and emulating each other (Bennett 1997). Indeed, most recent research on international interdependence relies on a specific set of causal mechanisms: policy makers learn, emulate and compete among one other (Weyland 2006; Dobbin *et al.* 2007; Gilardi 2012).

Given the assumption of adopters' rationality, spatial models focus on the macro-level of geographical and cultural proximity, whilst diffusion mechanisms underlie the micro-aspects of the decisional process. The difference, however, should not be overestimated. For instance, competition, emulation and learning underpin communication and policy network models. In addition, recent research has shown the need to improve theoretical design through the consideration that the broad array of diffusion variables can have an 'interactive impact' (Wejnert 2002). For instance, the pressures of isomorphism may mitigate or potentiate the impact of a fixed amount and strength of information on adoption (Strang and Soule 1998; Wejnert 2002; Jensen 2003). Accordingly, a careful reflection on both internal and external determinants is necessary in order to disentangle a complex phenomenon such as policy diffusion. In a quantitative framework, variables associated with different causal mechanisms are not easy to distinguish or test.

Within these explanations, the role of the OECD is not yet very well understood. As the role of the OECD in promoting, interpreting and rebranding the RIA policy 'label' is manifest, the three empirical analyses presented in this book provide an extensive overview of the extent of influence of transnational governance mechanisms (knowledge formation through publications; policy recommendation and peer review; and ranking data) on domestic politics.

2.4 The OECD policy networks and templates

Economic globalisation and regional integration have also led to the emergence of transnational policy communities composed of policy makers and experts who 'share their expertise and information and who form common patterns of understanding regarding policy through regular interaction' (Stone 2000a).[5] The transnationally established public management reforms revolve around the presence and role of change agents and mediators such as IOs, consultants and epistemic communities. Global communicative networks are carriers of policy processes and are involved in the diffusion of ideas, standards and policy practices (Stone 1999; Stone 2000a; Stone 2000b; True and Mintrom 2001; Sahlin-Andersson and Engwall 2002; Moon and Deleon 2005).

The emergence of transnational policy networks is explained by the simple assumption that it is more efficient for countries to tackle problems of common interest collectively than alone. Accordingly, transnational policy ideas and innovations are both cognitive and normative means for tackling complexity and they provide prescriptions for actions. Especially in the case of the OECD,

---

5. *See* also Haas 1992 and Rose 1993 on transnational epistemic communities.

these two purposive dimensions of discourse are interwoven. At the cognitive level, policy ideas denote the OECD's perceptions about the deficiencies, virtues and improvement of regulation. Furthermore, IOs such as the OECD rely on ideas, translated and incorporated into more concrete policy measures and recommendations, in order to constitute their authority and legitimacy (Ervik *et al.* 2009). Aspects of elite socialisation via the institutionalisation of norms have also emerged, impacting on national policy processes and outcomes (True and Mintrom 2001; Bearce and Bondanella 2007). Such mechanisms of institutionalisation energise the diffusion of a policy innovation (Lawrence *et al.* 2001) and transcend any single organisation's purposive control (Suchman, 1995). Although maintaining the analysis at the agency level, institutionalist scholars downplay the agency (as well as its decision-making process, its interconnectedness, and its influence from and on the other members of the social network) and emphasise the structure of the policy sectors (Suchman 1995). Normative pressures can even reinforce the 'reinventing government' movement: '[b]elonging to professional associations and being subject to periodic reviews, accreditation, and licensing appear to make government agencies less rigid and more flexible' (Frumkin and Galaskiewicz 2004).

Accordingly, combining the communicative and normative perspectives of policy networks, the OECD has mediative and inquisitive functions (Mahon and McBride 2009). Mediative functions refer to those activities that facilitate the construction of policy discussion among experts on the best policy solutions. It is due to such international expertise that standards and benchmarks emerge (Mahon and McBride 2009). Transnational networks are particularly capable of attracting the attention of national policy makers to administrative innovations through a process of packaging, theorisation and positive feedback. Inquisitive functions involve monitoring policy choices and outcomes through benchmarking and peer review, which in turn allows the auditing, comparison and ranking of member states (Lodge 2005; Mahon and McBride 2009). OECD member states generally comply with norms in order to reduce the costs of instrumental decision making, to legitimise their presence within transnational networks and to preserve their international reputation among peers. Within this framework, an IO is an 'organisational platform' from and through which 'norm entrepreneurs' promote their norms. Furthermore, and more importantly, IOs are 'agents of socialisation', capable of persuading their member states to adopt, implement and monitor new policies that adhere to international standards and peer country pressure (Finnemore and Sikkink 1998). This mechanism of socialisation urges national decision makers to achieve an international legitimation, to conform and belong to a 'group' of peers and to gain self-esteem (Finnemore and Sikkink 1998). The identity of member states is shaped by the OECD through the evaluative or prescriptive category of norms that are associated with the OECD's inquisitive tools, such as country policy evaluative reports and 'naming and shaming' charts and datasets. The collected data and shared information on member states are treated and summarised for comparative and ranking purposes.

The OECD's principal source of value lies in its role as an editor of ideas and experiences. The peculiar contexts and experiences of administrative reforms are inserted into broader theoretical frameworks with the aim of putting forward normative accounts and recommendations (Sahlin-Andersson 2001). Theorisation is a necessary means of constructing and legitimating 'modern' national states, which are founded on universalised notions of rationality, progress and evolution (Strang and Meyer 1993; Meyer *et al.* 1997). Moreover, administrative reforms are packaged together in more logically coherent modalities through a rhetoric of administrative rationality. Overall, '[a]s reforms and experiences are accounted for and narrated, they need to be framed and presented to others in terms of existing templates, examples, categories, scientific concepts, theoretical frameworks and widespread classifications that are familiar' (Sahlin-Andersson 2001).

Reform initiatives are promoted by designing, editing and disseminating the templates and prototypes of administrative innovations and reforms. The editing process involves and requires a change in the logic and rationale behind the origin of innovation: 'Developments may acquire a more rationalistic flavour. Causes and effects tend to be clarified, effects are presented as resulting from identifiable activities, and processes are often described as following a problem-solving logic' (Sahlin-Andersson 2001). Moreover, administrative reforms are packaged together in more logically coherent modalities through a rhetoric of administrative rationality. Experiences of reforms are narrated and presented through intelligible templates, examples, categories, scientific concepts, theoretical frameworks and widespread classifications (Sahlin-Andersson 2001).

Overall, the OECD's communicative and normative influences do affect, in different ways, national policy makers' decisions to adopt and legitimise the practice of policy innovations such as RIA. But the OECD has no means for placing its advice directly onto national agendas and cannot directly coerce member states to adopt its policy recommendations. However, transnational campaigns and policy processes trigger policy change at the national level (Orenstein 2008). Formulating and decontextualising cause-and-effect relationships, the OECD has been considered an 'ideational artist', capable of selecting, testing and promoting policy innovations. In so doing, the OECD is an enormous think-tank which continuously attracts the very best academics and actively takes steps in the learning processes of its member states (Marcussen 2004a).

The OECD is also characterised as an 'ideational arbitrator' which provides its members with a 'talking shop', a supportive environment in which national policy makers meet each other and develop their knowledge of policy as well as their personal and technical skills (Marcussen 2004a). Socialisation leads to more complex learning processes. National civil servants can develop a common language, examine problem-solving frameworks and frame 'reality' through the same kind of causal reasoning. Such socialisation is also supported by elements of indirect coercion or peer pressure. It could be argued that indirect coercion through powerful and regular peer review is the only means that the OECD has at its disposal in its attempts to execute multilateral surveillance (Marcussen 2004a).

The final role of the OECD as an 'ideational authority' is connected to implementation and evaluation practices. In this area, the OECD is perceived by its member states as a 'mythical, neutral, scientific and objective soothsayer that one cannot afford to ignore' (Marcussen 2004a). Indeed, the OECD's data, ideas and theories are used by national policy makers in order to legitimate reforms (Marcussen 2004a; Groenendijk 2011). The ideational authority of a policy network such as the OECD is related to the capacity of that network to influence its members, specifically in terms of whether its members are willing to subject themselves to its 'orders'. This is achieved mostly through the members' belief that such orders will be both appropriate and legitimate (Conzelmann 2010). A policy idea becomes powerful if the diffusers are conceived of as actors with expertise and policy-relevant knowledge. This implies that the OECD's analyses, criticism and subsequent recommendations regarding a set of problems must follow the criteria of clean, scientific analysis (Beyeler 2004). The OECD recommendations and best practices for all member states are, indeed, consistent throughout (Beyeler 2004). Therefore, its authority is in its capacity to induce a certain type of behaviour thanks to the legitimacy that stems from the appropriateness of its procedures, mission and capabilities (Conzelmann 2010). The OECD's ideational authority can be approximated through a set of indicators measuring 'the extent to which [it] is raising a specific form of consciousness among the many and varied actors in the national polity' (Marcussen 2004a). Policy convergence can be considered as the ultimate measure of authority and influence. Alternatively, an analysis of policy practices at the national level reveals whether the OECD's models of policy innovation are a constant reference in domestic politics and allows us to gauge the extent of conformity with transnational standards.

2.5 Conclusion

Economists, lawyers and political scientists have enriched the debate on the reasons for RIA. They tend to agree on three possible categories of explanations for what policy makers want and can potentially achieve with this administrative procedure: political control, democratic governance and economic rationality. Furthermore, supported by empirical evidence, rational choice theorists rightly show that RIA is not a politically neutral information device that provides more rational and transparent decision making. Whereas the rational choice model may explain the adoption of RIA at the agency level, it is not able to capture the reasons for adoption in the external environment. This raises the challenge of working in a comparative, as well as a longitudinal, mode with suitable research questions on: (i) the process of diffusion and the modes and extent of learning; (ii) the role of the OECD as a transnational change agency; and (iii) the variance – according to different policy stages – of the impact of the OECD's activities and functions concerning a transnational policy innovation like RIA on domestic policies.

The founding element of the proposed analytical framework is to recognise whether the phenomenon under analysis involves an innovation and a technological change. From this standpoint, the research can be developed comprehensively and coherently, embedding the attributes of innovation and innovators, as well as modes of policy interdependence. Overall, the literature on the globalisation of administrative reform has up until now neglected such a comprehensive perspective on policy interdependence. The analytical framework of the present study combines the epistemologically distinct elements of policy innovation diffusion, integrating functionalist explanations of RIA adoption with emulation and learning. Based on the consolidated but still separate literature on the global spread of administrative reforms and NPM, this book overcomes the lack of cumulative comparative evidence on transnational policy innovation, the related types of policy learning and their impact on domestic decisions to adopt, implement and evaluate.

The analytical model is comprehensive and integrates internal and external determinants of reform, as well as the horizontal and vertical dimensions of diffusion, by taking into account policy networks and the role of the OECD. Overall, there are two modes of policy interdependence facilitated by the OECD and affecting its member states: cognitive interaction and interaction through commitment (Gehring and Oberthür 2009). Conceived as inter-institutional learning, the former revolves around information, knowledge or ideas capable of modifying previous decision makers' beliefs and, in turn, affecting the national decision-making process. The latter is based on the power of international norms and the logic of appropriateness.

Empirically, however, this model has rarely been tested, either in qualitative or quantitative analyses. Within a functionalist theoretical framework, researchers tend to complement internal determinants with measures of the interconnectivity among countries and between the OECD and domestic politics.[6] By providing information and facilitating the role of scientific communities that legitimise the use of tools aimed at enhancing the rationality of decision making, the OECD alters the incentive structure of domestic policy makers and increases the probability of adoption and the establishment of policy appraisal practices. Although learning cannot be imposed through coercive pressures, both types of interaction are, nonetheless, facilitated and intentionally triggered by the OECD which acts as a transnational mediator, proselytiser and editor of ideas and NPM-style reforms (Sahlin-Andersson 2001).

In order to capture the complexity of the OECD's role and its impact on domestic policy, this research relies on a set of empirical evidence. Considering the variety of operationalisations of policy innovation discourses, decisions and practices heighten our understanding of the innovation-decision process which has similarities with the policy process (Mossberger 2000). Such cumulative knowledge provides a stronger framework for disentangling the concept of diffusion, highlighting the theoretical similarities across different stages of the

---

6.   There are essentially two approaches to the interlinking of countries. The first approach, the so-called 'additional variable', includes variables that measure the interconnectedness of countries, such as trade openness and foreign direct investments (Jahn 2006). Another additional variable solution relies on the idea of 'pairing' societies according to their geographic or cultural proximity in order to test the convergence of several policy outcomes (Franzese and Hays 2007).

policy cycle. This also contributes to a reconsideration of policy stages, such as implementation and evaluation, that seek to discern whether the unit of analysis is a (diffused) policy innovation. Indeed, if policy adoption studies enable us – through the analytical lens of diffusion – to take into account the interdependence of various governments' choices, this theoretical enhancement has still to be achieved in implementation and evaluation studies.

chapter three | RIA as an oversight mechanism

At the conceptual level, the literature on policy diffusion emphasises the compatibility of an innovation with a set of organisational and institutional attributes. The unit of analysis is not exclusively the innovation or the adopting organisation, but the interaction between an innovation and the type of organisation adopting it, given that the attributes of an innovation are defined by organisational perceptions (Downs and Mohr 1976). On the one hand, the innovation is reinvented in order to accommodate the organisation's needs; on the other hand, the adopting unit is rearranged to fit the innovation (Rogers 2003). Therefore, a better understanding of the complex phenomena of diffusion requires a clarification of this interaction by defining the intrinsic features of the innovation under analysis and then relating these to institutional attributes.

The aim of this chapter is twofold. It focuses on the political control of regulators as the main internal determinant and functional rationale of adoption. Relying on Elman's (2005) work on explanatory typologies, it firstly derives modes of regulatory review in order to achieve a better comparison of RIA systems adopted and implemented in different administrative contexts. To clarify, the typologies presented in this chapter are not explanatory, but support the main argument of the role of administrative institutions as preconditions for the adoptability and institutionalisation of regulatory governance innovations. Accordingly, the impact of regulatory process typologies on RIA diffusion is not exclusive. The extent and quality of communication and interdependence across countries also matter and are explored in the succeeding chapters. The argument is that RIA should be analysed in the broader context of administrative law that has common features in all democratic regimes: it attempts to combine the democratic accountability of the executive branch and the effectiveness and efficiency of public policies (Rose-Ackerman 2007a). This trade-off is resolved in different ways according to the various traditions of administrative governance and the extent of the executive's dominance over the other constitutional bodies.

By looking at the institutionalisation of RIA across a sample of pioneering countries – namely, Australia, Canada, Denmark, Germany, the Netherlands and the UK – the second objective of this chapter is to probe the political control interpretation which is conspicuous in the US. Since the role played by the OECD was irrelevant among the pioneers, this country selection is straightforward and justified in the attempt to determine which model of RIA emerged and whether the American model travelled. Political control theory has been extensively used to explain the relationships between the civil service and the executive.

In comparative studies, the reason for the wide use of ideal type models lies in 'the opportunity to compare not only the real world of one nation to the ideal world of the models but national systems to the models and then to each other' (Peters

1998). Drawn from the literature, these ideal types have been considered as the way out of the absence of an overarching theory for comparing public bureaucracy. Indeed, delegation and the consequent emergence of the administrative state have been explored by relying on P-A models that have been used to explain the adoption of administrative procedure in the US (McNollgast 1999) and to compare the administrative law of Western (Bishop 1990) and Asian (Ginsburg 2002; Baum 2007) countries.

There is, however, a caveat to bear in mind. P-A models, like many other political theories, have been applied in the US and then projected onto the rest of the world. This may cause conceptual flaws 'because the constructs, hypotheses, and theories are not necessarily representative of reality (valid) in other political and cultural contexts' (Peters 1998). But the centrality given here to US-inspired models is due to the emergence of RIA in that country. Consequently, an examination of American administrative law is deemed to be the necessary premise for developing an adequate baseline in order to derive other typologies. Indeed, as Peters (1998) put it, if we are to develop meaningful theoretical perspectives in the social sciences, we must examine each national experience in light of the experiences of other nations.

In the remainder of this chapter, Section 3.1 provides a brief overview of the American administrative state and argues for an institutional-based analytical framework. Successively, Section 3.2 defines RIA as a hierarchical procedure and proposes two dimensions for capturing the evolution of American regulatory process. Section 3.3 provides a property space for comparing RIA across different administrative governance systems. Section 3.4 shows that, across a sample of pioneer countries, the process of institutionalising RIA shares the common feature of becoming a mechanism for regulatory oversight. Section 3.5 concludes by summarising the main contributions of the interaction between attributes of innovation and organisational features in the analysis of diffusion.

3.1 Delegation and oversight mechanisms

With the aim of lowering the transaction costs of policy making, rational elected officials delegate because they lack the technical expertise that bureaucrats typically acquire through executing programmes. Furthermore, elected officials usually lack the time and financial resources for designing and realising public interventions. By reconstructing the delegation relationship between the political principal and the administrative agency, P-A theorists have modelled just such a dominant position of bureaucracy by relying on the economic concept of information asymmetry. Information asymmetry causes two types of problem for the political principal: 'adverse selection' concerns the political principal's insufficient information to choose the agent with the greatest expertise and with preferences closest to their own; and 'moral hazard' refers to the principal's incapacity to directly observe the agent's action. Thus, the level of effort that the agent engages in in pursuing the principal's interest cannot be determined. Rather, the agent may pursue the maximisation of his/her own budget and assure rents for private corporates. The elected officials, however, can attempt to minimise the costs of an agent's misbehaviour by designing institutions that modify the bureaucrats' incentive structure. Administrative rules and procedures are the most relevant for controlling bureaucratic policy-making and actions.

Indeed, in the US, administrative law refers to the 'procedural law of administrative process' concerning 'any practice that affects or is affected by government decision makers other than just the courts' (Koch 1997). This configuration of administrative law as a procedure coincided with the New Deal era in which the expansion of public intervention entailed the control of legislative power delegated by Congress to administrative agencies (Stewart 1975). With the enactment of the 1946 APA, administrative law has assumed a predominant role in the development of regulatory governance (Pierce *et al.* 2004).

After more than sixty years, '[t]he APA and its related statutes continues to provide an organizing vehicle for government intervention into private sector activities' (Pierce *et al.* 2004). In other words, the APA is the 'constitution of the modern regulatory state' (Croley 1996). Complying with the following four fundamental rules, the administrative rulemaking procedure allows the delegation of legislative power to agencies, within a respectful consideration of the constitutional principle of rule of law and separation of powers (Stewart 1975):

- administrative action must be determined by a precise mandate
- agencies' procedural decisions must comply with the authoritative legislation
- judicial review must be available to review agencies' actions
- agencies must facilitate judicial review

Within classical and liberal democratic theory, the American administrative and legal discussion focuses on whether the administrative system complies with these four rules. Indeed, more often than not, the American Congress delegates broader authority to agencies via vague and ambiguous statutes. Further, executive agencies are allowed to pursue 'negotiated rulemaking', an informal method which minimises judicial review (Pierce *et al.* 2004). As a result, the actual American administrative state is not totally consistent with the classical democratic model. These inconsistencies have facilitated the emergence of alternative administrative models such as: economic rationality, the neo-pluralist and the civic republican (*see* Section 2.2).

One can observe that the P-A model is founded on institutional checks and balances that aim to reduce the discretion of the bureaucracy and, ultimately, pursue accountability, within classical and liberal democratic theory. When it comes to establishing an analytical and comparative framework, institution-centred models have two enormous advantages. Firstly, it is easier and more feasible to compare stable administrative institutions and their mechanisms available for controlling and reducing the discretion of bureaucrats than it is to compare political phenomena and emerging pluralistic or deliberative policy tools (Peters 1998). Secondly, because they promote policy effectiveness and avoid bureaucratic arbitrariness, administrative procedures are common in all democracies (Moral Soriano 2002; Rose-Ackerman 2007a). Indeed, delegation and the consequent emergence of the administrative state have been explored by lawyers, sociologists and political scientists, and not only in the US.

The political principal has several options for obtaining information and controlling an agent's behaviour. An extensive literature has proposed different classifications of control mechanisms that have the common feature of attempting to internalise the principal's preferences into the bureaucrats' behaviour, limiting their discretion (Lupia and McCubbins 1994; Ginsburg 2002; Huber 2002). The political science literature identifies two categories of control mechanisms: *ex ante* mechanisms (such as statutory orders, appointments, and organisational and institutional checks) and *ex post* mechanisms (such as budgets, amending legislation and judicially supervised administrative procedure) (Huber 2002; Epstein and O'Halloran 1999; Epstein and O'Halloran 1994). The former group is composed of control mechanisms operating before regulators actually take actions. On the other hand, *ex post* control mechanisms operate after, rather than before, regulators take actions (Huber 2002). This classification, however, does not take into account the more recent evolution of administrative procedure in the US and Europe, where the bureaucratic agent's decisions are subject to a review that can be concurrent with the regulatory proceeding itself (Pierce *et al.* 2004). This is a third and peculiar modality for control of the bureaucracy, an *ongoing* control mechanism.

Looking at their institutional nature, Ginsburg (2002) proposes another three categories of control mechanism for reducing agency costs:

- perfect internalisation of the principal's preference, through professional indoctrination and training or through promulgation of a substantive political ideology
- hierarchical supervision, a *direct* manipulation of the agency's incentive through structures such as budgets, rules, procedures
- third-party supervision, that is, a judicially enforceable administrative procedure, in which the quality-control system of the agent's behaviour is delegated to the courts

Hierarchical and judicial supervision are particularly relevant for the analysis of RIA. Both refer, reshape and discipline the decisional criteria and process of an administrative agency and are common functions of appraisal systems such as EIA and RIA (Taylor 1984; McGarity 1991). But it is still necessary to understand in which category RIA falls. To do so, we need to recall the definition and functions of RIA through a brief exploration of American administrative rulemaking, within which RIA emerged.

3.2 RIA within the American administrative state

The main purpose of policy appraisal is to counterbalance informational asymmetries between the political principal and the bureaucratic agent, thereby preventing administrative drift (McCubbins *et al.* 1987; Bawn 1997). It follows that several economic methods and appraisal techniques have been used by American Presidents and Congress for overseeing and reducing the slack between them and bureaucratic agencies when the latter have a legislative function (Cohen and Strauss 1995; Posner 2001; Johnston 2002; Pierce *et al.* 2004).[1] In the case of RIA, since Nixon, every President has required agencies to submit a CBA to the Office for Information and Regulatory Affairs (OIRA). This agency of the Office for Management and Budget (OMB) has been specifically established for overseeing the regulatory process of executive agencies.

Presidential control is justified by the idea of getting better coordination and more efficiency from the administrative state. Overall and broader policy goals, such as a clean environment, low inflation or economic growth, are horizontal and cannot be achieved by one agency in isolation (Harter 1987; Kagan 2001). For the unitary doctrine, the President, as the head of the executive branch, has the duty to coordinate and oversee the government agencies, steering them towards the political goals for which he was elected (Shane 1995; Blumstein 2001). To do so, within the same hierarchy and institution (the American executive) the President enacts an executive order (EO) to directly influence the agency's incentive structure through the promulgation of internal rules that constrain administrative discretion. Accordingly, the American RIA is an ongoing regulatory review falling under Ginsburg's category of hierarchical supervision. Indeed, there are no parties involved in the American RIA administrative procedure other than the President, through his largest executive office, the OMB/OIRA, and his executive agencies. Presidential oversight does not, though, address independent agencies such as the Federal Communications Commission, Federal Trade Commission or the Federal Reserve.

However, the APA delineates a broader control mechanism that, involving public participation and judicial review, still legitimises regulatory delegation. As a fire-alarm mechanism activated by the main stakeholders, this Act alerts the political principal to the regulators' misbehaviour (Lupia and McCubbins 1994; McNollgast 1999), and has solved the constitutional puzzle of legislative delegation to agencies (Rosenbloom 2000; Rosenbloom 2002). Given the centrality of the APA in the American administrative state, all ongoing Presidential and Congressional regulatory reviews are additional and innovative steps of administrative rulemaking that were not originally required by the APA (Lubbers 1998; Rosenbloom 2002;

---

1. Congress has passed several acts that require agencies to provide an analysis of the specific impacts on information obligations (the Paper Reduction Act) and on small business enterprise (the Regulatory Flexibility Act). It is important to note that during the Clinton administration the Congress initiative, the so-called Regulatory Review Act, to extend CBA to the legislative process did not have enough support to be enacted.

Kerwin 2003). Ongoing control mechanisms such as RIA shape the rulemaking which is dynamic and has evolved according to administrative state modifications and regulatory reform in the US, accommodating changes in political goals and ideologies (Croley 1996). With the aim of reducing the President's information asymmetry, RIA has to be considered a hierarchical procedure that cannot be analysed in isolation from the administrative requirement for notice-and-comment and *ex post* judicial review established by the APA.

Table 3.1 presents the two dimensions for classifying American regulatory process: the presence of RIA as the hierarchical oversight and the presence of judicial review. The evolution of the American administrative state can be represented by shifts across the 'property space', composed of cells which capture 'a possible grouping of the attributes of the concepts being organized' (Elman 2005). In this case I rely on the property space as a systematic way to deductively combine the descriptive and classificatory features, expressed in dichotomous fashion (presence/absence), rather than to predict outcomes of the dependent variable and develop and test more precise hypotheses (Elman 2005).

Table 3.1: The evolution of American regulatory process as the interaction of RIA and judicial review

		Ex post judicial review	
		YES	**NO**
Hierarchical ongoing oversight	**YES**	RIA within a judicially enforceable administrative procedure	RIA without APA-type fire-alarm mechanism
	NO	The pre-RIA era	The pre-APA era

The pre-administrative state era was characterised by Congress being staffed by professional technocrats and experts on policy implementation, able to instruct agencies through precise and accurate statutes. In addition, courts safeguarded the fealty to statutory commands (Bignami 2001). With rulemaking and the enactment of the APA, the pre-RIA era was characterised by notice-and-comment requirements and the absence of hierarchical control (Pildes and Sunstein 1995; Coglianese 2002). At that time, federal agencies were in search of legitimacy and more often than not independently and voluntarily conducted economic analysis to support their decisions (Andrews 1984). Since the beginning of 1970s, economic analysis became a specific requirement of the President. It seems fair to conclude that the proposed property space can capture the longitudinal changes in American regulatory process. It also allows for the alternative scenario: the adoption of an ongoing control mechanism without administrative legislation on either public participation or judicial review of regulatory process. The next section shows that the latter case is common in many of the countries which adopted RIA.

3.3 RIA within other administrative systems

Based on the administrative law and categories of control mechanisms, the previous section has portrayed American regulatory process through a property space. In order to compare RIA systems implemented in other countries' administrative traditions, it is necessary to assess whether the category characterised by the exclusive presence of *ex post* judicial oversight still holds.[2] Among OECD countries, a judicially enforceable participatory regulatory process, as in the US, is found in Korea, Mexico and a few other parliamentary countries such as Australia and the Czech Republic (Jensen and McGrath 2010). In Korea, RIA is an integral part of the APA.[3] Therefore, in that country RIA is strongly based on a formal legal framework that is as broad as the American APA in regulating the regulators (OECD 2000; Ginsburg 2002).

Notwithstanding the spread of legislation to govern administrative procedure,[4] judicial review of the delegated legislation process is not a feature of parliamentary systems (Jensen and McGrath 2010). In other words,

> [t]he United States is unusual in having an Administrative Procedure Act that requires notice, hearings, and reason giving for rules and that permits judicial review of the rulemaking process. In Europe, most governments are not required to use popular, participatory procedures for the issuance of government rules and guidelines. (Rose-Ackerman 2007b)

The peculiarity of the American administrative rulemaking process stands in contrast to other countries' modes of reviewing the delegated legislation process in other countries in order to ensure the constitutional principle of separation of power. Accordingly, it is necessary to 'expand' the property space used for categorising the American regulatory process. Rather than judicial review as a fire-alarm mechanism, one can hypothesise the existence of a set of different constitutional powers that intervene in correcting a misuse in regulatory delegation. For instance, in the other common law countries the review of delegated legislation is conducted by parliament (*see* Table 3.2).

In the UK, as well as in other Commonwealth tradition countries, in order to ensure the separation of power and parliamentary supremacy on legislation, delegated legislations are scrutinised directly by parliament, as established by the

---

2. In an important case, the INS v Chadha, 462 U.S. 919 (1983), the Supreme Court declared unconstitutional the Congressional veto on the basis of the doctrine concerning separation of powers. As a result, once a regulatory agency has passed a regulation, only the courts can intervene to correct any invalid behaviour.

3. The 1997 Basic Act on Administrative Regulations contains requirements such as RIA and a sunset clause that makes Korean regulatory process among the most comprehensive and advanced (OECD 2000; Ginsburg 2002; Baum and Bawn 2005; Baum 2007; OECD 2007a).

4. Most of the OECD member states have adopted an administrative procedure law, usually applied to the adjudicative function of the administration.

1946 Statutory Instrument Act.[5] The Joint Committee on Statutory Instruments and the Commons Select Committee on Statutory Instruments are in charge of formally controlling for technical and procedural defects.[6] Another important parliamentary review is conducted by the House of Lords' Select Committee on the Merits of Statutory Instruments, which examines any statutory instruments or regulations that are subject to parliamentary procedure (Page 2010).[7] In order to facilitate this parliamentary scrutiny, the government has agreed to supply an explanatory memorandum for all delegated legislation. Within this context, the role played by governmental RIA is marginal (Page 2001).

Overall, in the UK, RIA, which is applied also to government bills,[8] is a 'policy' within the executive hierarchy, and, traditionally, consultation with the business sector is embedded within it (Froud *et al.* 1998). This consultation is a practice that 'is both assumed and assured' (Vogel 1986). It is possible to generalise this consideration to other common law and European countries that 'still rely on a more informal and "confidential" process of consultation where the bureaucrats mediate and bargain among conflicting interests' (Brickman *et al.* 1985; *see also* Rose-Ackerman 2007b).

In comparison with the UK, although parliamentary scrutiny of delegated legislation was established in the early 1970s during the Trudeau administration, the Canadian RIA system has had a greater impact on the delegated legislation process. RIA has been introduced within their Federal Government Regulatory Policy requiring federal departments to draft and publish a CBA – together with a regulatory proposal – in the Canada Gazette. In 1986, these general principles on regulatory governance were codified in the Citizens' Code of Regulatory Fairness, which seeks 'to authorize the courts to protect a set of fundamental civil liberties

---

5. As in the US, judicial review ensures the lawful exercise of the power given to the executive by an Act of Parliament by providing to an individual, or body of persons who is/are aggrieved by an administrative decision, and their rights adversely affected, the right to challenge this decision in the courts. However, the judicial review of regulatory process is limited in order to ensure that there has been no breach of statutory requirements, rather than procedural correctness. For instance, in the UK the courts seek, by judicial review, to ensure the following four principal objectives:
   - that the exercise of power by a public body does not violate human rights
   - that Acts of Parliament have been correctly interpreted
   - that discretion conferred by statute has been lawfully exercised
   - that the decision maker has acted fairly

6. Judgement on the merits of or policy behind the regulatory choice is excluded from parliamentary scrutiny.

7. In particular, through its reports, the Committee draws to the 'special attention of the House' any statutory instrument laid in the previous week which it considers may be interesting, inappropriate in view of changed circumstances since the enactment of a legislation framework, inappropriate in implementing EU legislation, or imperfect in achieving its policy objectives. According to its terms of reference, the Committee reviews in 'neutral terms' the policy intention and aims of regulatory proposals by reporting their deficiency and proposing questions which parliament may wish to pursue (Page 2001).

8. This is another difference between the US Presidential regulatory oversight and RIA enacted by parliamentary systems.

Table 3.2: An expanded property space of modes of regulatory review

		Ex post review of regulatory process		
	Judicial review	Parliamentary scrutiny	Council of state	Minimal
RIA as an ongoing hierarchical oversight	Australia Czech Republic US	Canada UK	Netherlands	Germany
RIA as a judicially enforceable oversight process	Korea		France Italy	

from the laws and actions of public sector agencies and officials by scrutinizing and limiting their actions' (Prince 1999). Thus, similarly to the American notice-and-comment procedure, the Canadian regulatory policy allows public participation. However, although open and transparent, the Canadian regulatory process 'is non-statutory, based on government policy, and supplements statutory requirements' (Elliott 2003). Further, it is doubtful whether the Charter has made an impact on regulatory process in either procedural or substantive terms (Prince 1999). The Canadian regulatory process, as a matter of fact, is still reviewed by parliamentary committees responsible for ensuring executive accountability (Weir 1997).

The separation of power and the rule of law are not exclusive constitutional doctrines of common law countries. They are the founding principles of the constitutions of many Western and civil law countries (Schwartz 2006; Singh 2001). However, looking at constitutional history, a substantial difference can be noted:

Anglo-American constitutional history is a record of attempts by legislature and courts to restrain excess by the executive branch. French constitutional theory, on the other hand, has been influenced by the memory of constant obstruction of the executive branch by the *Parliaments*—the common-law courts of appeal under the *Ancien Régime*. (Schwartz 2006)

These different historical patterns have led to different modes of judicial review. In France, as well as in other civil law countries, judicial review is conducted by a separate, specialised and – only with the evolution of the administrative state – *de facto* independent administrative court, the Council of State (Schwartz 2006). Although there is convergence towards similar administrative principles (Chiti 2004), the different historical patterns are still affecting the extent of judicial review, which is not as broad as it is in common law countries. Furthermore, under the doctrine of Acts of Government, the French Constitution of 1946 empowers the executive with an inherent power to enact regulation that goes beyond legislative delegation (Schwartz 2006).

The combination of different historical constitutional patterns, doctrines and distribution of authorities among constitutional institutions has led to a complementary *advising* role of the Council of State on regulatory proposals.[9] Indeed, in France, part of the regulatory process involves a hearing before the Council of State, in which a report (resulting from a previous meeting between a rapporteur from the Council of State and ministerial regulators) on a regulatory proposal is tabled. This advisory role of the judiciary is common in other civil law countries (for instance, Italy and the Netherlands) and is directly inspired by the French administrative model in which the Council of State has a relevant position in the regulatory process and must be consulted on all draft laws and many decrees[10] in order to assess their legal quality, consistency and administrative appropriateness.

At the end of the 2000s, the French Executive and Parliament extensively reformed the legal basis for RIA.[11] Within the constitutional amendment for disciplining the relationships between the executive and parliament, legal quality requirements were set. Specifically, the constitutional law of 23 July 2008 requires the conformity of draft laws with the condition laid down by the framework act, Organic Law No. 2009–403, of 15 April 2009. The latter stipulates that draft law provisions under which the executive asks parliament for authority to take certain measures by way of orders are subject to the obligation to produce prior evaluations of their economic, financial, employment relations and environmental consequences (OECD 2010b).[12] IA documents are appended and support legislative proposals and are tabled to the Council of State and parliament. The Organic Law also qualitatively details the contents of IA which, based on CBA, shall cover the objectives pursued by the bill, other possible options and the justification for new legislation. Accordingly, parliament and the Council of State are now entitled to assess the appropriateness and expediency of government legislative proposals by drawing up an assessment of the advantages and disadvantages of the legislation (OECD 2010b).

A legislative-based RIA system is also present in Italy where the Administrative and Regulatory Simplification Law 55 of 1999 requires ministries to conduct RIA on bills and regulatory proposals, providing the potential for review by the

---

9. 'Though the government does not have to follow the advice of the *Conseil d'État* it can only adopt either the original text or the text proposed by the *Conseil*, and the risk of legal challenge is high if it ignores the *Conseil's* advice, as the *Conseil* is also the legal appeal body where decrees and administrative actions can be challenged' (OECD 2004a).

10. In France, legislative acts often require that 'certain decrees which are necessary to their implementation, will be taken according to the Council of State, in order to better guarantee their legal quality' (OECD 2010b).

11. This reform considerably changed the previous French RIA system. Established in the mid-1990s through a *Circulaire*, a sort of Presidential executive order, the latter was a hierarchical administrative procedure with a marginal impact on other constitutional bodies.

12. There is no constitutional obligation to assess other legislative proposals, such as parliament-initiated draft legislation, draft constitutional legislation, finance scheduling legislation or draft decrees.

administrative court in cases of non-compliance. However, the Italian system has not triggered any substantial impact on the relationship between the executive and the other constitutional institutions within the regulatory process. By contrast, the Dutch RIA system has been established through a within-the-executive provision. It is composed of a series of tests of the environmental and economic impacts of proposed regulation, as well as a more specific assessment of administrative burden.[13] This fragmentation is also reflected in different guidelines set within the Prime Minister's directives on regulation which are defined as a:

> 'draftman's handbook' dealing with every important activity within the legislative issues e.g. how to prepare a draft, how to implement European legislation, what kind of legislative instruments to use, how to delegate legislative powers, how to attribute administrative authority, what kind of quality considerations are to be made, etc. (Voermans 2003)

Looking at the administrative and legislative contexts, there is a huge difference between the Dutch and the American RIA. The Dutch RIA has been entrenched within a regulatory process established by the Prime Minister's directives, which collectively form a 'handbook'; in the US the regulatory process is enacted by the APA, and considered as the constitution of the regulatory state.

Finally, moving on to the last column of Table 3.2, in Germany the review of regulatory process is minimal, notwithstanding the fact that the administrative courts are fully integrated in the judiciary and totally independent (Singh 2001). Contrasting the general purpose of German administrative law with the American one, Kagan[14] argues that:

> [t]he prescriptiveness of American statutes and regulations reflects politicians' and interest groups' desire to control regulatory agencies that they do not fully trust; the rules are designed to prevent the agency's 'capture' by regulated entities or, on the other hand, by regulatory zealots, and to facilitate judicial review that will check unwarranted administrative regulations. In Germany, in contrast, the detail of federal environmental regulations is designed to provide guidance to the state and local officials who are responsible for implementing federal law, and to *shield* regulatory administrators from judicial interference. (Kagan 2001)

Also, according to a comparativist lawyer, the main purpose of German administrative law is functional. It is:

> [...] not an isolated body of rules and regulations concerning the operation of the administration; it is concerned about the ordering of the society for the goals it sets forth itself. For this reason not merely control but also effectiveness and efficiency of the administration are important. (Singh 2001)

---

13. I thank Prof. Wim Voermans, who explained this to me during an interview held at the University of Exeter in November 2006 in the context of the ESRC project 'Regulatory Quality in Comparative Perspective'.

14. Quoting Kelemen (1998).

This difference in the overall scope of administrative law is ultimately reflected in the regulatory process. Germany has no general law for delegated legislation and there is no tradition or practice of prior consultation of the affected interests or subsequent scrutiny through procedure or through a parliamentary committee. (Singh 2001)

3.4 Institutionalisation of RIA as an oversight mechanism

The different attributes of RIA are also reflected in the variance in choices for the institutional design and economic methodology of regulatory oversight. Focusing on Australia, Canada, Denmark, Germany, the Netherlands, the UK and the US, and through a simple operationalisation based on the three reasons for adopting RIA (its functionalist logic), this section provides a qualitative and longitudinal analysis of this institutional variance.

Economic rationality and the wide application of the principles of welfare economics (Markoff and Montecinos 1993) can provide support if regulators are required to avoid failures (Howlett and Ramesh 2003). Once the need – in the case of market failures – and the efficacy – if a government has the capacity to correct, to supplement or replace the market (Stokey and Zeckhauser 1978; Vining and Weimer 1990) – of a regulatory intervention has been established, CBA is an essential technique for selecting the most efficient policy option (Arrow *et al.* 1996a; Arrow *et al.* 1996b; Howlett and Ramesh 2003).

Although regulatory legitimacy and accountability are not exclusive to RIA (Freedman 1978; Landy *et al.* 1994), this policy appraisal system is an analytic decision framework and communication device, capable of disciplining regulators and preventing the usurpation of their power. In other words, RIA is an opportunity for regulators to establish 'a formal analytic mechanism or set of conventions to collect, organize, summarize, and present information about alternative sets of outcomes to decision makers and the public' (Russell 1990). Shaping the concepts of legitimacy and accountability is a difficult enterprise. However, a solution is to refer to the undisguised principle that legitimacy can be achieved only when the bases of decisions are made explicit and open so that citizens can choose to exercise some oversight. Accordingly, the focus is on a subset of conditions for legitimacy and accountability, that is, transparency, and, specifically, an administrative requirement for publishing RIAs in some sort of official journal.[15] This requirement can be considered a benchmark of the institutionalisation of RIA as a transparent process, allowing the participation of affected parties as well as the general public.

The last reason considered for using RIA is the centralisation of control over regulators. The history of the American administrative system shows that presidents

---

15. Publishing is an essential element of public participation. It is a precondition for developing public participation through the collection of information and interaction. 'The quality of information collected and the level of appreciation of the policy process by citizens will be proportional to the amount of publicising' (Carley 1980).

have always struggled to assert a more centralised control over regulatory agencies (McDonald 1994; Pildes and Sunstein 1995). After an initial period of a light-touch form of institutionalisation aimed at enhancing coordination among executive agencies, a clear mandate was issued by President Reagan to establish a central unit, the OIRA, within the President's OMB, empowered to return regulatory proposals which were not satisfactory in terms of the quality of their economic analysis or which did not conform to the decisional criteria established by the general presidential regulatory policy. The presence of a central unit and its power to return a poorly assessed regulatory proposal are the variables concerning the extent of political control.

Table 3.3 clearly shows two different patterns of emergence, although the generalised absence of a substantial control mechanism and the lack of public disclosure and transparency (apart from Canada) must be borne in mind. Australia, Canada and the US have a similar pattern of emergence, with the choice of CBA and the establishment of a central unit. In the US, during the Nixon administration, a memorandum by the OMB Director, George Schultz, required all regulatory proposals of the newly created Environmental Protection Agency (EPA) and Occupational Safety and the Health Administration (OSHA) to be reviewed in an interagency coordination process, the so-called 'Quality of Life' review.[16] The agencies were required to prepare and submit to the OMB a summary of the benefits and costs of each proposed regulation and its alternatives (McGarity 1991). In Canada, the government required a 'socio-economic impact analysis' of the major social regulations for which regulatory costs were estimated to be over $10 million. The Canadian Treasury Board Secretariat (TBS) also demanded that departments publish a summary of the analyses in the Canada Gazette (Stanbury and Thompson 1982). The Australian RIA was introduced on a non-mandatory basis in 1986 and publication was not required.[17] As a result, 'ministers and regulatory departments/agencies routinely eschewed preparation of [a] Regulatory Impact Statement (RIS)' (Argy and Johnson 2003). Notwithstanding this non-mandatory basis, a regulatory oversight body was established when RIS was adopted (Argy and Johnson 2003). The methodology has always been CBA.

The European countries (in particular, Germany and the Netherlands) are characterised by a lean adoption. The regulatory appraisal system relies on checklists aimed at increasing awareness of issues affecting regulatory quality, a limited approach to rationality applied to problem solving. Further, coordination among regulators is not enhanced through the establishment of a central unit. In particular, together with the 'Joint Rule of Procedure' for the German federal ministries, the 'Blue Checklist', endorsed by the Cabinet in 1984, was intended

---

16. Under the Nixon, Ford and Carter administrations, the role of the central body 'was principally technical, consultative, and advisory' and the regulatory review was designed 'to increase interagency dialogue, coordination, and analytical precision' (Sunstein 1996).

17. As attested by the OECD database on formal policies of regulatory reform. Available at: http://www.oecd.org/dataoecd/48/13/1910817.pdf (accessed 1 March 2006).

Table 3.3: Patterns of emergence and institutionalisation of RIA

Country	Year	CBA	Publication on official journal	Central Unit[a]	Substantial review (power to return a regulatory proposal)
At the time of adoption					
US	1971	Yes	No	Yes	No
Australia	1985	Yes	No	Yes	No
Canada	1978	Yes	Yes	Yes	No
Denmark	1993	No	No	Yes	No
UK	1985	No	No	Yes	No
Germany	1985	No	No	No (1999)	No
Netherlands	1985	No	No	No (1989)	No
Actual institutionalisation of RIA					
US		Yes	Yes	Yes	Yes
Australia		Yes	No (b)	Yes	Yes
Canada		Yes	Yes	Yes	Yes
UK		Yes	No (c)	Yes	Yes
Denmark		No	No (d)	Yes	Yes (e)
Germany		No	No (f)	Yes	Yes (g)
Netherlands		No	No (h)	Yes	Yes (i)

[a] The year of establishment of the central unit is specified if it is subsequent to the adoption.
[b] There is, however, a single internet portal collecting all RISs.
[c] There is, however, a single internet portal collecting all RIAs.
[d] Public hearings and notice for comment on regulatory proposals are now publicised through dedicated websites such as the Consultation Portal (OECD 2010c: 62).
[e] But only on the part of RIA concerned with administrative burdens.
[f] Although the 2000 revised Joint Rules of Procedure stipulate that draft bills must include an explanatory memorandum (which should include an RIA) and an introductory summary sheet that are published on the internet.
[g] But only on the part of RIA concerning administrative burden.
[h] Although RIA supports the drafting of the explanatory memorandum.
[i] But only on the part of RIA concerning administrative burden.

to discipline the regulatory process,[18] but compliance with the guideline was not monitored or sanctioned. Similarly, in the Netherlands, a prime ministerial directive defined regulatory quality and the process for assuring the necessity, lawfulness, proportionality, legislative coherence, assessment of administrative burden and effectiveness of new legislation. The directive was the result of the work conducted by the Ministry of Justice for achieving a simplified regulatory environment, but the Ministry was not entitled to oversee the regulatory process.

Denmark and the UK, by contrast, immediately established a central unit for regulatory reform in order to enhance coordination among regulatory departments. The Thatcher Government, in adopting compliance cost assessment, set up the Enterprise and Deregulation Unit within the Department of Trade and Industry. However, 'the central Enterprise and Deregulation Unit which coordinated and supervised the exercise was given no power to review the substance of regulatory proposals' (Froud et al. 1998). Similarly, in Denmark, the main focus of the regulatory appraisal system was intra-governmental consultation on the likely economic and environmental effects of legislative proposals. In 1994, the government drafted guidelines for business impact assessments and created a committee of representatives of business and of the financial/economic ministries to monitor the aggregate impact of new legislation on competitiveness. The Danish RIA system was (and still is) composed of sectoral impact assessments on environmental and financial sustainability, as well as on business and public sector administrative burdens.

Turning to the actual stage of institutionalisation, the lower part of Table 3.3 shows that all pioneering countries have modified and strengthened their RIA institutions. There has been almost complete institutionalisation among the Anglo-Saxon countries that were eventually able to unify all three reasons for, and themes of, regulatory reform. Similarly, the Continental European countries have progressed towards a more substantial oversight of the regulatory process.

In the US, RIA has been confirmed (Pildes and Sunstein 1995) and institutionalised through the OIRA by successive presidents (Blumstein 2001; West 2004). In particular, President Reagan's EO 12,291 transformed the 'coordinating' appraisal strategy into an instrument for centralising the regulatory

---

18. Introducing 'a broad set of issues for regulators to consider when preparing new federal legislation' (OECD 2004b), the checklist comprised the following questions:
    - Is action at all necessary?
    - What are the alternatives?
    - Is action required at the federal level?
    - Is a new law needed?
    - Is immediate action required?
    - Does the scope of the provision need to be as wide as intended?
    - Can the length of the period for which it is to remain in force be limited?
    - Is the provision unbureaucratic and intelligible?
    - Is the provision practicable?
    - Is there an acceptable cost–benefit relationship?

relief efforts: 'Unlike its predecessors, EO 12,291 was intended to impose substantive restrictions on agency rulemaking as well as analytical requirements' (McGarity, 1991).[19] The same EO has strengthened the APA requirement guaranteeing regulatory transparency. Indeed, since 1981, the Federal Register has been detailing economic impacts at the stage of notice-and-comment and final rule publication, ameliorating the citizens' right to participate in the rulemaking procedure.

After a slow start and an almost ineffective implementation of socio-economic analysis, the Canadian Government, supported by various evaluation studies and an analysis of the American experience, enacted ten principles of regulatory quality (Stanbury and Thompson 1982). Since 1986, a regulatory impact analysis statement (RIAS) has been required for every proposal that has an economic impact and its pre-publication in the official journal was made compulsory (OECD 2002b). More recently, the Cabinet Directive on Streamlining Regulation clearly gave the TBS responsibility for ensuring analyses are consistent with the government's overall regulatory policy and coherent with existing policies as well as the government's policy agenda. In order to do so, the TBS 'is expected to review regulatory proposals, challenge departments and agencies on the quality of regulatory analyses, and advise them when the directions set out in the Directive have not been met' (Government of Canada 2007).

In Australia, it was not until 1997 that the administrative requirements within the regulatory process were strengthened and RIS made mandatory. The central unit, the so-called Office of Best Practice Regulation (OBPR) within the Department of Finance and Deregulation, has become a watchdog of the government's regulatory policy,[20] advising regulators on how to enhance the quality of their proposals. In 2010, the Australian Government strengthened the requirement (empowering the OBPR to oversee the regulatory process of ministries) by deciding whether a RIS is necessary, certifying the adequacy of analysis and drafting a one-page summary of the RIS for cabinet ministers. The Australian Government has agreed that a regulatory proposal likely to have an impact on business or the not-for-profit sector cannot proceed to the cabinet or other decision makers unless it has complied with the government's RIA requirements (Australian Government 2010). There is still no requirement to publish RIS in the official journal. However, RIS and the OBPR's adequacy assessment are now published on the oversight body's website.

In the UK, ten years after the adoption RIA, the Blair Government legitimised the regulatory appraisal system through CBA and joined the cluster of countries with more sophisticated regulatory governance. Further, the central unit set up since the early days of the CCA has been flanked by independent bodies, such as

---

19. The burden of proving the efficiency of a regulatory proposal shifted from the central unit to the executive agencies (McGarity 1991). The OMB could (and can) return a regulatory proposal to an executive agency if the accompanying economic appraisal is considered to be of poor quality.

20. The OBPR replaced the Productivity Commission as the body in charge of regulatory oversight. The latter is an independent and advisory body that has a role in reporting to the government on the overall quality of the regulatory environment.

the Better Regulation Task Force, recently re-labelled the Risk and Regulation Advisory Council, with the Small Business Unit now abolished.[21] The regulatory process has been modified since the introduction of an additional phase for monitoring the quality of regulatory proposals and analysis.

> All regulatory proposals likely to impose a major new burden on business require clearance from the Panel for Regulatory Accountability. [...] The Panel's consideration is based on a thorough RIA for the proposal being agreed by the Cabinet Office, before the proposal can be put to wider ministerial approval. (Cabinet Office 2006)

The publication of RIAs is limited to departments' websites. The central unit for RIA, now established within the Department for Business, Innovation and Skills, is also running an internet portal collecting RIAs. The government has recently drafted a regulators' compliance code based on the 2005 Hampton Report on administrative burdens and enforcement principles (such as: businesses should not have to give unnecessary information or give the same piece of information twice and regulators should use comprehensive risk assessment).

The other European cluster has clearly strengthened the control of the regulatory process through the parallel diffusion of the target to reduce the administrative burden by 25 per cent and the standard cost model (SCM). The latter is a Dutch regulatory appraisal model, a formula for quantifying the total cost borne by businesses for communicating with the public administration. The SCM is expressed as a formula comprising the multiplication of the numerical estimates of three factors: the number of businesses affected; the frequency of provision of information; and the cost of producing and transmitting the information required.[22]

In Germany, the Blue Checklist became mandatory in 1996 with a substantial revision of the joint rules of procedure for federal ministries (OECD 2004b). A further revision was necessary in order to demand that a summary of RIA be included within the explanatory memorandum. The memorandum, however, is not published in the official journal but on the internet as an accompanying documentation of bills approved by the federal cabinet and forwarded to the *Bundestag*. The current RIA system is based upon three types of analysis of intended and unintended consequences, namely, preliminary, concurrent and retrospective, that are performed at different stages of the regulatory process

---

21. With the creation of ACTAL, the establishment of independent task forces is also a trend observed in the Netherlands.

22. The cost of an information obligation is calculated by the hourly labour cost and the time spent dealing with a specific information obligation per regulation. The guidelines provide several suggestions on how the data might be gathered. For example, hourly labour costs can be determined from wage statistics, which can be validated in business interviews. Time can be estimated through business surveys. Alternatively, an objective method can be used, the so-called 'stopwatch method', in which time is actually quantified by a simulation of an administrative action (Legislative Burden Department 2003).

(OECD 2010d). Within a sustainable development framework, the ministries are called upon to 'describe' the economic, environmental and social impacts of the proposed legislations (OECD 2010d). Germany has adopted a strategy to reduce administrative burdens on business, as have the other European countries. That, however, has triggered the reform of the institutional framework of regulatory process. Two recently established institutions are now in charge of the RIA process: the Better Regulation Unit in the federal chancellery and an independent advisory body, the National Regulatory Control Council (NRCC). Both institutions support the federal programme to reduce the administrative burden on business. In particular, the NRCC functions as a gatekeeper in the federal law-making process: draft bills cannot be tabled before the Cabinet without first undergoing scrutiny by the NRCC, which, in a relatively short time, has become a well legitimated agency of regulatory governance. Since its opinions are published, ministries tend to follow its recommendations (OECD 2010d).

A similar pattern of institutionalisation has been pursued by the Danish and Dutch Governments through the empowerment of the ministries of finance as well as stringent measures to control the production of new regulations. Each ministry is now required to comply with a ceiling on administrative burden. This is a strong incentive to prevent additional administrative burdens because any increase in burden must be compensated for elsewhere.

Overall, this qualitative evidence has shown that the common pattern of RIA institutionalisation was (and is) characterised by two phases. In the first phase, RIA was used by the principal to enhance coordination among regulators. Such coordination was also achieved through the establishment of a coordinating unit. In Australia, Denmark, Canada, the UK and the US the establishment of such a body was simultaneous with the adoption of the administrative requirements of RIA. Germany and the Netherlands established central coordinating units well after RIA adoption. European countries also had a different modality to 'reinvent' rationality from that of Australia, Canada and the US, which preferred the welfare economics paradigm and CBA. In the European countries, on the other hand, rationality was conceived of as an analytical improvement of the problem-solving process, relying on a system analysis paradigm. In the second phase, RIA was used by the principal as a tool for controlling the regulators. In this phase there was a relevant change both in the administrative requirements and in the structure of the controlling bodies in order to devise control mechanisms for overseeing regulators.

3.5 Conclusion

The separation of powers is 'not purely a principle but a concept of constituting, allocating and balancing of state power' (Schmidt-Assmann 1998; quoted in Singh 2001). Accordingly, notwithstanding the wider application of the separation-of-powers and the rule-of-law doctrines, the definition, extent and application of the founding principles of an administrative regime vary. There are, indeed, different extents and modalities for balancing this trade-off between bureaucracy's discretion and respect for democratic principles and the control of bureaucracy in order to protect the public interest. For instance, '[i]n Great Britain, excessive delegations of Parliamentary powers are political concerns; in the United States, they are primarily judicial' (Weeks 1937; cited in Schwartz 2006). The practice of judicial review is an almost unique attribute of American regulatory governance. European countries rely on the scrutiny of a parliament or council of state and the absence of a constitution of the regulatory state makes it difficult to apply the pluralist and civil-republican models to European countries.

Within the broader context of administrative law and constitutional principles, the need to hold regulators accountable allows the application of a P-A model for analysing and comparing administrative states and regulatory processes (Bishop 1990). Considering RIA as a hierarchical and direct control mechanism, that is, an administrative procedure usually acting between the political principal and the administrative agent within the executive, this chapter has taken a systematic approach in comparing regulatory oversight and has developed a property space. The matrix includes cases of RIA either as a hierarchical control mechanism within the executive or as a judicially enforceable process, and the institution in charge of reviewing the regulatory process.

Moreover, the qualitative review of the process of emergence and institutionalisation among a sample of pioneer countries has shown that there is not a methodological model of RIA. The latter is instead an administrative principle which requires regulators to report – in a few cases in the official journal – costs or disadvantages and/or benefits or advantages. The empowerment of central units has transformed the coordination principle in a political control mechanism.

Given the absence of a unique model and the lack of evidence confirming policy transfer between the US and most European countries, one may be led to hypothesise a scenario of multiple sources of emergence. The European approach to regulatory governance is closer to a system analysis paradigm. Notwithstanding such differences with the Anglo-Saxon countries, almost all the pioneering European countries have shifted towards the purpose of controlling the regulators. Denmark and the Netherlands have strengthened political control over their regulators, focusing on administrative burden. Reduction targets and a methodology to measure administrative burden were important for this shift. A model for quantifying administrative burdens on business has now been adopted in many follower countries.[23] The reliance on a newer and limited economic paradigm focusing on the administrative burden for business still marks a relevant difference between the European pattern of institutionalisation, which revolves around the SCM and a reliance on internal checklists, with limited transparency and a lack of external control mechanisms, and the American 'cost–benefit state'.

In a diffusion research framework, the proposed typologies of RIA interaction with regulatory review are useful for setting expectations of patterns of diffusion and the extent of implementation, as well as for assessing the impact of RIA on the administrative state, bureaucrats' behaviour and, ultimately, politics. In particular,

---

23. Available Online: http://www.administrative-burdens.com (accessed 1 May 2010).

compatibility with the innovation is more pronounced in common law countries in which the review of regulatory process is conducted by the courts, as in the US, or by the parliament, than in countries with different administrative law traditions. There is a type of country in which regulatory process and its review are marginal since the administrative tradition privileges values of efficacy and efficiency over democratic accountability and political control. In Germany, and more generally in countries with a German legal origin, the adoption of RIA occurs in an administrative context that is not well suited to giving reasons. Finally, in between these two extremes there are countries with a French legal origin in which administrative courts review regulation and provide advice to the executive.

chapter four | framing a transnational policy innovation

This chapter explores the ideational role of the OECD. It gauges the OECD's activities in rearranging RIA into a transnational policy innovation. Indeed, the OECD has reframed the functional logic of RIA and de-emphasised its administrative, political and institutional settings. The argument here is that the 'RIA label', attached to different appraisal systems, and the discourse of economic rationality have formed an appealing strategy for spreading this policy innovation. The OECD has chosen this strategy notwithstanding the fact, as the previous chapter has shown, that there are theoretical and empirical arguments for the political control motive. In addition, the identification of best practice and the formulation of policy recommendations have been based on cases of regulatory reform congruent with the OECD's definition of RIA. This selection bias has resulted in a prototype or template for peer review. More recently, however, there has been a substantial revision of the OECD's organisational discourse on regulatory reform. Acknowledging that the one-size-fits-all approach has been ineffective in implementing RIA, the most recent publications call for the integration of actors, tools and processes into a coherent regulatory policy.

Bearing in mind the features of RIA and the reasons for its adoption, this chapter analyses the OECD's activities in producing discourses (Martens and Jakobi 2010) and developing cognitive interactions (Gehring and Oberthür 2009) among its member states. Data, knowledge, ideas and discourses are produced through semi-academic publications and working papers (Marcussen 2004b) which present the OECD's vision, values and mode of thinking. Publications are essential in order to identify emerging problems and responses, clarify concepts, frame cause-and-effect relationships, set agendas and define guiding principles (Martens and Jakobi 2010). Furthermore, publications translate concepts associated with policy innovations into a more familiar and rationalistic logic of regulatory reform. In other words, the OECD collects information, compares countries and analyses policy solutions, all of which are generalised into common templates and edited into prototypes (Sahlin-Andersson 2001; Sahlin and Wedlin 2010).

This chapter also demonstrates how the OECD's discourse on RIA has been simplified. RIA has been promoted as a decisional tool for evidence-based decision making. The next section analyses how the OECD identified emerging trends in regulatory reform. Section 4.2 remarks on how recommendations and best practice have enhanced the 'legibility' of RIA. Best-selling publications have also created a label for several methods of policy appraisal and a common language within the network of national experts (Section 4.3). Section 4.4 shows that, through an editing process, the administrative setting of RIA was omitted in order that it might also have a standardised peer review process. The latter is described in Section 4.5. Section 4.6 focuses on the recent shift of the OECD's discourse to regulatory policy and governance, and Section 4.7 concludes.

4.1 Regulatory reform trends

The OECD identifies policy innovations and best practices on the basis of international experience. By analysing and comparing different approaches to regulatory reform, the OECD appreciates the pressing issues faced by its member states and recognises emerging trends in policy solutions. The result of research and network activities is typically conveyed in a series of working papers.

Published by Public Management Committee (PUMA) in 1992, the first working paper on regulatory reform was an overview of the OECD member states' concerns, reactions and solutions to the complexity of regulation. The report comprised an introduction to the nature and role of regulation and an extensive section on regulatory issues faced by the OECD countries. The overall goal of the publication was to establish a general programme of work on the basis of a coherent and useful conceptual framework (OECD Public Management 1992). By rejecting the 'legal instrument' perspective for implementing and enforcing policy options, the OECD understood regulation as a set of incentives based on mandated actions and non-compliance sanctions (OECD Public Management 1992). This definition allowed policy makers to assess policy options according to their economic efficiency and cost-effectiveness. The definition of regulatory reform encompassed democratic and economic efficiency principles. Indeed, the review of international experience highlighted that regulatory reforms targeted both the process (in order to enhance accountability, participation and transparency) and the outcome (in order to ensure efficacy and economic efficiency for society as a whole) of regulation. Accordingly, that working paper was structured by sections on management and accountability, efficient allocation of resources, regulatory authorities and processes, and sectoral regulatory reform and deregulation.

Throughout that review there were also clear references to the theory of delegation and the trade-off between bureaucratic discretion and democratic accountability. 'Ongoing central oversights' were deemed to be necessary for improving the information flow from regulators to elected officials by establishing channels for policy direction and, ultimately, balancing competing social goods (OECD Public Management 1992). Feasibility, risk or cost criteria were indicated as the methods with which to limit and justify the use of regulatory authority – criteria that 'define a burden of proof that is expected to be met through analysis before action is taken' (OECD Public Management 1992).

The working paper referred to specific cases of regulatory innovation such as the American and Swedish experiences with measuring regulatory costs, the Australian 'sunset' provisions, which rendered regulation ineffective after a specific date and the German Blue Checklist (*see* Section 3.3). However, the administrative and political context was not provided. Neither was the RIA acronym ever mentioned. The neutral term 'analysis' was used instead. The three reasons for adopting RIA, i.e. reducing excessive quantity and cost of regulations; enhancing the centralisation of regulatory oversight through analytical tools; and strengthening legitimacy through public participation and consultation; were, however, well specified as regulatory reform objectives. Furthermore, the report observed two institutional models for centralising regulatory review. These were that oversight bodies are either centralised within the cabinets of ministries, presidential agencies and prime ministers' departments, or located within ministries (of economics, justice or finance) with responsibility for regulatory reform.

Based on a sound definition of regulation and concepts of democratic accountability and economic efficiency, this first OECD publication on regulatory reform also provided a comprehensive review of the role of the judiciary and the legislature, as well as the relationship between regulators and interest groups. Furthermore, the role of administrative bureaucracy in ensuring regulatory compliance was not neglected (OECD Public Management 1992). Training and oversight were considered to be the incentive to change regulators' behaviour (OECD Public Management 1992).

This research triggered the interest of member states in the use of checklists for improving the regulatory process (OECD Public Management 1992). In 1993, a Canadian consulting company reviewed the regulatory checklists used in Austria, Canada, the European Union (EU), Finland, Germany, Japan, the Netherlands, Spain, Sweden, the UK and the US. Defined as 'broadly applicable instructions or guidelines for the design, development, review, or substantive content of regulation' (OECD Public Management 1993), the report identified four functional categories of regulatory checklists. These functions were:

- to establish a procedural framework for grasping: (i) the need for government intervention; (ii) the preferred option of no regulation; and (iii) the appropriate level of governance
- to assess regulatory costs and benefits as well as the distributional and indirect effects of regulation
- to establish substantive criteria for the exercise of discretion on the basis of appropriateness and respect for the legislative mandate to regulate and procedurally safeguard through administrative procedure acts
- to check the lawfulness of regulatory proposals *vis-à-vis* international norms and agreements

Similarly to the previous working paper, this review of international experience underlined the common trends in member states' responses to the negative impact of regulation on economic performance. A regulatory checklist was defined as a flexible tool in terms of types of legislation to review, the purposes of such legislation and the extent of procedural openness and legitimacy. The report concluded by listing a set of lessons for implementation. As an administrative and control procedure, a regulatory checklist necessitates an appropriate time frame, financial resources, information and analytical expertise, as well as the establishment of a reward and sanction system. These are conditions which affect the scale, pace and costs of reform (OECD Public Management 1993).

Outcome and process framed the first proposal for a 'checklist of regulatory quality techniques' (OECD 1994). Within the OECD's Support for Improvement in Governance and Management (SIGMA) project, practitioners from member countries and the OECD Secretariat developed a checklist along seven dimensions: managing the regulatory system; ensuring public participation; ensuring legal quality; assessing regulatory costs and benefits; assessing compliance; implementation requirements; and communicating and codifying laws. In order to set the core principles of democratic administrative behaviour as well as the transparency and legitimacy of regulation, there were specific recommendations for the adoption of RIA and broader APA rulemaking. The next section shows, however, that the OECD's recommendations and checklist focused exclusively on the economic efficiency of regulation. Further, the quality standards of regulation were integrated with competition and trade policies, rather than with administrative procedures and rulemaking.

4.2 Best practice in regulatory quality

The variance within the international experience of regulatory reform was downplayed in the 1995 recommendation for regulatory quality. The OECD's strategy was to simplify the conceptual framework for regulatory quality. A 'uniform bureaucratic grid' facilitated the 'legibility' of local experiences (Sharman 2012). Principled beliefs stemming from international experience and causal beliefs in the positive relationship between economic growth and regulatory reform were consolidated.[1] The formulation of recommendation and best practice further enhanced legibility, enabling the OECD to promote a selected prototype of reform and strengthen its role as an ideational agency (Marcussen 2004a; Broome and Seabrooke 2012).

Acknowledging the lack of governments' capacity to undertake systematic regulatory reform, the main concern of the OECD was to reduce complexity by proposing best practice. In 1995, the reference checklist for regulatory decision making was approved as a formal recommendation of the Council of the OECD on improving the quality of government regulation (see Appendix B.1). Accordingly, regulation should be efficient, flexible and transparent. All levels of government were urged to pursue these standards and be aware that regulation had an impact on international trade and investment (OECD 1995). The checklist was composed of ten questions, 'a mix of technocratic, procedural and normative principles' (Pal 2012) on regulatory process. The objectives were to enhance the legal and factual basis for regulations, clarify options, establish a more orderly and predictable regulatory process, identify existing regulations that were outdated or unnecessary and make government actions more transparent (OECD 1995). Overall, this recommendation focused on the economic efficiency of regulation. The procedural safeguard to limit bureaucratic discretion was omitted.

---

1. As Marcussen put it, '[p]rinciple beliefs can be anything from visions and good practices to norms for appropriate behaviour, and causal beliefs can range from theories on the one hand, to facts and data on the other' (Marcussen 2004a).

In order to adopt and implement this checklist, further best practice (see Appendix B.2) concerning the regulatory quality system was presented in the two-volume *Report on Regulatory Reform*. Published in May 1997, it was accepted by the national ministers as the peer review standard for monitoring member states' regulatory reform (Carroll and Kellow 2011). This report relied on the belief that regulatory inflation has been an obstacle to economic and social welfare (OECD 1997c). With few references to countries' experiences, the report was nonetheless a coherent narrative of the economic benefits of deregulation and regulatory reform. The ideological elements of regulatory reform were rejected and these reforms were explained as governments' common reaction to external economic pressures, such as oil shocks and technological development. Further, government failures and regulatory capture were also identified as the causes of the obsolescence and ineffectiveness of regulation. Accordingly, regulatory reform was deemed necessary in order to increase productivity, lower prices and boost economic growth.

In the attempt to make regulatory reform more visible and legible, the proposed best practice was a crafted solution which provided an abstract interpretive framework (Broome and Seabrooke 2012; Sharman 2012). The OECD recommended the adoption of good-regulation principles as well as clear and concrete objectives on the basis of the 1995 checklist (Recommendation One). The regulatory process was to be carefully designed, allowing transparent and open consultation of affected parties (Recommendation Three). RIA was the recommended tool for reviewing regulations (Recommendation Two), and, finally, it was decided that regulatory policy should be integrated, such as taxation, employment, health and consumer protection (Recommendation Seven). The recommendations for sectoral reform were related to the need to strengthen competition policy by eliminating exemptions and enacting provisions against collusive behaviour, dominant positions and anticompetitive mergers (Recommendation Four). It was further recommended that competitiveness should be achieved through a strategy that, on the one hand, calls for deregulation of economic regulation restricting firms' freedom to do business, and, on the other, requires more regulation for breaking down abuses of market power (Recommendation Five). Recommendation Six stated that deregulation should also be pursued by eliminating barriers to international trade and investment.

The OECD soon realised that the challenge of comparatively evaluating the quality of competition and trade policies was rejected by member states. Indeed, the domestic political implications of such international standards were considered too significant (Carroll and Kellow 2011). Consequently, the *Report on Regulatory Reform* described specific institutional good practice in 'government capacity to assure high quality regulation' (*see* Appendix B.3). By focusing on the regulatory process, the OECD further attempted to render regulatory reform more neatly. It suggested that a regulatory management system should be designed on the basis of objectives, principles and standards. RIA, consultation, alternatives to regulation, and administrative coordination were the tools for achieving regulatory quality standards. Finally, a systematic review of existing regulations and red tape was also recommended.

Notwithstanding the wide and consensual review of a country's experience, best practice is not the lowest common denominator but, rather, an aspirational standard sometimes provided by the most advanced policy template (Sharman 2012). This is particularly true in the case of RIA. Its set of best practices were presented in a book published by the OECD in the same year (1997) as the regulatory reform report. This was a crucial publication in the development of the OECD's strategy for promoting regulatory reform through policy labels and peer review prototypes.

4.3 RIA as a policy label

The previous chapter as well as the first of the OECD's working papers on regulatory reform evidenced the emergence of two regulatory appraisal systems. On the one hand, common law countries have relied on welfare economics principles; on the other hand, Continental European countries have developed a systems analysis based on procedural checklists. Although the 1995 recommendations on regulatory quality were set on the basis of welfare economics principles such as the justification of regulation on the basis of its costs and benefits, the definition of RIA encompasses different methods (OECD 1997a *see also* Section 1.1).

By putting forward such a pragmatic definition, the OECD posited a general concept rather than a precise and neat model (Weyland 2006) for the adoption of RIA. In doing so, they have strategically chosen to label various techniques under a common and broader heading (Mossberger 2000; Sahlin and Wedlin 2010). Expressed in acronyms which are easy to remember, policy labels facilitate communication about reforms (Sahlin and Wedlin 2010). Moreover, the OECD has created a discourse community of policy makers engaged in disparate policy agendas, such as deregulation, business competitiveness and regulatory credibility and legitimacy (Pollitt 2001, Radaelli 2005b).

Notwithstanding the fact that a loosely bundled, even ambiguous, concept has been applied for a variety of purposes (Mossberger 2000), the common central element of the label has been firmly specified by the OECD: RIA is a method for improving the empirical basis for regulatory decisions (Jacobs 1997). Accordingly, the OECD orientated RIA towards its role in rationalising the regulatory environment. The technological rather than the programmatic or normative component of innovation was preferred in order to bring innovations and reforms to a broader audience of reformers (Sahlin-Andersson 2001; Sahlin and Wedlin 2010). Indeed, in its 1997 book, *Regulatory Impact Analysis: Best Practices in OECD Countries*, the OECD introduced RIA as good routine and practice in policy making. The other reasons for the adoption of RIA and the implications for regulatory process were understated.

Another feature of policy labels is their inherent symbolism (Mossberger 2000). RIA is a referential symbol, a way to name regulatory reform. It represents broader issues on regulation and reduces the information necessary to make sense of regulatory reform. Recommendations have always been centred on RIA. Indeed, it is the only regulatory innovation for which the OECD has drafted specific best practice (*see* Appendix B.4). The 2012 *Recommendation of the Council on Regulatory Policy and Governance* has further strengthened its relevance (see Appendix B.5, Recommendation 4). RIA is also a condensation symbol which communicates intentions and values. It exemplifies governments' association of regulation with poor economic and social performance (OECD 1997c; OECD 2011; OECD 2012). Ineffective regulation is an obstacle to be removed by enhancing the evidence base for regulatory decision making (OECD 1997a; OECD 2009). The symbolic value of RIA has been constantly reconfirmed and reinforced in the organisational discourse of the OECD, especially in its more recent publications (OECD 2006b; OECD 2008a; OECD 2008b; OECD 2009). This has occurred despite the fact that the positive effect of RIA on economic performance is still not proven (Cowen 1995; Radaelli and De Francesco 2010).

Overall, formulating a label for a policy innovation like RIA has produced two effects. Firstly, by merging two different but interdependent concepts of regulatory appraisal, such as CBA and systems analysis, the OECD has increased the compatibility of the innovation with different administrative and institutional settings. The OECD has also enhanced the relative advantage of RIA over other regulatory process innovations. Secondly, the creation of a policy label has created a common and simplified language which has facilitated the circulation of new policy ideas, best practice and templates for regulatory reform (Sahlin-Andersson 2001; Sahlin and Wedlin 2010). Chapter Five examines the extent to which the combination of both effects has promoted the diffusion of RIA.

4.4 Editing RIA contexts

Labelling is a part of the editing process through which the OECD emphasised policy similarities and downplayed the local settings of regulatory reform (Sahlin-Andersson 2001; Sahlin and Wedlin 2010). Whereas the first working papers on regulatory reform explicitly referred to accountability by analysis and regulatory oversight, the successive checklists advocated RIA for its widely accepted, dominant and celebrated values of rationality. Even though RIA labelled different appraisal methods, its legibility has been enhanced by a discourse centred on the need to enlighten and improve the analytical basis for decision making through CBA and welfare economics principles.

The executive summary of *Regulatory Impact Analysis* emphasised economic rationality and administrative transparency. Accordingly, RIA aimed at 'improving the quality and reducing the costs of regulations that are necessary to protect the public, and eliminating unnecessary regulation' (OECD 1997a). As an essential adjunct to decision making (Jacobs 1997), RIA has the potential to strengthen the quality of evidence. Although there was also an appreciation that RIA could have an influence on political discourse, its stated scope was to analytically demonstrate and communicate to the general public how specific government regulations benefit society.

Overall, the executive summary and the introduction to *Regulatory Impact Analysis* hugely downplayed the political control motive for introducing RIA.

Terms such as 'political commitment' and 'political leadership' were used instead and RIA was described as an accountability-to-citizens mechanism, rather than an ongoing central oversight mechanism within the executive. Administrative bodies were reviewed for their responsibility in implementing and controlling the quality of RIA. Its institutionalisation was perceived to be achieved through a cultural shift, whereby regulators would become more aware of the costs of action and more ready to take decisions to reduce costs (Jacobs 1997). The analytical burden on regulators to prove the economic efficiency of their proposals was overlooked. There was no mention of the impact of RIA on enhanced political steering capacity through centralised regulatory oversight. The chapter dedicated to RIA best practice considered oversight bodies to be a quality control mechanism for achieving a whole-of-government view on policy issues, rather than as a limit on the regulators' discretion (Deighton-Smith 1997).

Although the motive of political control re-emerged in the chapters dedicated to the American and Canadian experiences, that part of the book translated RIA as a means to achieve immutable policy goals, such as the maximisation of socio-economic welfare and the openness and transparency of the regulatory process. However, the empirical evidence proves that RIA is a means for achieving political goals that are constantly reset by different heads of government. By downplaying its constitutive purpose of political steering through analysis and information, this rationalistic reframing of RIA has been reflected in all recommendations and country reviews on regulatory reform.

The 1995 regulatory quality principles decontextualised RIA as a policy innovation prototype. The institutional and administrative context of regulatory process was barely recognised. The *Report on Regulatory Reform* ignored the emergence of RIA within the American administrative state. Consequently, the importance of the procedural safeguards of citizens' rights to participate in decision making was neglected. With the exception of the first working paper on regulatory checklists (OECD 1994), no recommendation has ever proposed the adoption of an administrative procedure on the basis of US and notice-and-comment rulemaking. Research on administrative procedure and rulemaking was scarce. Indeed, few comparative studies were conducted within the OECD's conference activities (OECD 2006a) or the SIGMA training programme (OECD 1997d; Rusch 2009). Furthermore, the reasons for the emergence of the Continental European model for regulatory appraisal were not investigated. No chapter of the book on RIA was dedicated to the European experience, although the previous working paper had reviewed the situation in Austria, Finland, Germany, the Netherlands and Spain (OECD Public Management 1993). The four countries, namely, Australia, Canada, the UK and the US, selected in order to describe the trend of regulatory reform experience, were consistent with the definition given to the RIA label.

To summarise, the unique and specific local prerequisites of policy innovation were de-emphasised or omitted in order that the labelled policy innovation could be imitated in every administrative and political setting (Sahlin-Andersson 2001; Sahlin and Wedlin 2010). References to political ideologies were also excluded. Usually, RIA has been nested into wider economic policy reform programmes:

the anti-inflation programme of the Carter administration; the deregulation and supply-side reforms of the Reagan and Thatcher administrations; the simplification initiative in Germany; and the Dutch regulatory reform programme to increase business competitiveness (Radaelli 2004). This aspect was not mentioned in the checklist, but clearly emerged in the reviews of regulatory reform in, for instance, Germany (OECD 2004b) and the Netherlands (OECD 1999). Furthermore, policy labels are generally silent on the institutional and political dynamics triggered by the adoption of RIA (Radaelli 2004). This decontextualisation culminated in the *Introductory Handbook for Undertaking Regulatory Impact Analysis,* in which the OECD proposed its own guidelines on how to conduct RIA based on welfare economic principles and CBA (OECD 2008b).

4.5 Peer review

De-contextualisation is also pursued through policy recommendations and checklists that generalise how reforms should be structured, managed and reviewed (Sahlin-Andersson 2001). This one-size-fits-all approach is indeed essential for having a standardised monitoring procedure. Indeed, the *Report on Regulatory Reform* established a set of checklists which was approved by member states in order to launch the peer review on 'government capacity to assure high quality regulation'. At the time of writing, twenty-nine reports had been published, for twenty-five countries, including non-members Brazil, China and Russia. Austria, Belgium, Iceland, Luxembourg, New Zealand, Portugal and the Slovak Republic, as well as Estonia, Israel and Slovenia were among the countries which joined the OECD in 2010 and had not been reviewed (Table 4.1 lists the OECD member states reviewed on regulatory reform). However, the EU 15 Better Regulation project, which started in 2008, covered Austria, Belgium, Luxembourg and Portugal.

Peer review is a distinctive mechanism of transnational governance (Martens and Jakobi 2010). It is a mechanism of accountability in public policy networks (Benner *et al.* 2004) and an informal instrument of pressure through which ideas and standards advocated by a majority of members gain agreement (Sullivan 1997). Peer review is defined as 'the systematic examination and assessment of the performance of a State by other States' (Pagani 2002). According to the OECD, peer review has the potential to improve policy making through the adoption of best practice and compliance with accepted good governance principles. The main features of this policy evaluation process are non-adversarial processes, mutual trust, accountability, learning, and soft law enforcement (Pagani 2002). Peer review requires the following elements: (i) a legal basis and subsidiary bodies; (ii) evaluation principles, criteria and standards; (iii) collaboration between the reviewed country, the examining country and the OECD subsidiary bodies; and (iv) a standardised procedure (Pagani 2002).

Regulatory review is voluntary. Member states apply for and financially support the process (Lodge 2005). In order to help governments set policy, self-evaluation is sent to the reviewed country at the beginning of the peer review

Table 4.1: List of OECD member states reviewed on regulatory reform

OECD member states	Year of publication of review
Australia	2010
Austria	EU 15 project
Belgium	EU 15 project
Canada	2002
Denmark	2000; EU 15
Finland	2003; EU 15
France	2004; EU 15
Germany	2004; EU 15
Greece	2001; EU 15
Hungary	2002
Ireland	2001; EU 15
Italy	2001; 2007 (regional level); 2010; EU 15
Japan	1999; 2004
Korea	2000; 2007
Luxembourg	EU 15
Mexico	1999; 2004
Netherlands	1999; EU 15
Norway	2003
Poland	2002
Portugal	EU 15
Spain	2000; EU 15
Sweden	2007; EU 15
Switzerland	2006
Turkey	2002
UK	2002; EU 15
US	1999

Available Online: http://www.oecd.org/gov/regulatorypolicy/countryreviewsonregulatoryreform.htm; and http://www.oecd.org/gov/regulatorypolicy/betterregulationineurope-theeu15project.htm

process. The questionnaire includes seventeen broad themes of regulatory quality (Lodge 2005). It is important to remark that the OECD's Regulatory Policy Committee has drafted another questionnaire in order to regularly collect data for the *Indicators of Management System* (*see* Section 7.3). By surveying the countries with the most developed evaluation practices, Chapter Seven shows whether and how collected data and indicators as well as the overall peer review mechanisms are used at the national level to reflect on RIA programmes.

Once the questionnaire is completed, OECD officials are involved in a one-week fact-finding mission that involves some sixty to eighty meetings with the national actors and experts involved in regulation (Lodge 2005). Further, the OECD Secretariat and working groups on competition, trade, telecommunications and regulatory reform maintain a constant dialogue with the national experts in order to revise the drafts of each sectoral report. The sectoral reports are then peer reviewed by two officials from other member states and discussed at the annual meeting of the *ad hoc* multidisciplinary group on regulatory reform in which the experts from the examined country have the chance to clarify specific issues. The government under review has no veto powers over the recommendations or the findings of the regulatory review report (Lodge 2005).

This peer review procedure ends with the publication of the approved final version of the report, which is written by the OECD in close cooperation with the national experts (Lodge 2005). Included in the same series of the OECD's books on regulatory reform, these reports are formally launched with a press conference within the member state under review. Each is composed of seven chapters. An introductory chapter provides the overall context of regulatory reform in the country under review. On the basis of Recommendations One, Two and Three, the second chapter is specifically dedicated to government capacity to assure high-quality regulation and RIA. Following the 1997 checklist on regulatory reform (Recommendations Four, Five and Six), two other chapters concern competition policy, market openness and trade. Two chapters are also dedicated to regulatory reform in the electricity and telecommunications industries. Finally, the concluding chapter summarises the specific policy recommendations. An important feature of the regulatory review is that there is no monitoring of compliance with the proposed recommendations. The OECD's overall aim is to support national champions of regulatory reform by accommodating their reform efforts in the process and prototyping of peer review. As a consequence, the OECD can prioritise those policy domains considered by the member state under review to be particularly problematic or pertinent (Lodge 2005).

The template for reviewing government capacity to assure high-quality regulation has been constantly structured on specific good practices (*see* Appendix B.3) and the RIA checklist (*see* Appendix B.4). Comparing the first 1999 report on the US with the recent 2010 review on Australia, there is no difference in report structure, which strictly adheres to the good practice and the RIA checklist. There are, though, differences in the extent of the information provided, in references to reviews conducted on other member states and in the attention paid to regulatory simplification. Specifically, the report on Australia provided a more detailed overview of the recent developments in regulatory reform and RIA by focusing on oversight bodies. Furthermore, there were references to comparable experiences with regulatory simplification in the UK.

The report on Australia contained quantitative measures of the number of regulations ('the stock') and of RIA conducted between 2000 and 2007. Furthermore, it was also more accurate in describing the regulatory process than the report on the US.

Given the consistency in the application of the peer review template, Chapter Six examines whether this 'multilateral surveillance system' (Marcussen 2004a) has been effective in increasing the similarity between national policy makers' choices for implementing RIA.

The peer review template has been updated for the EU 15 Better Regulation project.[2] This OECD and EU partnership is aimed at assessing 'better regulation' (a common term in Brussels and Paris circles) on the basis of the following core issues:

- policy for better regulation
- institutional framework and capacities for better regulation
- transparency, consultation and communication
- tools and processes – the development of new regulations
- tools and processes – simplification and measures to reduce administrative burdens
- compliance, enforcement and appeals
- the broader institutional landscape – sub-national levels of government; the interface with the EU; agencies
- the political economy of better regulation and the evaluation of regulatory management capacities

This review template is a substantial departure from that used previously by the OECD. The change is reflected in the analytical concept of this evaluation project. Regulatory policy is aimed at achieving objectives that vary among countries, rather than the maximisation of social welfare. There has been a clear focus on the procedural safeguards for citizens, who are allowed to have notice of, participate in, and appeal against rulemaking. The latter is defined as 'the process of making new regulations' (European Commission and OECD 2008). Particular emphasis has been given to the multilevel aspect of regulatory governance by assessing the effectiveness of the interface between national and sub-national levels as well as between member states and the EU. Further, independent agencies have also been taken into account.

To summarise, the institutional framework has been a fundamental aspect of the EU 15 review related to the governmental capacity to implement effective better regulation:

[the] institutional context for implanting effective management is complex and often highly fragmented. Approaches need to be customised, as countries' institutional settings and legal systems can be very specific, and range from systems adapted to small societies with closely knit governments that rely on trust and informality, to large federal systems that must find ways of dealing with high levels of autonomy and diversity. (European Commission and OECD 2008)

---

2. Online. Available: http://www.oecd.org/gov/regref/eu15 (accessed 18 October 2012).

Overall, this recent peer review project has attempted to bring the complexity of political dynamics and institutional settings back into the discourse of regulatory governance and RIA. It has overcome the one-size-fits-all approach pursued so far by the OECD. The next section tracks this ongoing change in the OECD's organisational discourse by analysing publications and working papers that have emphasised the concept of 'regulatory governance'.

4.6 Principles of regulatory governance

In 2002 and in concomitance with the establishment of the GOV(ernance) committee, regulatory reform became an important element of the OECD's initiative on governance. Another review of international experience, *Regulatory Policies in OECD Countries: from interventionism to regulatory governance* (OECD 2002a), signalled the OECD's new vision of regulation. Revolving around the concept of regulatory policy, this book lamented the inconsistency in international experience with regulatory reforms and the capacity to systematically and coherently frame objectives, tools and institutions.

This new perspective has allowed the OECD to take on policy objectives other than the maximisation of social welfare. For instance, *From Interventionism to Regulatory Governance* emphasised the importance of the rule of law and accountability as means of limiting regulators' discretion. The main contribution of the book was to reframe the discussion on regulatory reform around administrative law institutions, such as rulemaking, judicial review and affected parties' right to be heard. Centralised regulatory oversight was described as the institutional prerequisite for coordinating policy goals. Indeed, the OECD has observed that core executive bodies govern the regulatory process through requirements for impact assessment, measurement of administrative burden and consultation with affected parties (OECD 2002a). Furthermore, an increasing number of member states have put in place rewards and sanctions for constraining ministerial independence in the formulation of regulatory proposals (OECD 2002a).

Further publications have encouraged international policy communities to 'think big' on RIA. Drafted by the newly established Regulatory Policy Division in 2008, *Building an Institutional Framework for Regulatory Impact Analysis: guidance for policy makers* was the first working paper dedicated to developing countries (OECD 2008a). It paid particular attention to the necessary institutional conditions for integrating an RIA system into the regulatory process. Although not referring to any specific international experience, centralised oversight bodies were still presented as controllers of the quality of regulatory analysis. Published in 2009, *Regulatory Impact Analysis: a tool for policy coherence* renewed the OECD's comparative review of the most advanced countries in the institutionalisation of RIA (OECD 2009). According to the OECD, Australia, the Netherlands, the UK and the US provided lessons for enhancing policy coherence by dint of economic welfare principles.

Notwithstanding the emphasis on the maxim that estimated regulatory benefits must exceed the estimated costs, *a tool for policy coherence* also shed light on the political and administrative authority of central oversight bodies to limit ministerial discretion (OECD 2009). Furthermore, the review took into consideration the politics of RIA. This publication did not overlook the fact that RIA is 'often perceived as an unreasonable intrusion on the regulatory mandate' (OECD 2009). The latter aspect was further clarified in the working paper, *Strengthening the Institutional Setting for Regulatory Reform* (Cordova-Novion and Jacobzone 2011). The authority of regulatory oversight bodies, this working paper argued, stems from a political mandate to establish a coordination and monitoring system. As the quality of impact assessments is assessed, the oversight body is empowered to signal flawed regulatory proposals, either directly to regulators or indirectly to cabinets of ministers and the general public. This institutional dimension was also in the final milestone report on the EU 15 Better Regulation project. The key message of the 2011 review on *Regulatory Policy and Governance* was that the enhancement of economic growth, social welfare and democratic accountability requires 'institutional leadership and regulatory oversight to drive reform priorities and provide early warning to policy makers of regulatory issues that need to be fixed' (OECD 2011). At last, then, the OECD has comprehended the three reasons for the adoption of RIA. RIA is now understood as both a tool and a practice for achieving policy coherence and a united position on the part of the executive (Cordova-Novion and Jacobzone 2011; OECD 2011). Indeed, central oversight bodies not only assist policy makers in their evidence-based analysis, but also challenge and promote the quality of regulatory proposals, limiting ministerial regulators' discretion (OECD 2011).

This discourse on governance also influenced the updated versions of policy recommendations. The 2005 *Guiding Principles for Regulatory Quality and Performance*, however, retained all seven policy recommendations. Moreover, by making more explicit the connections with trade and investment, the explanatory notes and subordinate recommendations were expanded. In the same year, the Asia-Pacific Economic Cooperation forum and the OECD jointly adopted the *Integrated Checklist on Regulatory Reform*. Drawn from best practice on regulation, competition and market openness policies, this checklist is a self-assessment tool. Both policy recommendations have called for a coherent whole-of-government approach to objectives of competitiveness, market openness and regulatory quality. The OECD's new vision of regulatory governance has recently appeared in the 2012 *Recommendation of the Council on Regulatory Policy and Governance* (OECD 2012). There are now twelve elements for assuring an effective regulatory policy: maximisation of economic, social and environmental net benefits; transparency and participation in the regulatory process; mechanisms and institutions for regulatory oversight; RIA; review of existing regulation; systematic evaluation of regulatory policy; independent regulatory agencies; judicial review; risk management; regulatory coherence throughout multi-level regulatory governance; capacity and performance of sub-national levels of government; and international regulatory standards. In contrast to previous recommendations oriented to outcome, this new version of the principles of regulatory quality emphasises institutions, processes, standards and tools of regulatory policy (*see* Appendix B.5). The most relevant improvement in this recommendation is the acknowledgement of institutional elements of regulatory governance. Mechanisms and institutions for regulatory accountability, independent regulatory agencies and judicial review are now part of the common discourse and values of the international communities of regulatory reformers.

4.7 Conclusion

This chapter has shown that, over the last two decades, RIA has been central to the OECD's organisational discourse. Within the emerging narrative of regulatory governance, RIA has recently gained even more prominence, notwithstanding the fact that the OECD's vision of regulation shifted from reform to quality, and from management systems to governance. This chapter has also shown how the OECD has translated knowledge on a policy innovation such as RIA into the concept of economic rationality, which mirrors the aspiration that the transnational network be 'modern' (Lodge 2005). The OECD as an ideational agency is engaged in producing and promoting new policy ideas and innovative solutions, establishing principles and norms, and simplifying the policy discourse. In particular, politically acceptable attributes are emphasised in order to promote the adoption of a policy innovation. Furthermore, local administrative and institutional settings are understated. The crucial publications on regulatory reform tend to review countries with an English legal origin in which advanced solutions have been implemented.

The organisational discourse has, though, been flexible to accommodate the OECD's multiple targets. In order to promote RIA, the OECD attached the same label to different appraisal methods and experiences of regulatory reform. Recommendation and best practice established a prototype for peer review based on the maximisation of economic and social welfare. The actual process of peer review, however, allows the OECD a margin of flexibility in order to support policy champions and entrepreneurs within the national policy arena. The new emerging narrative on regulatory governance has conceded that RIA needs to be contextualised according to the mutable political purposes of regulatory reform. Also, because of frustrations experienced by several member states in the implementation of RIA, the administrative and institutional context in which an innovation is introduced is now taken seriously.

In a collection of key messages delivered at the 2010 regulatory policy conference, the OECD provided a description of its functions:

> Acting as a 'club of best practices' and a hub for global policy dialogue and exchange of experiences, the Organisation has played a pioneering role in bringing the issue of regulatory reform to the fore. Through its policy principles and guidelines, analysis, peer reviews, and now this major conference and flagship report, the OECD continues to make a real contribution in the field of regulatory policy. (OECD 2010a)

This interpretation is, however, too neutral and overlooks the OECD's role as a selective or biased booster of reform (Ervik 2009). The OECD has an influence in framing those reform agendas that are set according to a specific policy innovation such as RIA. Furthermore, the knowledge base and the interpretative framework of the policy discourse have been mostly set on the basis of evidence-based decision making and economic rationality. This facilitates the OECD's promotion of the innovation. The next chapters ascertain the extent of change (in national policies) induced by this international ideational agency in terms of governments' decisions to adopt, implement and evaluate RIA.

chapter five | influencing RIA adoption

The literature on the cross-national adoption of policy innovations has distinguished between prerequisites or necessary conditions for (Collier and Messick 1975; Bennett 1997) and different patterns and mechanisms of diffusion (Weyland 2006). Internal determinants, previous administrative innovations, types of regulatory review, spatial models and key events determining hierarchical information flows are all explanatory elements of governments' decisions to adopt RIA. Previous administrative innovations reveal the capacity of public administrations. The size of government and the extent of economic development are dimensions of adoptability, especially at the beginning of the cycle of diffusion. Spatial proximity as well as common administrative traditions and similar legal origins to those of previous adopters can be pertinent to patterns of diffusion. Furthermore, the previous chapter has shown that the OECD is the arena in which national policy makers interact and that it has played an essential role in forming the policy agenda for regulatory reform. It has shaped the political discourse and attributed a rationalist label to RIA. Overall, these different but combined layers of explanations can influence the adoption of transnational policy innovations.

Accordingly, this chapter tests a three-level framework for the formation of global trends in administrative reform and NPM, focusing on the probability of adoption by country i in year t. To recall, Salihn-Andersson (2001) identifies national (homogeneous but independent governments' responses to common global pressure), international (country-to-country interdependence) and transnational (interdependence through the OECD) explanations of administrative reform.

The challenge of this model in a large-n comparative analysis – of the thirty-eight EU and OECD countries – is to operationalise the different types of global trends, relying also on evidence for reconstructing the process of communication and interaction among international and transnational networks. Summarised in the explanations of hypotheses to test, preliminary findings confirm that these three levels of analysis are necessary for capturing the extent of interdependence of, and the role of, the OECD on RIA adoption, assessed through a discrete EHA. Chapters Six and Seven go beyond adoption to assess the extent of governments' interdependence concerning the implementation and evaluation of RIA.

This chapter is structured as follows. The next section formulates the hypotheses of adoption and diffusion of RIA, referring to the three levels of the theoretical framework. Section 5.2 highlights the methodological choices made in order to achieve accuracy in the statistical analysis. Section 5.3 summarises the results of the EHA and, finally, Section 5.4 remarks on the explanatory role of each internal and external determinant.

5.1 Levels of analysis and hypotheses

A comprehensive research strategy with three layers of explanation, such as the Sahlin-Andersson (2001) framework, is not novel in analyses of organisational innovations (Dobbin *et al.*1988). Starting from the internal determinants, the following hypotheses can be formulated.

5.1.1 Internal determinants

The first hypothesis concerns the adopter's rationality and institutional capacity. Adopting innovation is a complex process developed from a public organisation's accumulated stock of knowledge and skills (Boyne *et al.* 2005). This rationalist and functionalist perspective regards innovations as interconnected, contingent and complementary, following predictable patterns of adoption. 'Past experience and the cumulative stream of innovation will aid the process of innovation adoption' (Boyne *et al.* 2005). Accordingly, a hypothesis to test is that RIA is adopted only after other administrative innovations (such as environmental impact assessment (EIA) and freedom of information (FOI) law), have been considered as prerequisites for the adoption of RIA.

Hypothesis One: Previous adoptions of EIA and FOI increase the likelihood of adopting RIA.

Table 5.1 lists the years of adoption of EIA and FOI laws in each of the thirty-eight countries and shows that contingent and complementary innovations are a useful concept for capturing a broader sequence of adoption. Only eight countries adopted RIA before the adoption of an FOI law, i.e. Canada, the Czech Republic, Estonia, Germany, Hungary, Mexico, Switzerland and the UK. Only six countries adopted RIA before EIA: Denmark, Germany, Hungary, Norway, Sweden and the UK. It is important to note that Germany, Hungary and the UK, all pioneers, adopted RIA without having either FOI or EIA legislation. Overall, previous adoption of good-governance innovations is a necessary condition, especially among the later adopters. Correlations of adoption rankings are also significant. The Kendall's tau-b correlations are statistically significant at the $p < 0.05$ level for both innovations (with the following values: 0.25 for EIA, and 0.3 for FOI). The Spearman correlation is significant only for FOI (rho = 0.4229; $p = 0.0114$) and only marginally for EIA (rho = 0.2988; $p = 0.0861$).

The second hypothesis is twofold but with both parts referring to the extent of modernisation and economic development of a given country. As Bennett (1997) put it, the increasing complexity of modern systems requires a rational administrative system so as to enhance capacity and efficiency. Innovations in administrative law have often been appreciated as a necessary corrective to growing bureaucratic power and 'government obesity' (Bennett 1997). Ultimately, administrative legislation grants 'necessary new protections against bureaucratic bungling and abuses of power' (Rowat 1973). Administrative management needs

Table 5.1: Years and ranks of adoption related to RIA, FOI and EIA

Country	RIA	Rank of RIA	FOI	Rank of FOI	EIA	Rank of EIA
US	1971	1	1966	3	1969	1
Canada	1978	2	1982	8	1973	2
Germany	1984	3	2005	35	1990	13
Australia	1985	4	1982	8	1974	3
Netherlands	1985	4	1978	6	1978	6
UK	1985	4	2000	25	1999	30
Hungary	1987	7	1992	14	2001	34
Sweden	1987	7	1966	1	1998	29
Denmark	1993	9	1970	4	2004	37
France	1995	10	1978	6	1976	5
New Zealand	1995	10	1982	8	1974	3
Norway	1995	10	1970	4	1999	30
Estonia	1996	13	2000	25	1992	15
Mexico	1996	13	2002	31	1988	10
Korea	1997	15	1996	18	1981	7
Belgium	1998	16	1994	17	–	–
Czech Rep.	1998	16	1999	23	1992	15
Finland	1998	16	1951	2	1994	21
Latvia	1998	16	1998	22	1992	15
Austria	1999	20	1987	12	1993	18
Iceland	1999	20	1996	18	1994	21
Ireland	1999	20	1997	21	1989	12
Italy	1999	20	1990	13	1986	8
Switzerland	1999	20	2004	34	1988	10
Poland	2001	25	2001	29	2000	33
Slovak Rep.	2001	25	2000	25	1994	21
Bulgaria	2003	27	2000	25	1995	25
Lithuania	2003	27	1996	18	1997	27
Japan	2004	29	1999	23	1997	27
Spain	2004	29	1992	14	1986	8
Slovenia	2004	29	2003	32	1993	18
Romania	2005	32	2001	29	1995	25
Greece	2006	33	1986	11	1990	13
Portugal	2006	33	1993	16	1999	30
Turkey	2006	33	2003	32	1993	18
Cyprus	–	–	–	–	2002	36
Luxembourg	–	–	–	–	1994	21
Malta	–	–	–	–	2001	34

Table 5.1 *Sources*: Reynolds and Flores (2000); Sadler (1996); Seedern and Stroink (2002); GLOBALEX. Available Online: http://www.nyulawglobal.org/globalex, FAOLEX http://www. faolex.fao.org/faolex. Accessed 13 June 2007; Collection of Laws for Electronic Access of the World Intellectual Property Organization. Available Online: http://www.wipo.int/clea/en/index.jsp (accessed 13 June 2007); Swedish Agency for Administrative Development (2005). Available Online: http://www.freedominfo.org/index.htm (accessed 13 June 2007).

to be based on supervision and control through the standardisation of information and procedures, the main rationale for RIA, as the previous chapters showed. In other words, the greater the complexity and size of a government, the greater the need to enhance the flows of information and strengthen political control, solving all sorts of problems that involve transaction costs.

Hypothesis 2a: The likelihood of RIA adoption is positively associated with the size of a government.

The size of government is a multifaceted concept. It may refer, for example, to financial assets, annual expenditure, number of employees or the size of the client base (Hood and Dunsire 1981). Further measures, i.e. of the size of government, are composite. In order to measure and rank the freedom of economic activities across the world's countries, the term 'size of government' often labels indexes compiled by think tanks and research institutes such as the Fraser Institute and the Heritage Foundation. Correlations between the years of adoption and proxies for the size of government have been calculated in the attempt to select the most pertinent variable. The Fraser Institute's index[1] was chosen at the beginning (1970) and in the middle (1990) of the diffusion cycle; the Heritage Foundation's index[2] was preferred in 1995 and in the RIA adoption year of each country. A more traditional measure of government size is the general central government current expenditure as a percentage of GDP (Bennett 1997), and has been considered in 1971, 1990 and in the year of adoption of each country. Table 5.2 shows that only two measures are statistically significant: the general government final expenditure in 1971; and the Fraser Institute's size of government, which, however, has an opposite correlation with the 1990s index. These contrasting results lead to the necessity to choose for the EHA a measure of government expenditure that is negatively correlated with the years of adoption – meaning that countries with a higher level of government expenditure are earlier adopters.

The second part of the hypothesis is related to the level of economic development of a country. The chosen indicator is the World Bank's GDP per capita (constant 2000 US$) that at the midpoint of the diffusion cycle (year 1990) is significant and negatively correlated – meaning that later adopters have lower rates of economic growth – with the years of adoption ($r = -0.406$, $p = 0.0156$) Ackerman and Sandoval-Ballesteros (2006) argue that there is no clear relationship between economic development and wealth and the adoption of administrative innovations. However, as the diffusion process goes on, it is also plausible to predict that low-income countries would catch up with pioneer and richer countries in adopting administrative reform. This imitative process has

---

1. Varying from zero to ten (where ten represents the maximum level of freedom), this sub-index summarises four measures: general government consumption as a share of total consumption; transfer and subsidies as a share of GDP; government enterprise and investment as a share of gross investment; and top marginal income tax rate.

2. It varies from zero to 100, where 100 represents the maximum level of freedom.

Table 5.2: Pearson correlations between the years of RIA adoption, indexes of size of government, and general government final consumption expenditure as a percentage of GDP

	Fraser Institute 1970	Fraser Institute 1990	Heritage Foundation 1995	Heritage Foundation adoption year	Gov't expenditure % GDP in 1971	Gov't expenditure % GDP in 1990	Gov't expenditure % GDP adoption year
Years of adoption							
No. obs.	25	28	24	23	26	35	35
Pearson Correlations	0.557**	– 0.146	0.185	0.099	– 0.565**	– 0.290†	– 0.251

Significance levels †< 10%** < 1%

been described as 'hierarchical diffusion', that is, a tendency for each successive adopter to adopt at a progressively lower level of economic growth (Collier and Messick 1975).

Hypothesis 2b: The likelihood of RIA adoption is negatively associated with economic development and wealth.

Finally, the third national-level hypothesis refers to the extent of a government's accountability since the main purpose of administrative law is to strengthen the development of liberal democracy. Accordingly, new control mechanisms are necessary to keep the expanded executive institutions accountable to citizens and parliaments. As Peters (1992) argues, administrative institutions and their bureaucracies are important elements of the social and political environment and can trigger or hinder the search for efficient and accountable administration. In particular, administrative culture and state tradition 'play a role in defining the way in which administration is conducted, and the receptivity of the administrative system to change' (Peters 1997). How can one conceive external accountability and administrative culture? Regulators' external accountability refers to the regulatory review process. Chapter Three has shown that there are different modalities in which government regulations are scrutinised for their quality and lawfulness. To recall, in few countries was there a wide application of APA, with the courts functioning as external reviewers of the administrative rulemaking process. Instead, in common law countries, the quality control of delegated legislation is conducted directly by dedicated parliamentary committees. Civil law countries rely on an independent constitutional body such as the council of state. Finally, in Germany, there is a marginal *ex post* regulatory review. One may expect that the extent of external accountability is stronger in countries with direct and judicial review. It is relevant in countries where external review is conducted by the parliament and weaker in countries like Germany and civil law countries where the review is marginal or consultative. A further step would be to link the extent of external accountability with the adoption of RIA. Due to the lack of data regarding the different modalities of regulatory review, the categorical variable of legal origin – used by La Porta *et al.* (1999) as a determinant of countries' economic performance – would question the hypothesis of common administrative culture.[3]

Hypothesis 3: Countries with an English legal origin are more likely to adopt RIA than those with a French or German legal origin.

This variable can also be considered as a proxy of 'fixed regions' (Berry and Berry 2007), since it distinguishes between countries with an English, French, German, Scandinavian or socialist legal origin (La Porta *et al.* 1999). The concept of fixed regions or 'families of countries' (Castles 1993; Castles 1998) is widely used in political analysis and public policy. It tends to highlight how cultural commonality, historical connections (Weyland 2006) and shared geopolitical and economic characteristics matter (Brooks 2005). By applying Mooney's (2001) method for determining the running average of proportions of neighbouring countries that had previously adopted the innovation, Figure 5.1 shows that effects associated with legal origin are constantly positive, and mostly linear and unidirectional.

5.1.2 International interdependence

Turning to the international explanations and modalities of horizontal, country-to-country information exchange, an operationalisation is necessary to appreciate the importance of the US as a source of influence and to ascertain whether the idea of RIA has travelled from the US, the pioneer country. Adversarial modes of policy formulation are composed of complex transparency and disclosure requirements such as public notice and comment, open hearing, *ex parte* contacts, evidentiary standards and formal response to interest group arguments (Kagan 1991). Kelemen

---

3. Scholars interested in spatial diffusion have not taken geographical proximity and composition of country clusters for granted (Brams 1966; Kopstein and Reilly 2000). In this research strand, the focus on spatial dependence, defined as 'the extent to which behaviour in one state is a function of behaviour in adjoining states' (Kopstein and Reilly 2000), is comprised of two concepts:

- 'spatial stock', which encompasses 'assets, liabilities, or general qualities of a given unit [...] that shape the alternative available to decision makers' (Kopstein and Reilly 2000), and also shared membership of international organisations (Brams 1966) as well as the neighbours' internal characteristics (Kopstein and Reilly 2000)
- 'spatial flow', which represents instead 'the movement of information and resources between countries' (Kopstein and Reilly 2000), and which is captured by variables such as foreign direct investment, international trade (Kopstein and Reilly 2000) and diplomatic exchanges (Brams 1966).

   It is straightforward that the variables categorised as legal origin refer to the static concept of spatial stock.

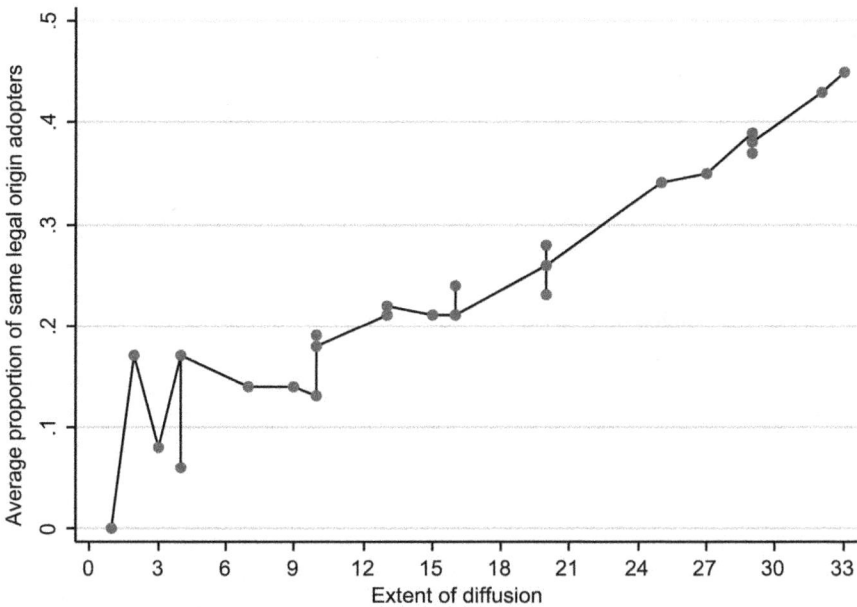

Figure 5.1: Observed average proportion of legal origin adopters

and Sibbitt (2004) have argued that US law firms played a significant catalytic role by exporting American approaches to law and regulation to foreign jurisdictions. They showed that between 1985 and 1999, the number of offices of American law firms in Western Europe more than doubled, benefitting also from the EU's single market (Kelemen 2011).[4] This surge was mainly driven by the presence of American multinational firms in Europe (Kelemen and Sibbitt 2004), which also directly hired US lawyers (DeLisle 1999). A one-year lag (to take into account problems of endogeneity) of the stock of US foreign direct investment (FDI) is used here as a broader measure of the extent of influence from the US in a given country to import RIA as an American-style administrative requirement.

Hypothesis 4: In a given country, the higher the stock of FDI from the US, the higher its likelihood of adopting RIA.

Another horizontal diffusion explanation is based on economic internationalisation (Garrett 1995; Garrett 1998), which compels national policy makers to react to the global conditions of markets rather than consciously deliberating in their own time over policy options (Dobbin *et al.* 2007). Specifically, the impact of increased trade competition on national policies is reflected in deregulatory initiatives.

---

4.   'American [law] firms have flourished in Europe because they had the size, forms of organization, and experience in legal fields that became vital for corporate clients in the increasingly liberalized market' (Kelemen 2006).

Costs related to unnecessary and unduly onerous regulations are implicit taxes on producers, decreasing the overall competitiveness of a country. RIA is interpreted by national reformers as an instrument to curb the excessive burdens on firms. A one-year lag of trade openness captures the country's position within international trade networks (Drori *et al.* 2006a) and indicates the extent of international pressure to rationalise regulatory governance.

Hypothesis 5: The higher the trade openness of a country, the higher is its likelihood of adopting RIA.

A spatial diffusion perspective would reveal that the probability of adoption decreases with the geographical distance from the previous adopters. Specifically, remoteness would cause smaller volumes of information and weaker awareness of the innovation and, consequently, its later adoption (Meir 1982).[5] As Gleditsch and Ward (2001) put it, '[d]istance is widely acknowledged to be a primary force shaping the opportunity for interaction among states in the international system'. Thus, the opportunity to interact declines with the increase in distance between countries. In other words, a 'spatial lag' links countries 'by using the value of their dependent variable as an independent variable for the focus country' (Jahn 2006). Furthermore, the inclusion of spatial variables in a fully specified model allows one to isolate purely spatial explanations from other informational influences (Simmons and Elkins 2004). The distances between capital cities constitute the most appropriate measure for interaction between reformers'. Accordingly, a symmetric connectivity matrix of distances weights the adoption of countries with closer capitals more heavily than countries with more distant capitals. Each value of the connectivity matrix has been inverted and row standardised for deriving a spatial lag which is the product of the one-year lagged dichotomic variable of the existence of RIA and the standardised connectivity matrix for each year.

Hypothesis 6: The closer a given country to previous adopters, the higher its likelihood of adopting RIA.

5.1.3 Interdependence through the OECD

The final level of explanation refers to the role of the OECD as a mediator, editor and evaluator of administrative reforms, the main focus of this book. Chapter Four showed how the OECD has been active in the promotion and dissemination of RIA. The OECD has a series of mechanisms to promote the adoption of administrative innovations, i.e. technical advice and assistance, peer reviews and reports on institutional frameworks, indicators, and drafting of handbooks and reference materials as a basis for training.

---

5.   Recalling the distinction between spatial stock and flow, this spatial dimension is unambiguously referring to the dynamic flow.

The first hypothesis to test is the OECD's mediative function in providing an arena for social interaction between national policy makers and, ultimately, in transferring knowledge, including beyond its members (Mahon and McBride 2009). Support for Improvement in Governance and Management (SIGMA) is a partnership project between the OECD and the European Commission that provides funds to the new EU member states. It was launched in 1992 to help countries in Central and Eastern Europe modernise their public governance but it was extended to support EU candidate administrations as well as European neighbours and partners. Administratively, the SIGMA project is led by the OECD directorate that is in charge of the thematic area of regulatory reform, namely the Public Governance and Territorial Development Directorate. Since 1996, this project has been promoting better regulation and RIA (OECD-SIGMA 1997a; OECD-SIGMA 1997b; OECD-SIGMA 1997c) by using the same learning mechanisms and tools for all OECD members. Networks of national experts have also been active within the EU. Information, knowledge and ideas produced in Paris have circulated in Brussels and a governance system similar to that proposed by the OECD has been adopted. Indeed, a group of Directors and Experts on Better Regulation (DEBR) was established in 1999 with '[t]he overall mandate...to promote and monitor progress on Better Regulation amongst Member States and to share experience and best practice (with the new Member States in particular)' (Allio 2008). The DEBR meets twice a year and is usually chaired by the state holding the entering presidency of the EU.

Hypothesis 7: Since 1995, the longer a country has participated in one of the OECD, EU or SIGMA networks of experts on regulatory reform, the higher its likelihood of RIA adoption.

Since the 1995 agreement on regulatory reform, the OECD has published peer review reports on countries' progress in this specific political economy. The process is a sort of naming-and-shaming mechanism, even if the report is approved by the member state under review. One can predict that a member state, in order to be considered smart, innovative and legitimate by its peers, will adopt RIA in the three years immediately before and after the publication of the report. SIGMA has carried out inquisitive functions since 2004 as it has been reviewing the regulatory management capacities of the ten new EU member states. Accordingly, the OECD monitoring and surveillance process has been widened to non-OECD member states.

Hypothesis 8: An OECD or SIGMA member state is more likely to adopt RIA three years before and after the publication of the OECD's regulatory reform report.

Table 5.3 summarises the models with the variables used to test each hypothesis via a discrete EHA as well as the descriptive statistics and data sources.

5.2 Event history analysis and its methodological issues

Since Berry and Berry (1990), the application of EHA has become established among policy innovation studies. The EHA model explains a hazard rate, which is the unobservable probability of a country adopting RIA in a specific year. However, the observed dependent variable is dichotomous: whether a country adopts RIA (ria = 1) or not (ria = 0). The dataset for analysis is called the 'risk set' and 'is a pooled cross-sectional time-series, being composed of an observation for each unit at each time period during which the unit is at risk of experiencing the event' (Berry 1994). Accordingly, once a country adopts RIA, no observation is made in subsequent years. The dataset starts in 1968, three years before adoption by the first country (the US), instead of making the common choice of starting the data collection after the first adoption as this would exclude the pioneer from the analysis. Exclusion of the first country is not justified in the baseline model of adoption based exclusively on internal determinants. Furthermore, a carefully conceived time frame is recommended by Heichel et al. (2005), who note that most of the diffusion studies overlook this important element of research design. To clarify, 1968 is considered a key year, indicating the start of the formation of neo-liberal ideas and ideology.

A further specification is necessary for the choice of the EHA model. The logit model has been preferred because it describes the event probability in a distinct observation time window (with the individual binary information 'event occurred: yes or no') whereas, in the Cox model, the response variable is given as the time elapsing before the event occurs, commonly called 'survival time' (Langner et al. 2003). This feature of the logit model allows for flexibility in the analysis. In particular, it can accommodate the complication related to the late entry of a country in the risk set because of its later independence (Beck et al. 1998). The Czech Republic, Estonia, Latvia, Lithuania, the Slovak Republic and Slovenia have been considered as late entries, entering the risk set when they gained independence. Further, in the logit model the standard treatment (for most statistical packages) for missing data is the deletion of any case containing them (Beck et al. 1998). This so-called 'case-wise' deletion has been implemented in this research, although this method reduces the sample size to 919 and 831 out of a possible 990 observations, representing 7 per cent and 13 per cent reductions, respectively.[6]

However, there are also three specific warnings or specification issues related to the logit model (Buckley and Westerland 2004). The first is related to the likelihood that the observations are temporally dependent. This issue is particularly relevant in an analysis which aims to assess how policy diffuses over time (Mooney 2001; Buckley and Westerland 2004). In order to consider 'time seriously' (Beck et al. 1998) and avoid the unrealistic assumption of a constant hazard rate, a simple precaution has been taken. Following Carter and Signorino (2010) and Buckley

---

6.   Beck et al. (1998) have argued that missing data on a logit model are not a problem so long as the
     correct time variable(s) is retained and thus there are no missing data on the dependent variable.
     Both conditions are respected in the risk set used for this analysis.

Table 5.3: Models of diffusion of RIA, descriptive statistics and data sources

Hps	Variable	Minimum	Maximum	Mean	Standard deviation	Source
Model 1: Internal determinants						
1a	EIA adoption dummy variable	0	1	0.31	0.46	Reynolds and Flores 2000; Sadler 1996; http://www.faolex.com (accessed 13 June 2007)
1b	FOIA adoption dummy variable	0	1	0.27	0.44	http://www.freedominfo.org (accessed 13 June 2007)
2a	GDP per capita (constant 2000 US$)/10000	0.13	5.46	1.31	0.91	WB development indicators
2b	General government final consumption as % of GDP	5.69	29.55	16.88	4.52	WB development indicators
3	Legal origin					La Porta 1999
	English	0	1	0.15	0.36	
	French	0	1	0.37	0.48	
	German	0	1	0.15	0.36	
	Scandinavian	0	1	0.14	0.35	
Model 2: Model 1 + horizontal diffusion						
4	Spatial lag	0	0.95	0.15	0.2	Calculated on the basis of a connectivity matrix of distances among capital cities
5	Trade openness (export plus import divided as % GDP) $(t-1)$	5.4	289.09	71.14	43.6	Penn World Table
6	Stocks of US direct investments abroad divided by 10000 $(t-1)$	-0.0004	8.36	0.46	0.95	US Bureau of Economic Analysis
Model 3: Full model						
7	No. of years of better regulation networking	0	12	0.77	2.12	Author's calculation

and Westerland (2004), I have inserted three time variables, t, $t^2/10$, $t^3/100$, in the discrete EHA. This cubic polynomial requires little effort to implement and is effective in avoiding the problem of quasi-complete separation[7] caused by the use of time dummy variables. It is important to note that, given the choice of considering the above mentioned newly independent countries as late entries in the dataset, the polynomial cubic count variables associated with such countries have been reset, associating a value of $t = 1$ with the year of their independence.

The second issue concerns the selection of an appropriate functional form that, according to Buckley and Westerland (2004), should be guided by appropriate substantive and statistical theory. The issue here has to do with the underlying distributional assumption within a logit model that the maximum marginal effect occurs at the value $\pi = 0.5$. This may lead to model misspecification when the distribution of the observed values of y is particularly skewed, with the presence of a few ones (as many as the countries that have adopted the innovation) but hundreds of zeros. This is precisely the case with policy diffusion, which is indeed an analysis of 'rare events' (King and Zeng 2001). In order to tackle this issue, alternative models, which control the degree of skewing in the error distribution, have been tested. Accordingly, robustness checks have been performed, testing the models through complementary log-log regression (Buckley and Westerland 2004). The coefficients and their statistical significance do not vary substantially, minimising concerns that the frequency of the dependent variable might skew the empirical results.

Finally, although the problems with both the logit and the discrete EHA models' assumption of temporal independence have been solved, diffusion studies are also about spatial dependency. A solution to relax the logit model's assumption of independent observations is to use '[r]obust variance estimation [that] allows for the relaxation of the assumption that the error terms are identically distributed, and clustering allows the further relaxation of the assumption of independence between observation in the data' (Buckley and Westerland 2004). Robust standard deviations have been computed clustered by countries, not by regions, because the model already takes into account the cultural and legal proximity with the dummy variables for legal origin.

5.3 Empirical results

The previous section has specified the preference for the discrete EHA model and the issues related to the model specification and robustness checks. Table 5.4 presents logistic regression coefficients for the three models specified in Table 5.3. The maximum-likelihood method was used to predict adoption of RIA from the model of internal determinants (including variables such as GDP per capita,

---

7. This is a major problem in logistic regression because the coefficients of predictors almost perfectly determine the value of the dependent variable, determining the non-existence of maximum-likelihood estimates (Allison 2008).

government expenditure, EIA, FOI law) and fixed regional effects (including a set of variables featuring the legal origin).[8]

Three variables are statistically significant predictors of RIA adoption: French legal origin at the level of $p < 0.001$, FOI law at the level of $p < 0.005$ and Scandinavian legal origin at the level of $p < 0.01$. Two other variables are marginally significant (at the level of $p < 0.1$), that is, EIA and government expenditure. The logit regression results can be interpreted using discrete change of predicted probabilities when these dichotomous predictors change their values from 0 to 1 (see Table 5.5). With all other variables held constant at the mean, the discrete changes of predicted probability associated with the prior adoption of FOI law and EIA are 0.0234 and 0.0115, respectively. The discrete changes of predicted probabilities related to French and Scandinavian legal origins are both negative, -0.0233 and -0.0117, respectively. The marginal effect, the change in the predicted probability because of an infinitesimal change in the value of the predictor of government expenditure, is equal to 0.001.

The relevant predictors of the first model are French legal origin and previous adoption of an FOI law. These findings strongly support the hypothesis of administrative capacity and rationality: governments do not adopt RIA without previously adopting complementary innovations, in this case FOI law. It is important to note that the high level of significance of FOI law overshadows the other tested innovation, EIA, which, as expected, has a positive relationship with RIA adoption.[9] Belonging to a specific legal origin cluster based on common administrative tradition explains the delay in adopting RIA, although, unexpectedly, the German countries are closer to common law countries and quicker to innovate than the Scandinavians.

Turning to the second model, three other independent variables have been added to the first model, these are: stocks of US direct investments abroad, the extent of trade openness and the spatial lag. Although there is a relevant reduction in the percentage of adjusted correct predictions to the level of 0 per cent, the overall fit of the model is reasonable. There are improvements in the Wald χ^2, log likelihood and pseudo-R^2. The Hosmer-Lemeshow χ^2 (2.66, p = 0.9537) also indicates a relatively good fit. Through a Wald test on the restriction that the added variable coefficients are 0, we can observe that neither trade openness nor US FDI mattered for the adoption of RIA, rejecting the hypotheses of countries' interconnectedness with the US and economic internationalisation. Among the horizontal diffusion variables, only the spatial distance is a relevant predictor (p < 0.01), as evidenced by the marginal effect of 0.03, the most significant of all the predictors.

---

8. Countries with a socialist legal origin are the reference group. This choice is justified by the fact that the formulation of the hypothesis relies on the concept of the extent of transparency and judicial review, concepts that were not common among socialist regimes.
9. Although the two innovations do not exert the same effect in the adoption of RIA.

Table 5.4: Discrete Event History Analysis of RIA adoption

Variables	Model 1 (robust standard errors)		Model 2 (robust standard errors)				Model 3 (robust standard errors)			
EIA	0.919†	0.5365	0.658	0.546	0.685	0.623	0.74	0.624	0.666	0.554
FOIA	1.520**	0.519	1.35*	0.585	1.0386	0.649	1.047	0.642	1.399*	0.628
GDP/10000	0.284	0.288	-0.812	0.523	-0.965†	0.542	-0.944†	0.556	-0.826	0.518
Gov't expenditure	0.118†	0.062	0.146**	0.056	0.178**	0.059	0.181**	0.057	0.149**	0.055
English LO	-0.541	0.611	0.89	0.66	1.481*	0.677	1.435*	0.675	0.906	0.638
French LO	-2.294***	0.624	-0.757	0.768	-0.566	0.886	-0.662	0.887	-0.71	0.785
German LO	-1.302	1.008	1.01	1.047	1.402	1.089	1.283	1.077	0.996	1.006
Scandinavian LO	-1.888*	0.932	0.895	1.218	1.429	1.263	1.339	1.263	0.945	1.201
Trade openness (t - 1)			0.004	0.01	0.006	0.006	0.006	0.006	0.005	0.006
US FDI/10000 (t - 1)			0.363	0.263	0.412	0.273	0.424	0.277	0.359	0.266
Spatial lag			3.793**	1.181	0.909	1.98			3.661**	1.209
Networks					0.402†	0.221	0.47**	0.153		

(Cont'd.)

Table 5.4: (Cont'd.)

Variables	Model 1 (robust standard errors)		Model 2 (robust standard errors)				Model 3 (robust standard errors)			
OECD report					0.048	0.682	0.0646	0.678	0.202	0.629
t	0.259	0.211	0.308	0.377	0.0976	0.428	0.0736	0.411	0.314	0.364
t2/10	-0.148	0.111	-0.123	0.183	0.0405	0.237	0.06	0.225	-0.128	0.176
t3/100	0.029	0.017	0.017	0.027	-0.016	0.04	-0.02	0.037	0.018	0.026
Intercept	-7.7***	1.57	-10.2***	2.588	-10.3***	2.502	-10.3***	2.432	-10.3***	2.379
No. of observations	919		831		831		831		831	
Log-likelihood	-109.5		-93.14		-91.39		-91.45		-93.09	
Wald Chi2	110.88		178.72		221.31		211.77		181.62	
Pseudo R2	0.264		0.313		0.326		0.325		0.313	
% of adjusted correct prediction	5.7		0		6.25		6.25		-0.031	

Significance levels:
† < 10%
* < 5%
** < 1%
*** < 0.1%

Note: Standardised logistic regression coefficients with robust standard errors (clustering by countries: 38 in Model 1; 37 in the others)

Analysing the internal determinants, the significant predictors are FOI law (with a discrete change in predicted probabilities of 0.015, p < 0.05) and government expenditure (with a marginal effect equal to 0.001, p < 0.01).[10] The level of significance and the change in predicted probabilities of variables for French and Scandinavian legal origins drops significantly because of the combined effect of US FDI and spatial lags. Indeed, excluding both variables results in French and Scandinavian legal origins maintaining their significance at the levels of the previous model.

In the last comprehensive model, two variables are added to the previous model, namely, network and OECD report. Network measures the length of time for a given country's participation in the OECD, SIGMA and EU networks on regulatory reform. The counting starts in 1995 for the OECD network, in 1996 for the SIGMA network and in 2002 for the EU network. For several countries, membership in the OECD, SIGMA and EU overlapped, but the network years are not cumulative. The model fits the data fairly well. The Wald χ^2 and the pseudo-R^2 are higher than those for the previous models. This is also reflected in the percentage of adjusted correct predictions attested at the level of 6.25 per cent, as well as the Hosmer–Lemeshow χ^2 (4.68, p = 0.79).

Government expenditure and an English legal origin are the statistically significant internal determinants. The former keeps the same extent of marginal effect (0.0012) attested in the previous models; the latter has the most relevant change of predicted probability (0.0192). The significance of an English legal origin is related to years of networking: excluding the latter predictor from the model, this variable is not statistically significant. In a different manner, FOI loses its significance level for the effect of the network years. Excluding the latter, FOI keeps its significance at the level of p = 0.026. Among the diffusion variables, the network coefficient is significant only at the level of p < 0.1, with a marginal effect of 0.0029. Contrarily, despite the larger marginal effect (0.0065), the spatial lag variable is not statistically significant. These two diffusion variables are highly correlated (χ^2 = 0.806, p < 0.001) because of the limited geographical distance among the majority of the OECD members (situated in Europe). The high standard error of the spatial lag and the tolerances (0.1352 for the spatial lag, 0.1161 for the network years) and the variance inflation factors (7.40 for the spatial lag, 8.61 for the network years) for both variables detect a marginal multicollinearity problem. Dropping each variable in turn from the model, one can observe that the model with network years performs better than the one with the spatial lag in terms of adjusted correct predictions, Wald χ^2 and pseudo-R^2. Furthermore, in the model with only the network years, the magnitude of coefficients as well as their standard errors and levels of significance are very similar to the ones of the comprehensive model. In a different manner, in the model with only the spatial lag the coefficients vary significantly. The spatial coefficient itself is almost 3.5 times bigger. This

10. Government expenditure has raised its significance level given the fact that this variable and U.S. FDI exert a similar effect on the adoption of RIA: $W = 0.61, p = 0.43$.

Table 5.5: Discrete changes in predicted probabilities and marginal effects

Variables	Model 1		Model 2		Model 3		Model 3 without spatial lag		Model 3 without networking	
	PP change 0→1	Confidence interval	PP change 0→1	Confidence interval	PP change 0→1	Confidence interval	PP change 0→1	Confidence interval	PP change 0→1	Confidence interval
EIA	0.0115	[-0.0064, 0.0293]	0.0059	[-0.006, 0.01776]	0.0056	[-0.0067, 0.0178]	0.006	[-0.0064, 0.0184]	0.0059	[-0.006, 0.0178]
FOIA	0.0234	[0.0021, 0.0448]	0.0148	[0.0006, 0.0290]	0.0095	[-0.0038, 0.0228]	0.00946	[-0.0036, 0.0225]	0.0155	[-0.0002, 0.0311]
English LO	-0.0047	[-0.0142, 0.00477]	0.00987	[-0.0099, 0.02973]	0.0192	[-0.012, 0.0504]	0.018	[-0.012, 0.048]	0.01	[-0.0094, 0.0295]
French LO	-0.0233	[-0.0399, -0.0067]	-0.0057	[-0.0164, 0.00494]	-0.0039	[-0.0148, 0.007]	-0.0045	[-0.015, 0.006]	-0.0053	[-0.0163, 0.0057]
Scand. LO	-0.0117	[-0.0211, -0.0024]	0.0099	[-0.0282, 0.04798]	0.018	[-0.0378, 0.0737]	0.016	[-0.0356, 0.0675]	0.0106	[-0.0281, 0.0493]
	Marginal effect	Confidence interval	Marginal effect	Confidence interval	Marginal effect	Confidence interval	Marginal effect	Confidence interval	Marginal effect	Confidence interval
GDP	0.00295	[-0.0026, 0.0085]	-.00644	[-0.0166, 0.00373]	-0.0069	[-0.0169, 0.003]	-0.0067	[-0.01671, 0.0033]	-0.0065	[-0.0165, 0.0035]
Gov't expenditure	0.00122	[0.00015, 0.0023]	0.00116	[0.0001, 0.0022]	0.00128	[0.0002, 0.0023]	0.00128	[0.0002, 0.0023]	0.0012	[0.0001, 0.0022]
Spatial lag			0.03007	[0.0001, 0.0601]	0.0065	[-0.0214, 0.0344]			0.0288	[-0.0004, 0.0581]
Networks					0.0029	[-0.0011, 0.0069]	0.0033	[-0.00015, 0.00681]		

Note: Confidence intervals at 95 per cent; other variables held constant at their mean

means that the network years' variable is a more stable predictor than the spatial lag. In addition, the model with the network clarifies the mode of communication behind the adoption of RIA and the role of the OECD, which has been effective in reducing governments' uncertainty about such an administrative innovation. The spatial model, instead, relies on the strong assumption that each adopting unit has the same capacity to receive communication about an innovation, communication that is modulated only by distance from previous adopters.

Overall, this comprehensive model stresses the importance of the transnational networks for the transfer of administrative innovations. The role of the OECD is, however, limited to its mediative function. Regulatory reform inquiries on OECD member states' regulatory management capacity do not affect the probability of adopting RIA. Together with the lack of a unique model of RIA and, more broadly, the absence of a global paradigm of administrative reform, these results demonstrate that adoption is, in this case, driven by the extent of governments' interaction with the OECD and EU networks. The latter are 'facilitators' of good lessons rather than 'norm teachers' (Finnemore 1993). The predicted direction of government expenditure and its constant marginal effects throughout the three models proves the hypothesis that the political control of regulators is rooted in the rise of complexity in public administration.

5.4 Conclusions

This chapter has provided evidence for the diffusion of RIA among EU and OECD countries. The hypotheses rely on a three-fold explanatory model in order to capture the null hypothesis, as well as on international and transnationally formed patterns of diffusion. Following the literature on the diffusion of administrative reform, the fixed regional model was assumed to be based on administrative cultural tradition, together with geographical proximity and interconnectedness. The latter aspect has been captured through specific measures of horizontal and vertical modes of diffusion. Being a US commercial partner and open to international trade did not have any effect on a given country's probability of adopting RIA. No empirical finding supports the hypothesis that countries more exposed to trade competition or better positioned in 'world society' also have a significant probability of adoption. The role of the OECD as a promoter of administrative reform has been confirmed by countries' length of time and total number of years spent in networks of regulatory reform. The normative pressures of peer review mechanisms for enhancing regulatory reform did not have a major impact on governments' choice to adopt RIA.

The results show an unclear picture with regard to the internal determinants of adoption. The relationship between administrative capacity to innovation has been a relevant explanation only in the first and second models. On the other hand, government expenditure emerges more strongly as a predictor in the last two models, questioning the political control hypothesis. The legal origin variables set out to capture the administrative tradition and did so significantly in the first and, more marginally, in the comprehensive model. Overall, the explanatory framework holds reasonably well considering the complexity, as mentioned by Sahlin-Andersson (2001), of discerning and associating each specific measure with one of the three levels of explanation. The major finding is that the transnational networks have provided governments, which were already aware of the need to overview their regulatory process, with cognitive shortcuts (set up by the theorisation, promotion and relabelling of regulatory reform) to taking the decision to adopt RIA.

Two further analyses could improve these empirical findings of the role of the OECD in the diffusion of RIA. Firstly, detailed information about the activities and engagement of each government within the OECD network could better specify the IO's role. Secondly, an analysis of what has been adopted and implemented, and ultimately whether and how RIA has been evaluated (and whether and what governments have learned from this regulatory governance innovation) could feed back the alternative explanation of diffusion. These are the objects of the next chapters.

chapter six | modelling RIA implementation

The previous chapter has shown that the OECD, by constructing and reframing policy discourses around the concept of policy innovation, has had a tangible effect on governments' decisions to adopt RIA. However, has the OECD also played a role in the way governments implemented this transnational policy innovation? How and to what extent have the OECD's recommendations been observed by its members? Or, in other words, to what extent have governments gone through a process of adaptation and selection of the reform package designed by the OECD?

This chapter answers these questions by relying on the scope of implementation, an aggregated indicator based on OECD surveys and two additional data sources. This indicator is introduced in terms of its relationship with categories of adopters and adoption timing. This chapter also aims to highlight the importance of the relationship, too often neglected, between the OECD and policy interdependence at the stage of implementation. Indeed, the literature on the OECD and, more generally, transnational policy networks tends to focus on ideational rather than actual policy change. Policy diffusion research tends to opt for discovering patterns or probabilities of policy adoption, implicitly assuming that 'all states adopt exactly the same policy' (Clark 1985). Few theoretical papers promote the study of diffusion as a dynamic process (Downs and Mohr 1976; Downs 1976; Lamothe 2004; Lamothe 2005) and a few empirical studies have looked at the extent of adoption and reinvention (Clark 1985; Glick and Hays 1991; Hays 1996a; Hays 1996b).

Taking into account the role of the OECD and the categories of adopters enables us to put aside such an unreasonable assumption and formulate specific hypotheses on the extent of normative pressure and institutional capacity. Transnational best practice for implementing policy innovation should ultimately lead to a desired convergence toward universal standards (Pal 2012). However, pioneer countries are assumed to have, across time, greater resources to invest in policy formulation and, consequently, given the incrementalism effect, they tend to have the most extensive policy at any point in time (Clark 1985). An institutionalist interpretation would differentiate the pace of implementation according to administrative tradition and legal origin.

Furthermore, the characteristics and attributes of RIA, related to governments' capacity to adjust, adapt and mould this administrative innovation, are also considered (Rogers 2003). Accordingly, the different reasons for its adoption and institutionalisation are depicted through the 'implementation dimensions' of clarity of the regulatory policy and legal mandate to pursue regulatory reform; organisational resources and procedures; the strategic use of RIA and its integration to other policy goals; and overall legitimacy. These dimensions are not exclusive. On the contrary, one can argue that governments with greater implementation are willing to achieve simultaneously different and sometimes contrasting goals.

This chapter is structured as follows. Section 6.1 attempts to link the emerging concepts of transnational governance with the implementation of policy innovations. Section 6.2 reviews the few available studies on the scope of change and policy reinvention and, relying on theoretical insights, formulates the main expectations of the extent to which implementation should be tested. Section 6.3 illustrates the methodology for deriving the implementation score. Section 6.4 presents the major results from the implementation scores and highlights whether countries pursue political control rather than economic rationality or regulatory governance legitimacy. The relationships between implementation and the groups of adopters, the year of adoption and effectiveness of administrative innovation are also provided. Section 6.5 concludes, arguing that the impact of the OECD's peer review on national choices for implementation was marginal.

6.1 The OECD and the implementation of policy reform

Establishing a causal relationship between the ideational roles of the OECD and policy change (Marcussen 2004a) is not an easy task (Armingeon and Beyeler 2004; Jakobi and Martens 2010; Pal 2012). So far, cross-sectional analyses have relied on the analysis of congruence or convergence to extricate this complexity. The former is a qualitative method which, over time and between countries, entails establishing concordance between the OECD's recommendations and the content and effectiveness of policy reform. In particular, the lack of compliance with the *Economic Survey* recommendations has been considered an indication of deficiencies in the OECD's ideational authority (Armingeon and Beyeler 2004). This method has, however, two caveats. Firstly, it is difficult to isolate the effect of the OECD from the influence stemming from other IOs and from national policy dynamics and determinants. Secondly, the extent of concordance could be overrated because of an excessive length of time considered in the analysis, as well as the bias in coding as concordance any small change in the direction of the OECD's policy recommendations. A more recent study attempted to overcome the first methodological flaw through a matched comparison of the impact of the EU's and the OECD's pension policy recommendations for Norway and the UK. This comparative analysis traced and gauged the ideational influences stemming from neighbouring countries as the main rationale for pension policy reform (Ervik 2009).

Other studies have attempted to establish the relationship between OECD governance mechanisms, i.e. generation and dissemination of ideas, peer review and the production of data, and policy implementation by relying on the concept of policy convergence (Jakobi and Martens 2010). Cross-sectional analysis assessed the variance of macro- and meso-level education policy indicators through sigma-convergence. This method, however, cannot isolate the OECD benchmark effects from other sources of policy change. Indeed, the moral suasion argument of the Job Strategy peer review is overdetermined when other convergence drivers, such as market integration and domestic policy dynamics, are also taken into account

(McBride and Williams 2001). Based on the assumption that the more a country's policies were at variance with Jobs Strategy norms, the more recommendations for reform it received, a reduction in the number of OECD recommendations is a crude measure of convergence (McBride and Williams 2001). In a later analysis, this simple measure was used to rank a sample of OECD countries and provided evidence of the presence of two clusters of countries: the neo-liberal and the 'flexicurity', within the OECD's employment strategy (McBride *et al.* 2008).

Single case studies on public management reform disagree on the OECD's influence. On the one hand, Pal collected evidence through academic assessments; a survey of academics and practitioners; and an analysis of the OECD's own evaluation of policy impact and effectiveness. He concluded that 'it is hard to imagine a world of governance and public management reform without the OECD as a key player' (Pal 2012). On the other hand, in a review of the Irish National Better Regulation Programme, Lodge (2005) found only limited evidence of the OECD's role as a standard setter capable of combining demands and dispositions for change.

In a similar vein, qualitative single case studies on other policies do not provide a neat picture of the OECD's influence. There is little evidence of the impact of the OECD's ideas on Danish employment policy, which was seen to be mainly dependent on domestic policy dynamics (Grinvalds 2008). Domestic dynamics, on the other hand, were marginal in the case of the reforms promoted by the OECD on the control of currency exchange and restrictions on foreign direct investment (Williams 2008). Further evidence pointing to the OECD's influence refers to emerging public policies and innovations such as the licensing of genetic inventions, urban development policy and the reconciliation of work and family life, an area in which the OECD has been effective in forming the policy agendas and persistent in exhorting their implementation (Bradford 2008; Drouillard and Gold 2008; Mahon 2008).

Overall, analyses of the OECD's impact on national policy implementation differ according to the selection of policy sectors (traditional policy sectors *vs* emerging policy issues) and countries, causing evident selection bias. Another major problem is related to the analytical framework which should integrate both the transnational and the domestic policy dynamics. Furthermore, the issue of temporality is too often overlooked. Turning to these dimensions, the next section argues that policy innovation is a useful standpoint from which to assess the OECD's influence and to formulate hypotheses on the implementation of national reform.

6.2 Implementation in the literature of policy diffusion

Although most policy diffusion literature tends to explain or test why countries waited so long before adopting a certain policy innovation, theoretical contributions recommend analysis of what is happening after the time of adoption (Rogers 2003). Later stages are relevant for understanding if and how an innovation has been reinvented (Hays 1996a; Hays 1996b; Hays 1996c; Hays and Glick 1997) and institutionalised (Lawrence *et al.*2001), and when an innovation would mature and then become obsolete, both being preconditions for further innovations (Rogers 2003).

Notwithstanding the fact that empirical evidence of the OECD's influence is patchy, an innovation framework enables us to clarify the relationships between the scope of implementation, on the one hand, and the OECD as well as other external and internal determinants, on the other. Indeed, the previous chapter's empirical findings confirm the soundness of a model that envisages the null hypothesis of diffusion, assessing the strength of internal determinants, together with modes of country-to-country and transnational interdependence. Each of those three levels of analysis can be associated with certain hypotheses and degrees of implementation.

Starting from the functional perspective, different contexts and purposes of regulatory reform lead to different modes of implementation. Accordingly, combining each reason for RIA with a sub-component of the extent of implementation, one can simply assume that the extent of an RIA programme is broader when governments want to achieve simultaneously diverse and (sometimes) contrasting goals, such as political control, economic rationality and external accountability. Furthermore, scholars interested in administrative reforms have shown that reforms in public administration rest on institutional path dependency (Melo 2004; McGuinn 2004) and administrative traditions (Peters 1997; Peters 2008), resulting in a great variance in the institutional choices for RIA (Radaelli 2005a; De Francesco *et al.* 2012). For instance, Smith (1996) emphasised the difference between the US and the European Union's approach to regulatory reform: 'Regulatory reform in Europe has been debated more in the context of competitiveness, a perennial European concern, than in the context of deregulation, cost/benefit analysis, and risk assessment'. Accordingly, a strong impact of internal determinants on adoption, such as legal origin, would determine a large part of the variance in RIA implementation and, consequently, maintain the persistence of national features. From another internal standpoint, pioneers generally have more resources, administrative capacity and information, and, given the usual effects of incrementalism, their policy may be more extensive than those of laggards at any point in time (Clark 1985).

Turning to the transnational level of diffusion, the role and influence of the OECD can lead to two different implementation modes. The proposition of a neat and precise policy model would require a much greater degree of centralisation in policy advice as well as use of the inquisitive function through intensive peer-reviewed benchmarking activities (Lodge 2005; Weyland 2006), especially for the followers and laggards (Marcussen 2004a; quoting Aubrey 1967). Yet the mediative function conducted through the provision of technical advice and expertise networks would facilitate the promotion of general principles and variety in implementation.

Finally, horizontal diffusion is characterised by the extent to which an adopting unit is connected to the US and other leading countries. This emulative mode of diffusion can lead to homogenisation. In other words, 'if laggards typically borrow the programs of leaders in order to simplify their decision making environments, then there may be little interstate variance in program breadth' (Clark 1985).

Another expectation can be derived from the literature on 'policy reinvention', defined as a general tendency to increase the scope of legislation along the diffusion process. Accordingly, subsequent adopters are in the relatively more advantageous position of learning from the collective experiences of all earlier adopters (Hays 1996b). Hays (1996b) tested the relationship between comprehensiveness of policy, measured both at the time of adoption and at the current time, and the year of adoption.

A positive slope indicates increasing comprehensiveness over time, and a negative slope indicates decreasing comprehensiveness over time. A very low or zero slope indicates that there is no support for any linear trend in the law's comprehensiveness. The absence of any linear trend would suggest that, while reinvention may still be present, it probably results not from a temporal learning process but from factors particular to each adopting. (Hays 1996b).

Similarly to Clark and Hays' works, this chapter focuses on a measure of the *de jure* dimension of the extent of implementation. Although a database of laws and regulations (enacted in all thirty-eight EU and OECD member states) concerning regulatory reform, as well as RIA guidance, does not exist, in 2007 and 2009 the OECD published the results of its surveys on the OECD member states' capacity to produce high-quality regulations (Jacobzone *et al.* 2007a; Jacobzone *et al.* 2007b; OECD Regulatory Policy Committee 2009), making it possible to extrapolate measures to assess the extent of implementation across countries. This set of indicators has been elaborated by the OECD with reference to the accepted approaches for good practice in regulatory management developed over more than a decade of regulatory reform reviews (OECD Regulatory Policy Committee 2009). Although this index differs from the congruence procedure which is based on policy recommendations specifically formulated by the OECD for each government within its regulatory review mission, it provides an indication of the extent of conformity among peers as well as a straightforward measure of the extent of improvement or reinvention over a short period of time.[1]

---

1.   Although the OECD conducted three rounds of surveys in, 1998, 2005 and 2008 respectively, the 1998 survey is of no use since the answers are not detailed and it is impossible to understand how a given country implemented RIA. As a result, the time span covered is only a small portion of the overall diffusion period, 1971–2006. The data presented in this chapter are therefore not able to represent the entire process of reinvention after the initial efforts of the pioneers.

In order to integrate data concerning the new EU member states that are not OECD countries, two additional data sources are used. These datasets are the outcome of two research projects: Evaluating Integrated Impact Assessment (EVIA) and European Network for Better Regulation (ENBR, *see* Appendix C for further details of these two research projects). These projects have developed country microfiches and databases on RIA, covering the contents of guidelines as well as broader and structural measures of implementation, such as legal mandate, financial resources and the extent of institutionalisation. Since EVIA and ENBR databases are not longitudinal (for each country a single set of observation data were collected in 2007), their integration with the 2005 implementation and the years of adoption. However, since most of the EU countries adopted RIA in the last decade, and assuming a limited degree of 'reinvention' in such a short time span, this should be enough for drawing major conclusions. Specifically, a positive relationship, meaning that later adopters implemented RIA more extensively than first adopters, suggests that the 'early majority' and 'laggards' learn or emulate the leaders, thanks partly to the role of the OECD. On the other hand, a negative relationship suggests a selective mode of learning based on internal and administrative features. Overall, this *de jure* index of good practice in RIA institutionalisation allows the relationship between the OECD and national RIA programmes to be assessed through theoretical expectations and the methodological insights of policy innovation research.

6.3 The implementation score

6.3.1 Theoretical insights for constructing the implementation score

Following Williams (2002), the implementation score revolves around three dimensions of institutional innovation:

- The legal dimension is concerned with rules and procedures stemming from 'ministerial mandates which assign legal responsibilities and delineate those who can make authoritative policy decisions from those who cannot'. This dimension 'alters policy procedures and organizational position in ways that enhance autonomy, agenda control, and ability to contest alternative policy proposals'. An example is a presidential decree establishing a central unit with a clear and overarching mandate for the promotion of regulatory reform;

- The organisational and decisional dimension refers to how 'technocratic appointees construct new bureaucratic entities'. Their 'decision rules [...] specify who can participate in the decision-making process and how collective choices are reached when legitimate participants disagree'. This dimension of implementation 'centralizes decision making authority in single-purpose units [,] alters organizational position and enhances [the technocrats'] autonomy; [it] displaces conflict over reform initiatives' and ultimately changes the way regulators think and behave. An example is the institutional arrangement of the regulatory process: the central unit has the authority to veto a regulatory proposal or to review and, ultimately, oversee decision making through an economic methodology such as CBA;

- The strategic dimension concerns standards to 'maximize the efficiency of resource expenditure required to secure procedural changes or create effective new policy instruments'. This dimension 'alters institutional arrangements in ways that ensure [a] future stream of preferred outcomes via [the] most efficient expenditure of resources'. Examples of this strategic dimension are: the use of CBA to review existing regulations, the creation of a regulatory budget to limit the flow of new regulation, and *ex post* review of regulatory reform and better regulation programmes.

In short, the first dimension is about the legal and political mandate for regulatory reform and regulatory quality management; the second refers to the central oversight unit and its independence; and the third looks at the capacity of an embedded innovative framework to maximise benefits of established administrative rules and procedures.

Another theoretical modality for arranging the analysis of implementation is consideration of the three principal reasons for RIA: enhancing the empirical basis of decision making; controlling and increasing the internal accountability of regulators; and improving regulatory legitimacy. The contributions to the implementation score from the first two of these reasons are derived by rearranging the three implementation dimensions described above (legal, organisational and strategic). A 'legitimacy' (fourth) dimension is then added to the implementation score to account for the third reason.

6.3.2 Elements of the implementation score

The items comprising the four different dimensions of RIA implementation are summarised in Tables 6.1–6.4, which also list the data sources, the implementation score sub-component values (usually dichotomous values, zero or one), maximum values of each sub-index (eight for the strategic dimension; five for all the others) and the countries not covered by the datasets.

The items of the legal dimension (Table 6.1) refer to the existence of an explicit policy for better regulation, the establishment of regulatory reform objectives, principles of good regulation, ministerial responsibility for better regulation and the degree of compulsory RIA. The available data sources omit two observations, those for Bulgaria and Romania.

The organisational and procedural dimension (Table 6.2) is crucial for understanding how the incentive structure within the bureaucracy has changed as a consequence of the legal mandate given by the political agent to technocrats or high-level civil servants. Essentially, this dimension measures the institutionalisation of a central unit and its authority to oversee the regulatory process, as well as more general measures (of the presence of criteria to select proposals, the presence of guidelines and the requirement to rely exclusively on CBA).

Table 6.1: Legal dimension of RIA implementation

Indicators	Items and data sources			Countries not covered	Functional rationale
	OECD	ENBR	EVIA		
Explicit regulatory reform or better regulation policy	Is there any explicit, published regulatory policy promoting government-wide regulatory reform or regulatory quality improvement?	Is there an explicit policy (adopted by the government, cabinet or in law) promoting government-wide regulatory reform or regulatory quality improvement (i.e. a 'better regulation' policy or programme?	Key documents, law(s) and decree(s) establishing RIA framework	None	NA
Objectives of regulatory reform	Does the regulatory policy establish explicit objectives of reforms?	Do(es) the regulatory policy(ies) establish explicit objectives to be achieved by improving regulatory quality (e.g. reducing costs on business, improving compliance, etc)?	The rationale for and the aims of RIA: Explicit = 1 Implicit = 0	None	ER
Principles of regulatory quality	Does the regulatory policy set out explicit principles of good regulation?	Are the following principles explicitly included in the regulatory quality/reform programme(s)		Bulgaria and Romania	ER

(Cont'd.)

Table 6.1: (Cont'd.)

Indicators	Items and data sources			Countries not covered	Functional rationale
	OECD	**ENBR**	**EVIA**		
		None = 0; Otherwise = 1			
Responsibility and accountability at ministerial level	1) Does the regulatory policy establish specific responsibilities for reform at the ministerial level? 2) Is a specific minister accountable for promoting government-wide progress on regulatory reform? Both present = 1 Otherwise = 0	Is an individual minister responsible for ensuring progress on regulatory quality/reform against measurable benchmarks?		Bulgaria and Romania	PC
Mandatory RIA	Is RIA formally required by law or by a similar binding legal instrument? 'Always' or 'only for major regulation' = 1 'In other selected cases' or 'No' = 0	Is IA compulsory at the national level?	Mandatory or voluntary IA: 'Mandatory for all proposals' or 'Mandatory for some proposals' = 1 'Purely voluntary' = 0	None	PC

ER = Economic Rationality; PC = Political Control; NA = Not Applicable. Maximum value of this sub-index is 5.

Table 6.2: Organisational and procedural dimension of RIA implementation

Indicators	Items and data sources			Countries not covered	Functional rationale
	OECD	ENBR	EVIA		
Central Unit responsible for regulatory reform	Is there a dedicated body (or bodies) responsible for promoting the regulatory policy and monitoring and reporting on regulatory reform and regulatory quality in the national administration from a whole government perspective?	Is a specific administrative body(ies) (for example, a central 'regulatory quality unit' in the cabinet office) explicitly responsible for overseeing progress on regulatory quality/ reform against measurable benchmarks?	Presence and role of the coordination unit: 'Present with guidance role' or 'Present with guidance and control role' = 1 'Not present' = 0	None	PC
Central Unit monitoring RIA quality	Is this body entrusted with the authority of reviewing and monitoring regulatory impacts conducted in individual ministries?		Presence and role of the coordination unit: 'Present with guidance role and control role' = 1 'Present with guidance role' = 0.5 'Not present' = 0	None	PC
Selection of proposals to analyse	Is there a clear 'threshold' for applying RIA to new regulatory proposals?	Does the written guidance contain explicit criteria (other than the word 'significant') to select those proposals deserving less and more extended IA?	Coverage and selection criteria of proposals subject to IA: 'All policy initiatives including broad strategies or 'Only legal proposals' = 0 'Most important proposals' or 'Only policy initiatives that can have significant burdens for firms and/or public administration' = 1	None	NA

(Cont'd.)

Table 6.2: (Cont'd.)

Indicators	Items and data sources			Countries not covered	Functional rationale
	OECD	ENBR	EVIA		
Guidance	Is general guidance on the regulatory policy and its underlying objectives published and distributed to regulatory officials?	Is there written guidance on IA?	Availability and implementation of guidelines: 'Guidelines are poorly implemented' or 'Guidelines available and implemented' = 1 'Guidelines do not exist' = 0	None	NA
CBA as the only method	Does the RIA require regulators to demonstrate that the benefits of new regulation justify the costs? 'Always' or 'Only for major regulations' = 1 'In other selected cases' or 'no' = 0	Does the written guidance on IA mandate use of a specific methodology to select the preferred policy option? 'CBA only' = 1 Otherwise = 0	Methods and models used for assessments: 'CBA' = 1 Otherwise = 0	None	ER

ER = Economic Rationality; PC = Political Control; NA = Not Applicable. Maximum value of this sub-index is 5.

Table 6.3: Strategic dimension of RIA implementation

Indicators	Data sources			Countries not covered	Functional rationale
	OECD	ENBR	EVIA		
Multi-level regulatory policy	a) Are there formal coordination mechanisms between National/Federal and State/Regional government? b) Are there formal coordination mechanisms at the supra-national level (i.e. as a consequence of membership of international bodies, such as the EU)? 2 = both present 1 = one of the two present 0 = none	Does regulatory quality policy extend to the sub-national level?	Vertical integration among different decision making levels: Assessments consider input from higher or lower level. 0 = 'no/only marginally' or 'varies between IAs' 1 = 'to some extent' or 'yes/substantially'	None	ER
Consultation and RIA	Are the views expressed in the consultation process included in the RIA? Subordinate regulation	Does the written guidance on IA prescribe that consultation should inform the assessment of different options?		Bulgaria and Romania	PC

(Cont'd.)

Table 6.3: (Cont'd.)

Indicators	Data sources			Countries not covered	Functional rationale
	OECD	ENBR	EVIA		
RIA and competition	Is the RIA required to include assessment of impacts on competition? Always' or 'Only major regulation' = 1 'In other selected cases' and 'No' = 0	Does the written guidance on IA analyse options in terms if their impacts on competition?		Bulgaria and Romania	ER
Review of regulations	Are there standardised evaluation techniques or criteria to be used when regulation is reviewed?	Does the written guidance on IA contain procedures for monitoring and evaluation *ex post* the extent to which the regulation meets its objectives?	Monitoring and *ex post* evaluation	None	ER

ER = Economic Rationality; PC = Political Control. Maximum value of this sub-index is 5.

The strategic dimension (Table 6.3) refers to the sophistication achieved in implementation, i.e. whether RIA requirements and regulatory quality concepts can be extended to the supranational and/or regional level of governance; the presence of a systematic review of existing regulations; the comprehensiveness of economic analysis to include the impact on competition; and the extent of integration with other administrative requirements of the regulatory process (such as consultation). Again, the available data sources omit two observations, those for Bulgaria and Romania, which are therefore excluded in order to avoid bias.

The sum of these three sub-indexes provides the first indication of the extent of implementation. This index relies on the OECD 2005 survey and covers twenty-six OECD member states. Having only adopted RIA in 2006, Greece, Portugal and Turkey are not included in the 2005 index, notwithstanding their survey response. RIA programmes in these countries are assumed to be incomplete. These three countries' responses to the OECD's survey may be based on the RIA system which was still at the proposal stage, rather than the actual *de jure* implementation. However, these countries are included in the 2008 index. Relying on the same methodological approach used by the OECD in the construction of the index of regulatory management systems (OECD Regulatory Policy Committee 2009), the few missing data of these OECD surveys have been assigned zero in the calculation of the indexes.

The last column in Tables 6.1–6.3 indicates whether the implementation measure can be associated with the justification for achieving economic rationality (ER) or with political control (PC). In few cases the measure can be regarded as not applicable (NA), since the element of implementation cannot be related exclusively to a specific rationale of adoption. The rationality index is composed of elements of the legal dimension (objectives and principles of regulatory reform are specified), and the strategic dimension (multi-level regulatory policy; RIA and competition policy; and criteria to review regulations). CBA is the only appraisal method used. The maximum value of this sub-index is seven. The political control index encompasses the accountability of the minister, the obligation to conduct RIA, the functions of the central unit and the integration of consultation within the RIA process. The maximum value of this sub-index is five.

Finally, the last dimension of implementation considered concerns the degree of legitimacy that regulatory quality policy and RIA have achieved in the institutional context. This is measured with reference to activities conducted by other constitutional bodies (parliaments and courts) and to different features of regulatory consultation, e.g. notice-and-comment procedure, openness and the public disclosure of RIA reports (Table 6.4). The legitimacy data are drawn exclusively from the OECD surveys since the other datasets overlooked this aspect of institutionalisation. Adding legitimacy to the legal, organisational and strategic dimensions results in the comprehensive implementation index, with a maximum score of thirty-six.

Table 6.4: Legitimacy dimension of RIA implementation

Indicators	OECD	Data
Parliamentary Committee	Is there a dedicated parliamentary committee or other parliamentary body with responsibilities that relate specifically to the regulatory policy/regulatory reform policy?	Data on OECD countries only
Parliamentary Committee 2	Is this body also entrusted to review quality of subordinate regulation? (i.e. lower level rules?)	Data on OECD countries only
Parliamentary Committee 3	Is the review process, if it exists, explicitly guided by regulatory quality criteria?	Data on OECD countries only
Parliamentary Committee 4	Does this body review and report on progress on regulatory policy/regulatory reform across the administration?	Data on OECD countries only
Courts	Are elements of the regulatory policy subject to judicial review (e.g. If RIA or consultation requirements are legislatively based, can the validity of laws be challenged if these requirements are not met?)	Data on OECD countries only
Citizens	What forms of public consultation are routinely used? Public notice and comment?	Data on OECD countries only
Citizens 2	Can any member of the public choose to participate in the consultation?	Data on OECD countries only
Citizens 3	Are RIA documents required to be publicly released for consultation with the general public?	Data on OECD countries only

Maximum value of this sub-index is 8.

6.4 Empirical results

Tables 6.5 and 6.6 list the values of the implementation scores for each country (classified according to adopter categories and legal origin). In 2005, as many as eleven countries scored over the mid-range of the overall index: the UK, the US, Canada, Korea, Mexico, Italy, Australia, New Zealand, Poland, Switzerland and Ireland. Most of these countries are pioneers and early followers and also had high scores on the legal, organisational and strategic dimensions of implementation. The UK, the US, Canada and Korea performed markedly better on the legitimacy score than the remaining countries. Among this group of top-scoring countries, there is also a relatively surprising group of late followers. Italy and Poland have the highest score on the legal dimension, whereas Ireland performed better on the organisational dimension and Switzerland had an even implementation. Just below the mid-range, Germany, the Netherlands, Spain, Austria, Denmark and Belgium formed a cluster of countries characterised by their strategies for cutting bureaucratic red tape.

Table 6.5: 2005 OECD and 2007 ENBR and EVIA implementation scores

Country	Adopter type	Legal origin	Legal	Organisational	Strategic	Subtotal	Legitimacy	Overall index	Ec. rat.	Pol. cont.	Effect. impl.
				2005 OECD survey							
UK	Pioneer	English	4	5	4	13	8	21	6	4	1
US	Pioneer	English	5	5	4	14	7	21	6	5	1
Canada	Pioneer	English	5	4.5	4	13.5	7	20.5	6	4.5	1
Korea	Early follower	German	5	5	4	14	6	20	7	4	1
Mexico	Early follower	French	5	5	5	15	3	18	7	5	1
Italy	Late follower	French	5	3.5	4	12.5	3	15.5	5	4.5	0
Australia	Pioneer	English	4	4.5	3	11.5	3	14.5	5	3.5	1
New Zealand	Early follower	English	2	4.5	4	10.5	3	13.5	5	2.5	1
Poland	Late follower	Socialist	5	3.5	3	11.5	2	13.5	4	4.5	1
Switzerland	Late follower	German	3	3	3	9.5	3	12.5	4	3.5	0
Ireland	Late follower	English	4	4	3	11	1	12	4	4	1
Germany	Pioneer	German	4.5	3	3	10.5	1	11.5	5	3.5	0
Netherlands	Pioneer	French	2	3	4	9	2	11	3	4	1

(Cont'd.)

Table 6.5: (Cont'd.)

Country	Adopter type	Legal origin	Legal	Organisational	Strategic	Subtotal	Legitimacy	Overall index	Ec. rat.	Pol. cont.	Effect. impl.
Spain	Laggard	French	5	1	2	8	3	11	4	3	0
Austria	Late follower	German	4.5	1	3	8.5	2	10.5	4	2.5	0
Denmark	Pioneer	Scandinavian	4	2.5	2	8.5	2	10.5	3	3.5	1
Belgium	Late follower	French	3	3.5	2	8.5	1	9.5	3	3.5	0
Finland	Late follower	Scandinavian	1.5	2	4	7.5	2	9.5	4	1.5	1
Czech Rep.	Late follower	Socialist	4	3.5	1	8.5	0	8.5	4	2.5	0
France	Early follower	French	4	2	2	8	0	8	5	1	0
Norway	Early follower	Scandinavian	1.5	1	3	5.5	2	7.5	3	1.5	0
Japan	Laggard	German	4	1	0	5	2	7	2	2	0
Hungary	Pioneer	Socialist	1.5	0.5	2	4	1	5	2	2	0
Slovak Rep.	Late follower	Socialist	1	1	3	5	0	5	2	2	1
Sweden	Pioneer	Scandinavian	0.5	1	2	3.5	1	4.5	1	1.5	1
Iceland	Late follower	Scandinavian	0	1	0	1	1	2	0	1	0

(Cont'd.)

Table 6.5: (Cont'd.)

Country	Adopter type	Legal origin	Legal	Organisational	Strategic	Subtotal	Legitimacy	Overall index	Ec. rat.	Pol. cont.	Effect. impl.
2007 ENBR and EVIA survey											
Estonia	Early follower	Socialist	1	0	1	2	1	1	NA	NA	0
Latvia	Late follower	Socialist	1	1	1	3	1	1	NA	NA	0
Lithuania	Laggard	Socialist	5	2	0	7	2	2	NA	NA	0
Slovenia	Laggard	Socialist	4	0	0	4	2	1	NA	NA	0

Turning to the 2007 ENBR and EVIA datasets which cover only four additional countries, namely, Estonia, Latvia, Lithuania and Slovenia, one can observe that the implementation has been essentially legalistic, although with a high level of variance. Indeed, on the one hand, Lithuania and Slovenia had a comprehensive legal dimension of implementation; on the other hand, Estonia and Latvia were still lagging behind. At the time of the surveys, the aims of both economic rationality and political control were only marginally developed, with Lithuania scoring the highest (two).

Turning to the 2008 OECD implementation score (Table 6.6), as many as fifteen countries were above the mid-range score. Compared with the 2005 score, this group of leading countries was joined by Denmark, Sweden, France, the Netherlands and Japan. By reducing its implementation score by one point, Switzerland then came below the mid-range. Similarly, there were only a few other countries, i.e. Korea, Mexico and Belgium, which had a negative difference between the two scores. This may be due to a different interpretation of the questions in the OECD's survey, which was peer reviewed by foreign national officials tutoring the responding governments.

The greatest improvers were Sweden (10.5), a pioneer, France (7.5), an early follower, the Slovak Republic (8.5), a late follower, and Japan (8), a laggard, all of which possessed the characteristic of having notably enhanced the legal design of RIA implementation. Through regulatory reform review, the inquisitive influence of the OECD might have targeted not only late followers and laggards but also early adopters such as Sweden, which was able to reform its regulatory management system comprehensively by improving the organisational and strategic dimension as well as the legitimacy of RIA. These improvements were driven by the 2006 general election and were partly a response to the OECD's 2007 report. The new government adopted the SCM, with the target of reducing administrative burdens by 25 per cent; it also strengthened regulatory quality principles and revamped the RIA system through the broader Action Plan for Better Regulation (OECD 2010d). In other words, the strategy for cutting red tape presented an opportunity for a broader reconsideration and enhancement of regulatory quality governance which also affected the pre-existing RIA system. As a result, Sweden, as a pioneer country, joined the leading countries in terms of implementation.

Beyond the legal dimension, the Japanese Government improved its strategic use of RIA. This improvement appears to have been a result of the two rounds of regulatory review published in 1999 and 2004 (*see* Table 4.1). Whereas the first report attested to the absence of a central overview of regulatory requirements and the absence of administrative requirements, the 2004 publication acknowledged the commitment of the Japanese Government to adopt RIA and guided the initial steps of implementation by suggesting a gradual process.

Turning to Slovakia, no OECD review has been conducted. However, within the SIGMA project, the inquisitive influence of the OECD could be exercised on new OECD and/or EU members, including the Czech Republic, Hungary, Poland and the Baltic states. The review conducted, however, did not follow the same template used by the OECD to formulate specific policy recommendations (*see*

Table 6.6: OECD 2008 implementation scores and differences compared to the 2005 scores

Country	Adopter type	Legal origin	Legal	Org.	Strat.	Subtotal	Legit.	Overall index	Ec. rat.	Pol. cont.	Diff. from 2005
UK	Pioneer	English	5	5	4	14	8	22	6	5	1
US	Pioneer	English	5	5	4	14	7	21	6	5	0
Canada	Pioneer	English	5	4.5	5	14.5	6	20.5	7	4.5	0
New Zealand	Early follower	English	2	4.5	5	11.5	8	19.5	6	2.5	6
Korea	Early follower	German	5	5	4	14	5	19	6	5	-1
Mexico	Early follower	French	4	5	5	14	3	17	7	4	-1
Italy	Late follower	French	5	4	5	14	3	17	7	5	1.5
Poland	Late follower	Socialist	5	3.5	4	12.5	4	16.5	5	4.5	3
Australia	Pioneer	English	5	4.5	3	12.5	3	15.5	5	4.5	1
Denmark	Pioneer	Scandinavian	5	3.5	3	11.5	4	15.5	5	3.5	5
France	Early follower	French	4	3.5	4	11.5	4	15.5	7	2.5	7.5
Ireland	Late follower	English	4	4	3	11	4	15	4	4	3
Japan	Laggard	German	5	3	4	12	3	15	6	4	8
Netherlands	Pioneer	French	5	3	5	13	2	15	6	5	4
Sweden	Pioneer	Scandinavian	5	3	4	12	3	15	5	5	10.5
Czech Rep.	Late follower	Socialist	5	4.5	3	12.5	2	14.5	5	4.5	6
Greece	Laggard	French	5	4	4	13	1	14	6	5	NA
Finland	Late follower	Scandinavian	5	3	4	12	2	14	6	4	4.5

(Cont'd.)

Table 6.6: (Cont'd.)

Country	Adopter type	Legal origin	Legal	Org.	Strat.	Subtotal	Legit.	Overall index	Ec. rat.	Pol. cont.	Diff. from 2005
Slovak Rep.	Late follower	Socialist	5	2.5	3	10.5	3	13.5	4	4.5	8.5
Germany	Pioneer	German	5	3	3	11	1	12	5	4	0.5
Spain	Laggard	French	5	1	2	8	4	12	4	3	1
Portugal	Laggard	French	5	1.5	3	9.5	2	11.5	4	4.5	NA
Switzerland	Late follower	German	3.5	3	2	8.5	3	11.5	3	3.5	-1
Austria	Late follower	German	4.5	1	4	9.5	1	10.5	5	3.5	0
Turkey	Laggard	French	4.5	3	2	9.5	1	10.5	4	2.5	NA
Belgium	Late follower	French	4	3	2	9	0	9	3	3	-0.5
Hungary	Pioneer	Socialist	1.5	2.5	3	7	2	9	2	4	4
Norway	Early follower	Scandinavian	1.5	1	3	5.5	2	7.5	3	1.5	0
Iceland	Late follower	Scandinavian	4	2	0	6	1	7	2	2	5

OECD 2007b). With the exclusion of Hungary (which is still lagging behind, notwithstanding its being a pioneer and an OECD member subjected to regulatory review in 2000), the mediative influence and the desire to be 'modern' is expected to play a greater role on the regulatory reform and RIA systems of these new OECD members, categorised as late followers. This is also evidenced by the Czech Republic's adoption of the 1995 OECD recommendation, *Improving the Quality of Government Regulation* (OECD 2001).

Although reviewed in 2004 and 2008, within the EU 15 regulatory review initiative, France has strengthened the legitimacy aim through the constitutionalisation of the RIA system, a nationally generated solution that goes well beyond any recommendation from the OECD. Further, the most recent OECD regulatory review lamented the lack of an overall regulatory governance strategy in France. Moreover, it held that all measures intended to improve regulatory quality needed to be coherently integrated into a clear policy goal (OECD 2010b). By contrast, in Italy the adoption and the *de jure* institutional design of RIA have been guided by several regulatory reviews, electronically published in 2001, 2007, 2010 and 2012. However, this observance of international standards was not accompanied by effective implementation (Natalini and Stolfi 2012).

Similarly to Sweden, the relatively large increase in the implementation scores of Denmark and the Netherlands can be explained by the governments' choice to rely on the SCM as a strategy to revamp better regulation policy. This strategy to reduce administrative burden was mainly driven by the autonomous choices of national decision makers.[2] In these two countries, the OECD regulatory reviews were conducted at the end of the 1990s. Furthermore, the OECD has been rather sceptical about a regulatory quality policy mostly based on the measurement of administrative burden (OECD 2010c; OECD 2010f). However, the possibility of a marginal influence of the OECD cannot be excluded. On the basis of OECD recommendations, SCM can lead to the institutionalisation of principles, objectives and a regulatory oversight body concerning RIA procedure (*see* Section 3.4). On the other hand, it is fair to conclude that New Zealand, a country with an English legal origin, steadily improved its implementation of RIA by improving its legitimacy without any OECD influence. Similarly, Iceland enhanced its legal implementation score without any inquisitive pressure from the OECD. No report has been drafted on these two countries.[3] And Ireland, which improved its overall implementation score by three points, was assessed only in 2000, though it gives further evidence of the compatibility of an English legal origin with RIA and the consequent autonomy of these countries in their decisions concerning the implementation of RIA.

---

2. Indeed, '[m]any of these issues [concerning evidence-based analysis] had already been raised in the OECD's 1999 report, which drew specific attention to the need for effective quantification, the need to consider alternatives, and the need to consult. There has been progress on some fronts since then, notably the quantification of administrative burdens for business, but not enough to generate an effective approach.' (OECD 2010f).

3. *See* http://www.oecd.org/countrylist\0,3349,en_2649_37421_1794487_1_1_1_1,00.html (accessed 25 May 2012).

Korea and Switzerland were also reviewed in between the two OECD surveys. However, their implementation scores were lower in the later survey. Their overall OECD index of the extent of the RIA process did not vary substantially (OECD Regulatory Policy Committee 2009), indicating the marginal impact of regulatory reform reviews in countries with an already well consolidated system of regulatory governance. The review of Korean regulatory reform concluded by highlighting that the government was investing in the RIA system and remarked on potential improvements that could be made by managing regulations stemming from both parliament and regional regulators (OECD 2007b). In a similar vein, the focus of the review of Switzerland was on the coherence of its multi-level regulatory governance. The discussion of RIA was marginal and the report was not structured around the usual template, with a specific chapter dedicated to government capacity to assure high-quality regulation (OECD 2006c).

Overall, in between the two OECD surveys, the countries that markedly improved their implementation scores (a rise of at least three points) were mainly Scandinavian and post-socialist countries, but represented a mix of categories of adopters (four pioneers, two early followers, six late followers and a laggard). With the exclusion of Sweden and Japan, there was also a lack of OECD inquisitive influence. The latter was marginal on the Central and East European Countries (CEECs) which joined the SIGMA project, and indirect on the European countries that embarked on the SCM model.

A further interpretation of these implementation scores can be derived from Table 6.7 which reports the average implementation scores according to the categories of adopters and legal origin. Estonia, Latvia, Lithuania and Slovenia scores (based on ENBR and EVIA data) are added to the average for a check on robustness. This table questions whether pioneers and English legal origin countries tend to have the most extensive implementation across all sub-indexes and to converge towards the highest overall level of implementation. On the other hand, if the OECD's influence is stronger, the other adopter groups are expected to implement extensively and converge towards high scores.

Starting from the 2005 OECD survey, the averages partially confirm the incrementalism explanation of the extent of implementation: pioneer countries score higher than late followers and laggards but not higher than early followers. The latter group includes Korea, Mexico and New Zealand (which have high scores) in all implementation dimensions except legitimacy and political control. Averages calculated by taking into account ENBR and EVIA data reduce the scores among early and late followers. It is important to note the high level of variance within the same legal origin and adopter category countries, as signalled by the large values of the standard deviation and the standard deviation of the mean.

The overall tendency of the early followers to implement better than the pioneers on several implementation dimensions is also confirmed in the 2008 OECD survey. Pioneers, however, are characterised by an even implementation of RIA. Indeed, political control has progressed mainly among the pioneers (only Germany and Hungary have relatively low scores), while it is not yet consolidated among followers. Similarly, high economic rationality scores are common among

Table 6.7: Averages of implementation sub-indexes and variance, standard deviation and standard deviation of the mean of the overall implementation score. Scores and variance measures calculated according to legal origins (LO)

Type	Legal	Organ.	Strat.	Legit.	Econ. rat.	Pol. contr.	Overall average	Min.	Max.	Var.	Std. dev.	Std. dev. of mean
2005 OECD survey												
In parenthesis, averages comprehensive of Estonia, Latvia, Lithuania, and Slovenia (ENBR and EVIA data).												
Pioneers	3.39	3.22	3.1	3.5	4.11	3.5	13.28	4.5	21	41.8	6.5	2.16
	(3.08)											
Early followers	3.5	3.5	3.6	2.8	5.4	2.8	13.4	7.5	20	32.17	5.7	2.5
		(2.92)	(3.17)		(4.67)	(2.5)						
Late followers	3.15	2.6	2.6	1.5	3.4	2.95	9.85	2	15.5	16.06	4.01	1.27
	(2.95)	(2.45)	(2.45)		(3.18)	(2.77)						
Laggards	4.5	1	1	2.5	3	2.5	9	7	11	8	2.8	2
	(4.5)	(1)	(0.5)		(2.5)	(2)						
English LO	4	4.58	3.67	4.83	5.33	3.92	17.08	12	21	17.5	4.2	1.7
French LO	4	3	3.17	2	4.5	3.6	12.17	8	18	14.47	3.8	1.5
German LO	4.3	2.6	2.6	2.8	4.4	3.1	12.3	7	20	22.8	4.78	2.1
Scandinavian LO	1.5	1.5	2.2	1.6	2.2	1.8	6.8	2	10.5	12.45	3.5	1.6
Socialist LO	2.875	2.125	2.25	3	3	2.75	8	5	13.5	16.17	4.02	2.01
	(2.8)	(1.437)	(1.14)		(2.25)	(2)						

(Cont'd.)

Table 6.7: (Cont'd.)

Type	Legal	Organ.	Strat.	Legit.	Econ. rat.	Pol. contr.	Overall average	Min.	Max.	Var.	Std. dev.	Std. dev. of mean
OECD 2008 survey												
Pioneers	4.61	3.78	3.78	4	5.22	4.5	16.17	9	22	18.56	4.31	1.4
Early followers	3.3	3.8	4.2	4.4	5.8	3.1	15.7	7.5	19.5	15.7	4.85	2.17
Late followers	4.5	3.05	3	2.3	4.4	3.85	12.85	7	17	10.67	3.27	1.03
Laggards	4.9	2.5	3	2.2	4.8	3.8	12.6 (13.5)	10.5 (12)	15 (15)	3.425 (4.5)	1.85 (2.12)	0.83 (1.5)
English LO	4.33	4.58	4	6	5.67	4.25	17.36	12	22	14.3	3.8	1.4
French LO	4.61	3.11	3.55	2.2	5.3	3.83	13.5 (14.25)	9 (9)	17 (17)	8.3 (9.97)	2.9 (3.16)	0.96 (1.3)
German LO	4.6	3	3.4	2.6	5	4	13.6	10.5	19	11.92	3.45	1.5
Scandinavian LO	4.1	2.5	2.8	2.4	4.2	3.2	11.8	7	15.5	17.57	4.2	1.9
Socialist LO	4.125	3.25	3.25	2.75	4	4.375	13.375	9	16.5	10.06	3.17	1.6

Greece, Portugal and Turkey are included in the 2008 averages. The descriptive statistics in parenthesis do not consider these three countries, facilitating the comparison of the same sample of countries from the 2005 OECD survey.

pioneers and early followers. Among the latter, in 2005, Mexico and Korea had the highest scores (seven); Iceland and (surprisingly) Sweden the lowest (zero and one, respectively).

Turning to the late followers and laggards, these two groups have similar overall scores. However, laggards focused on the legalistic dimension by getting the highest score among all the adopter categories. In 2008, although increasing the extent of implementation, these two categories are not converging towards the highest best practice model. Consequently, the hypothesis of a concluded process of homogenisation towards the highest level of implementation can be excluded. Indeed, laggard countries increased the extent of implementation in organisational and strategic dimensions but still lagged behind in terms of legitimacy. The late followers scored relatively low on the organisational, strategic and legitimacy dimensions of implementation. Overall, the 2008 OECD survey shows a broad reduction of variation in the implementation index across adopter categories. Variation which is, however, still considerable, especially among early followers.

Whereas the sub-index averages of adopter categories do not provide a clear pattern of implementation, the averages related to legal origin are straightforward: apart from the legal dimension, countries with an English legal origin always have the highest implementation scores. Both in 2005 and 2008, those with a French or German legal origin scored very similarly, but the French legal origin group is the most, and only relatively, homogenous group. In 2008, although improving considerably in terms of the extent of implementation, especially on the legal dimension, countries with a Scandinavian legal origin still lagged behind and are characterised by the highest level of variation.

Convergence patterns are more discernible if one considers each dimension of implementation. Table 6.8 summarises the descriptive statistics of the six sub-indexes for each data source. The legal is the most developed of the implementation dimensions, while legitimacy is less common among the twenty-six OECD countries surveyed in 2005. The organisational and strategic dimensions are similar, both in terms of means and variations. Turning to the function of RIA, the indexes of economic rationality and political control are also notable. It is important to note that the legitimacy scores have the largest variance, the strategic and the political control scores the least.

Notwithstanding the inclusion of Greece, Portugal and Turkey, the 2008 OECD sub-indexes show a consistent increase in the extent of implementation and a reduction in its variation. Compared with the 2005 index, on the legal dimension countries are converging to the highest score, by an increase of one point. The strategic dimension also has a remarkable increase in similarity among the twenty-nine OECD countries. Turning to the indexes associated with the three functional rationale of RIA, it is evident that the legitimacy score still has the largest variation and the lowest score, whereas the political control index is converging towards a higher value.

A further test is to assess the relationship between years of adoption and the implementation scores (Table 6.9). A negative and significant correlation indicates the constant leading role of the early adopters and the marginal emulation of later

Table 6.8: Descriptive statistics of implementation scores

Sub-indexes	Obs.	Min.	Max.	Mean	Variance	Std. deviation	Std. dev. of mean
2005 OECD survey							
Legal	26	0	5	3.4	2.54	1.59	0.31
Organisational	26	0.5	5	2.86	2.43	1.56	0.31
Strategic	26	0	5	2.85	1.57	1.25	0.246
Legitimacy	26	0	8	2.54	4.74	2.18	0.43
Econ. rationality	26	0	7	4	3.04	1.74	0.34
Political control	26	1	5	3.08	1.53	1.24	0.24
2008 OECD survey							
Legal	29	1.5	5	4.4	1.096	1.05	0.19
Organisational	29	1	5	3.31	1.49	1.22	0.22
Strategic	29	0	5	3.45	1.33	1.15	0.21
Legitimacy	29	0	8	3.17	4.22	2.05	0.38
Econ. rationality	29	2	7	4.96	2.106	1.45	0.27
Political control	29	1.5	5	3.91	1	1	0.18
2007 ENBR and EVIA surveys							
Legal	4	1	5	2.75	4.25	2.06	1.03
Organisational	4	0	2	0.75	0.92	0.96	0.48
Strategic	4	0	1	0.5	0.33	0.58	0.29
Econ. rationality	4	1	2	1.5	0.33	0.58	0.29
Political Control	4	1	2	1.25	0.25	0.5	0.25

adopters. The result confirms this expectation, especially when the legitimacy motive is included and implementation scores for Estonia, Latvia, Lithuania and Slovenia are integrated with the 2005 OECD data.

Thanks to the OECD and EVIA datasets, it is possible to derive another dependent variable: the number of RIAs conducted in the EU and OECD countries per year. This variable better reflects the effectiveness of the implementation. The last column in Table 6.5 summarises the countries with an effective RIA system in place, distinguishing them from the countries with a symbolic adoption or a policy that was still to be developed. Through a quick check, it is fair to say that most of the countries with high overall implementation scores are also the countries with effective implementation, with the exceptions of Belgium, the Czech Republic, Germany, Italy, Spain and Switzerland, which have a relatively high score but lack effective adoption of RIA. Apart from Spain, a laggard, all those countries fell in the followers category. Hungary was the only country among the pioneers with ineffective implementation. The other puzzling cases are Finland, the Slovak Republic and Sweden, which, notwithstanding their low scores, had

Table 6.9: Correlations between implementation scores and years of adoption and effective production of RIA

	OECD 2005		OECD 2005 and 2007 ENBR-EVIA	OECD 2008	
	Subtotal	Overall index	Subtotal	Subtotal	Overall index
Obs	26	26	30	29	29
Adoption years	−0.3280	−0.4288	−0.3803	−0.3454	−0.4505
Sign. level	0.1018	0.0288	0.0382	0.0665	0.0142
Effective RIA		0.4232	0.4766		
Sign. level		0.0198	0.0138		

relatively efficient RIA implementation. On the other hand, Portugal represents an interesting case of fast institutionalisation, although its impact analysis concerns only administrative burdens.

A further statistical analysis (Table 6.9) confirms the correlation between implementation effectiveness and the implementation scores standardised by their maximum values. The output shows that effective implementation is positively related to the standardised implementation scores with coefficients 0.4232 and 0.4766, significant at levels 0.0198 and 0.0138. It is important to remark that this dimension of the effectiveness of the implementation captures only the production of RIAs, without appraising the quality of the single RIA or the overall quality of the RIA system, an aspect that is well beyond the scope of this research.

Another useful indication of the extent of the RIA programme's implementation is the number of staff employed in the oversight central unit. The report on the 2005 OECD survey provides this important piece of information. Furthermore, the EVIA survey and the recent OECD review on the fifteen 'old' EU member states as well as an OECD report on the quality of regulatory oversight bodies provide additional data on the central unit staff that are summarised in Table 6.10, (Cordova-Novion and Jacobzone 2011). Table 6.10 provides a crude measure of the extent of implementation and government commitment. Furthermore, the EVIA survey, an OECD report on the quality of regulatory oversight bodies (Cordova-Novion and Jacobzone 2011) and the recent OECD review on the EU-15 provide additional data on the central unit staff that are summarised in Table 6.10.

Table 6.10: Number of staff employed in the regulatory oversight central units

	2005 OECD review	EVIA	Cordova-Novion and Jacobzone
Australia	20		50
Austria		NA	
Belgium		20	16
Bulgaria		NA	
Canada			30
Czech Rep.	20	9	
Denmark	7	NA	7
Estonia		NA	
Finland		NA	
France		No information	
Germany		Small resources	12
Greece		NA	
Hungary		No information	
Iceland			
Ireland		1.5	
Italy	4	1.5	
Japan			10
Korea	40		44
Latvia		No information	
Lithuania		No information	
Mexico	16–20*		
Netherlands		No information	40 + 18
New Zealand	4		
Norway			
Poland		10	
Portugal		No information	10 + 8
Romania		6	
Slovak Rep.			
Slovenia			
Spain		No information	
Sweden		Not applicable	9
Switzerland			
Turkey			
UK	70	No information	
United States	50		

Source: NA = No answer
* (1999 OECD Review)

6.5 Conclusion

While evaluative studies have been conducted on the quality of implementation, scoring and benchmarking, single RIA reports (Hahn 1999; Hahn *et al.* 2000; Cecot *et al.* 2008) and more recent studies have explored the process of implementation (De Francesco *et al.* 2012) within a macro-economic and political context. This chapter has focused on the systematic meso-dimensions of implementation brought forth from theoretical insights and a consideration of the reasons for adopting RIA. Although not performing a dynamic analysis of policy reinvention, the creation of a set of implementation scores disentangles the different aspects of the implementation of a transnational policy innovation.

Firstly, there is no comprehensive implementation across the different dimensions of RIA. By and large, only the legal and organisational dimensions have been fully developed. In particular, the laggards have higher scores on the legal dimension, indicating a symbolic adoption of the overall principles of regulatory reform. Symbolic adoption is also indicated by the lowest variance in the legal score.

Secondly, among the three reasons for adopting RIA, political control has the higher mean values only within the pioneer category. This indicates that political control needs the institutionalisation of the administrative innovation, a finding already suggested in Chapter Three, on the process of institutionalisation among a sample of first adopters. Economic rationality has less variance and the scores of the pioneers and followers are similar, indicating that this aim is easier to transfer, especially thanks to the mediative activity of the OECD, which has promoted RIA as a decisional tool for enhancing evidence-based decision making. It is not surprising that, as democratic doctrines such as pluralistic and representative models of regulatory process have not developed beyond the US, the legitimacy score has the lowest average. Across countries, RIA has not been developed to enhance the democracy of regulatory governance.

Thirdly, the high variance across and within the overall implementation scores of categories of adopters and legal origin countries suggests the importance of the internal determinants and circumstances of the particular countries and the absence of a concluded process of emulation and homogenisation. An incrementalism explanation is evidenced by the higher means of the pioneers in the overall implementation score and by an even implementation across its dimensions. Furthermore, early followers have higher scores than late followers and laggards. Administrative tradition matters: English legal origin countries tend to implement RIA extensively.

Fourthly, the role of the OECD's inquisitive function was marginal, as also suggested by the qualitative findings on the impact of regulatory reform reviews on implementation scores.

Finally, the negative correlations between time and implementation indexes imply that laggards did not learn from pioneers. A comprehensive learning process, based on the experiences of previously adopting countries and best practice, can therefore be excluded as a plausible diffusion mechanism. The latter finding is confirmed by the OECD itself. In the *In-depth Evaluation of the Group on Regulatory Policy* the OECD evaluators stated that reviews of:

> Regulatory Reform are viewed by the vast majority of reviewed countries as having a significant policy impact, though limited use has been made of them by Members as a means of drawing lessons from across a broad range of national experiences. (Council of the OECD, 2009)

The systematic analysis of implementation provides a four-fold conception of effective and efficient innovation. There are significant correlations between the extent of implementation and effective performance of the innovation. Governments choose different patterns of implementation. Pioneer countries tend to have the most comprehensive implementation, while later adopters have chosen a more prudent approach. Overall, governments' interdependence seems not to affect implementation. Considering the two modes of diffusion, there is no strong evidence of horizontal communication. Furthermore, the role of the OECD is limited to promoting homogenisation of the legal and economic rational dimensions through mediative and cognitive interactions.

chapter seven | evaluating RIA programmes

The principal contribution of this book is to assess the influence of the OECD on domestic policy throughout the institutionalisation of RIA. Defined as 'the attainment of long-term viability and integration of innovation within organizations' (Goodman and Steckler 1989), institutionalisation is the final stage of the diffusion process (Goodman and Steckler 1989; Steckler *et al.* 1992; Lawrence *et al.* 2001; Rogers 2003). In the case of public policy, it refers to the permanence of an innovation which endures through elections and changes of governments (*see* Chapter Three for a qualitative account of the extent of institutionalisation in a sample of pioneer countries). Policy innovation eventually becomes a routine and loses its character of novelty (Rogers 2003; Steckler *et al.* 1992). Indeed, through the confirmation of previous adoption decisions, an innovation is integrated within most organisational subsystems (Steckler *et al.* 1992) and eventually reaches the point of 'maximum feasible expansion' (Rogers 2003).

The empirical findings produced so far refer to the role of the OECD in setting a transnational regulatory quality agenda which influenced the adoption of RIA in various countries and provided a model for its implementation. Considered as 'passages', the stages of adoption and implementation represent an incipient degree of institutionalisation and 'are highly symbolic events to those involved with an innovation' (Steckler *et al.* 1992). This chapter concludes the empirical investigation by focusing on the policy innovation confirmation stage, in which governments acquire additional information on and recognise the benefits and costs of RIA. Granted that governments exchange information on criticism of the innovation; evaluation research; and the experiences of other adopters (Mossberger 2000; Mossberger and Wolman 2003; Weyland 2006; Dolowitz 2009), the chapter discusses whether and how governments (and in some cases stakeholders) measure, monitor and evaluate the performance of RIA. It further provides an account of the OECD's experience with the development and management of tools aimed at assessing regulatory quality. Its main goal is to find out whether governments learn exclusively from their direct experience or use information and knowledge from both, other countries and the OECD (Levitt and March 1988) in order to situate their experience within a broader international context.

This chapter proceeds as follows. The next section links concepts of learning, policy diffusion and evaluation. Section 7.2 summarises the results of several surveys which probed governments on their experiences in evaluating regulatory policy, better regulation and RIA. It shows that only one-third of the countries which adopted RIA reported having an evaluation system in place. How do these countries reflect on their experience? After a brief description of the OECD peer review and benchmarking indicators on regulatory quality (Section 7.3), the remaining sections attempt to assess the extent of interdependence on RIA evaluation practice and search for evidence of the use of the OECD peer review and benchmarking systems at the national level. By looking at Australia, Belgium, Canada, Denmark, Sweden, the UK and the US, countries with a consolidated *ex post* review of the RIA system, Section 7.4 illustrates the main types of institutions and stakeholders involved in RIA performance review and Section 7.5 resumes the examination of quantitative and qualitative measures associated with the evaluation of RIA programmes. Section 7.6 concludes.

7.1 Linking learning, evaluation and policy diffusion

Learning is one of the mechanisms of policy diffusion (*see* Chapter Two; *see* also Dobbin *et al.* 2007; Meseguer 2009; Gilardi 2010). It is a micro process that involves interaction among policy makers on goals, values, structures and outcomes (Zito and Schout 2009). In addition to direct experience, governments can learn 'through the *transfer* of encoded experience in the form of technologies, codes, procedures, or similar routines' (Levitt and March 1988). From the perspective of those who formulate and design policies,

> '[i]nternally, they may learn about the preferences of the public, the goals of interest groups and other politicians, and the effects of previous policy. Externally, they may learn about what policies have been successful at meeting the needs of similar governments elsewhere' (Volden *et al.* 2008).

In other words, policy learning is about 'updating beliefs about key components of policy as the result of *analysis* and/or *social interaction*' (Radaelli 2009) [author's emphasis].

There is a clear link between instrumental policy learning and policy evaluation. Instrumental learning 'entails new understandings about the viability of policy interventions or implementation designs [...] [and] concerns improved designs for reaching existing policy goals' (May 1992). It results from the feasibility testing carried out through systematic policy experiments or implementation evaluations (May 1992). Although policy adaptation and redesign constitute only prima facie evidence of instrumental learning (May 1992), in a policy diffusion research framework it would be possible to distinguish true instrumental learning from mimicking socialisation. A large-n comparative analysis of evaluative practices has the advantages of avoiding: (i) the selection on the dependent variable, testing also the null hypothesis of no learning; (ii) the consideration of a narrow time-frame; and (iii) a focus restricted to a typology of learning, compounding the different concepts, mechanisms and micro-foundations of learning (Radaelli 2009).

Figure 7.1 summarises the set of hypotheses tested in this chapter. The first test contrasts the existence of evaluation activities and institutions, a precondition for policy learning, with the null hypothesis of governments not performing any evaluation. The absence of policy evaluation suggests adoption has been only symbolic. Accordingly, the operationalisation would proceed through an assessment of the existence of evaluation elements such as systematic evaluation of RIA programmes, active watchdogs and quality assurance programmes and indicators.

Granted, governments' capacities and efforts to evaluate the implementation of RIA policy transfer refers not only to ideas and policies but also to the means for measuring success and the identification of what counts as evidence (Dolowitz 2009). Focusing on knowledge generated by evaluation, different types and degrees of learning can be distinguished. The argument here is that an analysis of policy interdependence and diffusion should be completed by a careful observation of learning from IOs and other countries' evaluative experiences and practices. This reinforces the previous findings on patterns of policy interdependence and OECD influence.

The micro-foundations of policy learning can be different (Radaelli 2009). Following Dolowitz (2009), one can argue that actors who voluntarily engage in policy transfer – through a comprehensive analysis of all available evaluative practices – are able to learn (hard) forms of knowledge updating. By contrast, coercive and emulative mechanisms rely on the accumulation of soft forms of information in the post-transfer implementation process. Therefore, a further set of hypotheses can be derived. One regards the non-existence of governments' interaction on evaluation practices (the second hypothesis in Figure 7.1). In other words, governments design and operate their evaluations relying exclusively on their internal information and direct experience. This circumstance means that the diffusion process is essentially limited to adoption and implementation of policy innovation and does not pay attention to evaluation practices. Governments do

Figure 7.1: Linking policy evaluation, policy learning and diffusion mechanisms

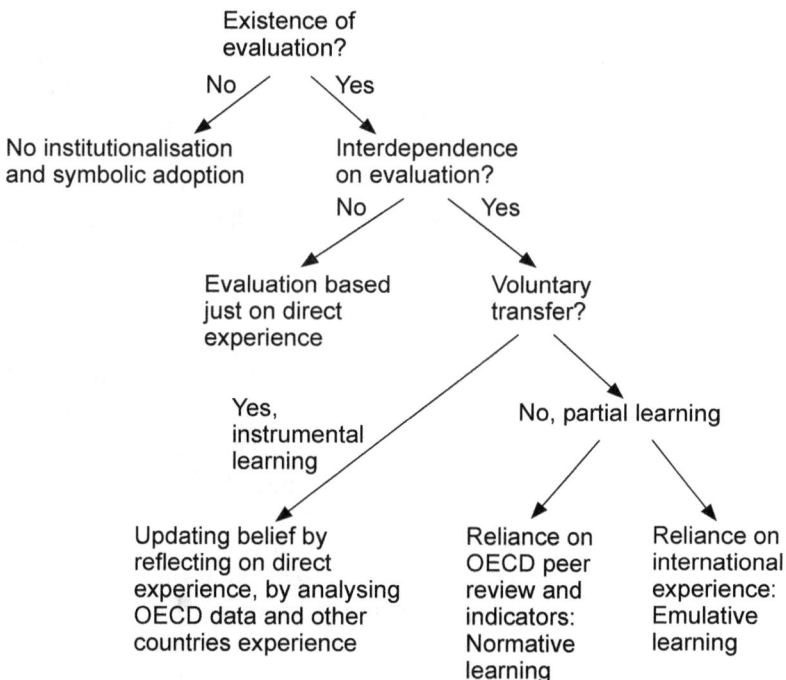

not learn how to evaluate RIA programmes from each other. On the other hand, a government could conceive policy evaluation by relying on both internal and external information. The results and experiences of evaluative practices in other countries and IOs would be fully acknowledged and adjusted to the national administrative context.

A yet more limited approach to learning how to evaluate and redesign policy innovation is also plausible. A hypothesis of the transfer of evaluative practices through the mechanism of mimetic emulation could be tested through evidence of common indicators and targets, models of oversight bodies and overall common evaluation practices agreed through country-to-country influence. This is the case where a country is observing a successful case of innovation and wants to achieve similar results by duplicating all elements of the reform package designed by the leading countries. Furthermore, a normative emulation mechanism would be proved through the impact of the OECD's norms and recommendations, imposing a unique model of policy evaluation and benchmarking.

The next sections provide qualitative evidence of the types and extent of learning achieved among OECD and EU member states. At the outset, it is useful to make a distinction between fully fledged systems of evaluation, such as the OECD regulatory peer review system which is based on the use of indicators and benchmarks, and simpler quality assurance mechanisms which routinely check whether RIA conforms to the government's principles and requirements. While several countries have introduced formal mechanisms to oversee and monitor the quality of RIA implementation, experience with performance measures is still limited. Another distinction concerns what is measured. Indicators of design refer to the planning and utilisation of bureaucratic capacity and resources in the appraisal system. Activities (also often referred to as policy outputs) cover two elements: (i) oversight activities carried out by bodies in the executive (cabinet office and/or departments), such as training, drafting guidelines and monitoring departments; and (ii) regulatory analyses produced. Finally, real-world outcome indicators are associated with the long-term and purposive impact of the programme, including the betterment of the regulatory environment for business and citizens.

7.2 The cross-national experience

The OECD has surveyed its member states on the composition of RIA programmes (Jacobzone *et al.* 2007a; Jacobzone *et al.* 2007b; OECD Regulatory Policy Committee 2009). Several items of this survey were dedicated to governments' capacity to evaluate regulatory policy and RIA, complementing a previous and more specific survey on the *ex post* evaluation of RIA (OECD 2003). Also, scholars surveyed EU governments on their capacity to evaluate better regulation policies (Radaelli and De Francesco 2007). This set of surveys is an excellent assessment of whether governments are engaged in evaluating their RIA programmes. Jacobzone *et al.* (2007) reported on the capacity of countries to assess 'compliance with key requirements of regulatory policy'. Among the

OECD member states, only twelve out of thirty OECD member states[1] responded by reporting that they were engaged in assessing compliance with regulatory policy. Further, the OECD survey distinguishes between RIA and consultation procedures in which compliance is controlled, showing that governments have usually established both.[2] The report also lists those countries that made attempts 'to measure the impact of regulatory policy on outputs or outcomes' (Jacobzone et al. 2007a): Finland, Hungary, Japan, Korea and the US responded by reporting that they had established measures to assess the impact of regulatory policy.

The 2008 OECD survey assessed governments on their capacity to calculate yearly regulatory inflation (OECD Regulatory Policy Committee 2009). Austria, Belgium, Canada, France, Italy, Korea, Luxembourg, Mexico, Norway, Poland, Portugal, Sweden and the US indicated that they were capable of estimating the extent of regulatory inflation. In addition, several other governments were also attempting to measure trends in the aggregate burden of regulation over time. These were: Australia, Austria, Belgium, Denmark, France, Germany, Greece, the Netherlands, Spain, Sweden, Switzerland, the UK and the US.

In 2005, Radaelli and De Francesco (2007) surveyed several EU member states in order to assess how widespread the concept of regulatory quality was. They found that twelve countries out of the twenty EU member states surveyed responded by reporting that they had set quantifiable targets, a precondition for *ex post* evaluation via appropriate indicators (Radaelli and De Francesco 2007).[3] Radaelli and De Francesco also questioned EU governments on the linkage between better regulation policy and the overall performance management systems. Half of the respondents were required to measure the performance of better regulation policy, usually within budgetary policy and through a central RIA overseeing unit. This is an indication of the formal commitment of a given government to performance measurement, but it does not show whether departments had actually complied with such a requirement. These survey results can also be compared with the 2003 OECD survey on the *ex post* review of regulation policy which reported that only nine out of twenty-two surveyed member countries[4] activated any explicit strategy/policy to evaluate regulatory tools and institutions, and ten countries established institutions responsible for monitoring regulatory policy. Overall, the surveys found a limited spread of evaluative activities within a third of

1. Australia, Canada, Denmark, Hungary, Japan, Korea, Mexico, New Zealand, Poland, Switzerland, the UK and the US.
2. With the exception of Japan, which does not perform any compliance assessment on RIA.
3. 'There were three groups of quantifiable targets. The first group covered administrative burden (four countries). The second group was composed of another five countries targeting administrative simplification through the reduction of procedures or time to get licences. The last group aimed at full compliance with the requirements of RIA; two countries had set this specific target' (Radaelli and De Francesco 2007).
4. Australia, Belgium, Canada, the Czech Republic, Denmark, Finland, Germany, Greece, Hungary, Ireland, Italy, Japan, Korea, Mexico, the Netherlands, New Zealand, Norway, Spain, Sweden, the UK and the US.

the governments that had adopted RIA; the majority of governments did not design RIA to include a form of evaluation and/or performance measurement, which in turn suggests, especially among later adopters, a lack of institutionalisation of RIA and its symbolic adoption.

7.3 OECD regulatory quality indicators

In the last two decades, the OECD has attempted to causally link good governance and the quality of institutions to economic growth and performance, as well as to living standards and social development (Holmberg *et al.* 2009; Dellepiane-Avellaneda 2009). In order to sustain the theory that economic growth can be achieved partly through high-quality institutions, the OECD has been engaged with the conceptualisation, design and assessment of several government performance measures (Arndt and Oman 2006; Porter 2009; Erkkilä and Piironen 2010).

An increasing number of indices have been created for ranking and benchmarking governments in relation to specific policies. These good governance indices provide governments and policy makers, as well as the mass media and citizens, with comparative information by ranking policy process and outcome. Comparative knowledge and expertise on policies, standard setting, professional/peer accountability, and naming and shaming are soft instruments of influence used by the OECD (Benner *et al.* 2004; Pal 2009). Furthermore, the use of these types of indices usually occurs within transnational networks that are composed of OECD administrators, national policy makers, independent experts and consultants (Benner *et al.* 2004; Groenendijk 2011; *see also* Section 4.5).

Indices and benchmark systems have considerable autonomy (Porter 2009). They are 'devices' of governance which create connections within and between the OECD, national governments, the mass media and the general public (Porter 2009). The main purpose of the measurement is to improve performance, accountability and, ultimately, the legitimacy of member states' public policies (Groenendijk 2011; Porter 2009). 'Measurement functions as a source of authority in order to inform, to legitimate and to control managerial decisions... [introducing] new control modes within a performance-oriented climate' (Noordegraaf and Abma 2003). This attention to measures has been coordinated by a web of transnational organisations and national agencies (Drori *et al.* 2006b). Administrative accountability, regulatory quality and transparency have become key priorities for IOs, and their diffusion is nowadays often seen as a necessary condition for economic growth and development (Delacroix and Ragin 1981; Bardhan 1997; Goldsmith 1999; World Bank 2002).

Over time, the OECD's Group on Regulatory Policy has been updating the guidelines and recommendations for regulatory reform which provide the template for peer review of regulatory reform efforts in member countries. 'The OECD operates with a special mix of research and country participation' (Pal 2009). Governments broadly set the OECD's research agenda and are usually involved in reviewing country reports before they are published. The OECD's special strength is that it can draw on the willing support of its members to provide 'inside' information about what governments are doing in specific fields. Through peer review, the OECD regularly collects information on members' behaviour or performance and assesses this information in the light of shared standards, norms and principles (Conzelmann 2010).

Comparative statistics, rankings and best practice not only produce 'a constant enticement to encourage "laggards" to catch up to "leaders"' (Pal 2009) but also structure multilateral surveillance on the implementation of policies (Marcussen 2004a). The most relevant aspect of this process of networked governance is 'mutual education'. In a nutshell, the OECD's ambition is 'to hardwire indicators into an ongoing global conversation among practitioners about good governance, in order to facilitate lesson-drawing mechanisms' (Pal 2009).

There are two modes of measurement used by the OECD for assessing regulatory reform and quality: indicators of product market regulation (IPMR) and indicators of regulatory management systems (IRMS). Although both systems are compilations of best practice and rely on information gathered by the OECD through national high-level civil servant surveys, they differ in several respects.

IPMR are a compilation of measures of 'the extent to which policy settings promote or inhibit competition in areas of the product market where competition is viable' (IPMR website).[5] These economy-wide indicators summarise a wide array of different regulatory provisions across the OECD countries (including state control, barriers to entrepreneurship, international trade and investment) (Conway *et al.* 2005). IPMR are composite and the aggregation is conducted through a random weighting technique to test the sensitivity of summary indicator values to different weighting schemes. Furthermore, the IPMR are objective in the sense that the questionnaire given to the high-level civil servants asks for factual information on specific regulatory measures (Conway *et al.* 2005).

IRMS, instead, are drawn from a checklist based on recommendations for regulatory reform and governance. The checklist is then used to generate peer review procedures and reports on governments' efforts in reforming regulatory governance and achieving regulatory quality. The measurement system is aimed at showing trends in countries' strategies and the sequence of reform strategies (OECD Regulatory Policy Committee 2009) in order to empower regulatory reform across OECD member states. The system is participatory, given that governments have agreed on a set of recommendations. Rather than focusing on the extent of regulation, IRMS measure the institutional quality of regulatory reform strategy, based on: cooperation between regulatory oversight bodies and other departments; a reduction in administrative burden; effective consultation and public participation; CBA and IA; and indicators of regulatory performance and outcomes. In other words, the measurement system focuses on the processes for generating new regulations and for managing the stock of existing regulations. IRMS are supposed to be a powerful means of communicating reform trends,

5. Online. Available. http://www.oecd.org/eco/regulatoryreformandcompetitionpolicy/indicatorsof-productmarketregulationpmr.htm (accessed 28 October 2012).

achievements and gaps to national policy makers. They highlight priority areas for further action, demonstrate consistency between regulatory policy actions and regulatory quality outcomes, enhance the legitimacy and accountability of regulatory reform, and raise awareness of regulatory policy issues among regulators (OECD Regulatory Policy Committee 2009). The aggregation is conducted only to meso-areas of regulatory management institutions and recently the OECD ran a principal component analysis in order to derive patterns and clusters of countries (Jacobzone *et al.* 2010).

7.4 Evaluation institutions

At the national level, one manifestation of a 'quality assurance culture' is the presence of a consolidated structure in charge of the systematic assessment of that country's RIA programme. The quality assurance system typically involves bodies within the executive (often a central unit in the prime minister's office) and bodies at arm's length from the executive, as well as independent auditors reporting to parliament. The task of reviewing the delivery and accomplishment of an RIA programme is commonly performed by the same central unit in charge of overseeing regulatory departments. In several countries there are also independent auditing institutions and stakeholders reviewing the impact of RIA on regulatory governance. A further important feature is the integration of RIA and, more generally, of regulatory quality in governments' performance review activities.

7.4.1 Oversight units

The IRMS show that in fifteen member countries the minister responsible for better regulation is required to report to parliament on progress in regulatory reform (OECD Regulatory Policy Committee 2009). For instance, the American Congress receives an annual report issued by the Office for Information and Regulatory Affairs (OIRA) on the total annual regulatory costs and benefits – in aggregate, by agency and programme, and by the most relevant regulations – as well as the overall impact of regulation on the public sector. This mode of evaluation is unique and confirms the US as the leader in RIA practices.

In Australia, there is an annual compilation and reporting by departments and agencies of 'regulatory performance indicators'. Furthermore, the Productivity Commission reports annually and advises on the strategy to reduce administrative burdens.[6] More recently, this Commission has undertaken a study to benchmark the efficiency and quality of the Australian RIA processes. Although the consultation and issue paper refers extensively to the OECD's regulatory quality principles and recommendations, the Productivity Commission is also intended to 'go further to look at other indicators of effective and efficient RIA processes as implemented, in

---

6. Available Online: http://www.pc.gov.au/projects/study/regulatoryburdens (accessed 21 June 2010).

order to highlight leading practices' (Productivity Commission 2012). As a result, the proposed range of performance indicators are based on questions surrounding the consistency of RIA processes with international and national good practice and effective implementation. The other issue considered is the actual impact of RIA on decision making, regulatory outcome and administrative transparency. In other words, although the 2010 OECD review triggered an ongoing review of the RIA processes, the Australian Government tends, on the one hand, not to extensively exploit the OECD indicators (there is no reference to the IPMR) and, on the other hand, to go beyond them by attempting to find evidence of improvement in regulatory outcome. Contrarily, Access Economics Pty Limited, an Australian consultancy company, drafted a report for the Department of Treasury and Finance of Victoria which relies on IRMS in order to review the effectiveness of RIA. In doing so, the consultancy firm was able to select the most useful international experience associated with a specific best practice. For instance, the Netherlands was selected in relation to the provision of training and advice (Access Economics Pty Limited 2010).

Nevertheless, the latter evaluative methodology is an isolated case. Usually, governments' reports on RIA tend to refer to the OECD indicators in order to provide overall evidence of the extent of implementation and to make this comparable with international practice (HM Treasury 2005; Argy and Johnson 2003). There is also a tendency to refer to the OECD initiatives on RIA as a general background to national policies (Italian Presidency of the Council of Ministries 2011). The British Regulatory Policy Commission (RPC), in the four annual reports published so far, has never referred to the OECD's peer review system and indicators. In a similar vein, the Belgian Federal Government's annual reports on administrative costs published by the *Bureau fédéral du Plan* revolve around the specific methodology of quantification through business survey (Kegels 2008).

In countries where governments pursue a specific target reduction in administrative burdens, usually of 25 per cent, an annual report on the achievement of this target is presented to parliament. This occurs in Denmark, Italy, the Netherlands and Sweden. A specific target facilitates monitoring and auditing. The formula to compute administrative burden (*see* Section 3.4) is easy to understand and control. This type of approach facilitates the involvement of parliaments and prime ministers in the design and reorientation of better regulation policy. For instance, in Sweden a 2002 parliamentary resolution called for effective simplification and required the government to review and simplify business regulations, setting a quantitative target for simplification. Alongside the publication of an influential report on administrative burdens and regulatory enforcement,[7] the British Prime Minister publicly endorsed the *Less Is More* (Better Regulation Task Force 2005) approach that draws explicitly on the standard cost model (SCM),[8] recommending

---

7.   The so-called 'Hampton Review' (HM Treasury 2005) was flagged up by the British executive as an example for improving the business environment.

8.   One chapter of *Less Is More* is entirely dedicated to the Dutch methodology.

the setting of quantitative targets for the reduction of administrative burdens. This 'recalibration' was a consequence of a new focus on targets for simplification and burdens, creating a case of convergence with the other countries that have adopted the SCM, notably with the 25 per cent target for the reduction in administrative burdens – possibly in connection with a successful campaign by the 2004 Dutch Presidency of the EU to adopt a common method across the member states and at EU level.

7.4.2 Evaluation networks

What distinguishes the evaluation experience across governments is the presence of a network in which data, information and research are generated by different actors, strengthening the analysis of regulatory quality. In the US, where the OIRA monitors the compliance of executive agencies with the federal regulatory policy, the institutional framework is completed by the Government Accountability Office (GAO), the auditing and investigative arm of Congress, which has produced several reports on the effectiveness of regulation.[9] Although these reports do not quantitatively assess regulatory quality and performance, some evaluation activities of the GAO are innovative. For example, one report assessed the impact of information and communications technology on regulatory accessibility and transparency and the quality of RIA (General Accounting Office 2001). Other studies focused on economic analysis and methodologies, with reference to performance measures and procedural standards, such as peer review mechanisms, for comparing programmes across government and enhancing the credibility of regulatory analyses (Government Accountability Office 2005).

In a similar vein, the UK approach to the design of quality control mechanisms is based on different layers of monitoring, evaluation and quality appraisal. The internal layer of quality assurance mechanisms, based on departmental units and coordination activities conducted by the Better Regulation Executive (BRE), is supported by the RPC and National Audit Office (NAO) which has enhanced the openness and transparency of the *ex post* review and assessment exercise. Established in 2009, the RPC provides an external and independent challenge to the evidence and analysis presented in RIAs. Every year, it presents a report on the overall quality of the analyses scrutinised through a 'traffic light rating method': opinion on each RIA has been prefaced with a red ('not fit for purpose'), or amber or green ('fit for purpose') rating. This method was previously experimented with by the NAO in the quality assurance process. In 2001, the NAO produced a report on good RIA practice, drawing some lessons from a review of a sample of twenty-

---

9.　It has investigated the federal regulatory process, reviewing and reporting on: (i) the whole regulatory process as designed by EO 12,866 (General Accounting Office 2000); (ii) more specific aspects of American rulemaking, such as regulatory agencies' failures to comply with the OMB's guidance (General Accounting Office 1998); (iii) the OIRA and its role in reviewing agencies' draft rules (General Accounting Office 2003); and (iv) the OIRA's annual report (General Accounting Office 1999).

three RIAs (National Audit Office 2001). The NAO has also assessed the quality of RIA guidance (National Audit Office 2005). One interesting feature of the work conducted is that desk analysis of specific RIAs is accompanied by semi-structured interviews with staff within the departments at the Better Regulation Executive.

In Canada, the Auditor General reviewed federal health and safety regulatory programmes, recommending objectivity in the appraisal of regulatory outcomes through the best available methodologies. As Canadian regulatory policy requires the protection of Canadians' health and wealth to be balanced against the achievement of budgetary, economic and trade objectives (Regulatory Affairs and Orders in Council Secretariat 2002), another recommendation concerned the overall effectiveness of health and safety regulatory programmes, to be reported annually to parliament, and the extent to which they have the necessary financial and human resources. A similar audit of regulatory programmes is also performed by the Australian National Audit Office, suggesting a trend among common law countries in the mode of evaluating regulatory policy.

Alternatively, the Netherlands provides an example of a specifically dedicated and independent advisory body, the Dutch Advisory Board on Administrative Burdens (ACTAL), which guides departments in assessing administrative burden and which proposes improvements when quality is weak, especially with reference to estimates.[10] This solution of an independent advisory body is also common in the UK, through the experience over the last two decades of various bodies at arm's length from the Cabinet Office (such as the Better Regulation Task Force, whose mission was to make the voice of stakeholders heard in the UK's regulatory process. The task force was later re-branded the Better Regulation Commission, and, more recently, the Risk and Regulation Advisory Commission). The latter is a body established in 2008 with the mission to develop a better understanding of public risk and foster a more considered approach to public risk and policy making. This model of an external and independent contribution to government better regulation policy has been adopted by thirteen OECD member states (OECD Regulatory Policy Committee 2009).[11]

In several countries there has been a spontaneous involvement of stakeholders in the appraisal of regulatory quality. In Sweden, stakeholders have provided fresh ideas by turning the Swedish principles of better regulation into indicators. Through a scorecard, the Board of Swedish Industry and Commerce for Better Regulation (NNR) periodically reviews how agencies, committees and commissions of enquiry,[12] as well as government offices, comply with Swedish regulatory policy. The NNR's analysis includes an account of existing problems, the aims

---

10. In the period September 2003 – December 2004, this advisory body planned to review 150 RIAs (ACTAL 2003) and proposed thirty-five recommendations to reduce administrative costs.

11. *See* Table A.1. in Appendices.

12. These bodies examine the issue or problem the regulation aims to solve. The findings of the analysis, together with consultations, are the basis of the government's proposal for new regulation.

of the proposal, alternatives to regulation and the financial impact on companies affected by the proposal (Board of Swedish Industry and Commerce for Better Regulation 2002). The British Chambers of Commerce collected information on the aggregated costs and benefits quantified in RIAs (Ambler *et al.* 2003). The report shows the total sum of costs and benefits identified by RIA in a year.[13] This analysis leads to simple measures of output, such as percentages of RIAs that present a summary of consultations, consider non-regulatory options, or quantify costs and benefits. In the US, the American Enterprise Institute has been assessing OIRA's activities through such scorecards[14] (Hahn 1999; Hahn *et al.* 2000). Section 7.5.3 provides more insights into this evaluative method. Overall, neither national auditors and independent advisory bodies, nor stakeholders have exploited the OECD's benchmarking template or its measures to assess the quality of regulatory reform and RIA implementation. Instead, national evaluative networks reflected on regulatory quality on the basis of an independently conceived evaluation methodology.

7.4.3 Integration of RIA in evaluation systems

Another feature to bear in mind is the extent of integration of RIA evaluation with the overall government performance review. This provides evidence of stronger institutionalisation of RIA, since agencies and departments are reviewed and awarded for their regulatory analyses and performance. For instance, in the US, regulatory quality is embedded in 'performance budgeting', a 'government-wide initiative designed to better align spending decisions with expected budgeting' (General Accounting Office 2004b). Specifically, the OMB, whose predominant mission is to assist the US President in overseeing and coordinating the preparation of the federal budget, has developed a performance measurement and coordinating programme, the Program Assessment Rating Tool (PART), in order to assess competing funding demands among agencies and to set funding priorities. PART is 'a diagnostic tool meant to provide a consistent approach to evaluating federal programs as part of the executive budget formulation process' (General Accounting Office 2004a).

Similarly, in the UK (where better regulation policy has evolved around the principle of net benefit), appraisal systems for new regulations as well as for the simplification of existing regulations are specified in the Cabinet Office's 'Public Service Agreement' through specific quantitative targets. But governments also successfully link the strategy of reduction of administrative burdens to their budgetary policy. Through the so-called 'zero-base measurement', an inventory of all information obligations and administrative activities grouped according to the responsible ministry, the Dutch and the Danish governments encourage departments to respect ceilings of administrative burdens that 'are being created

---

13. The study collected 165 of 197 RIAs performed by government departments.
14. Also used to compare EU and US regulatory quality (Cecot *et al.* 2008).

for all departments as a fixed component of the budget and accountability system' (ACTAL 2003). This integration of the strategy for cutting red tape in budget policy enhances the monitoring role of the Ministry of Finance in the Netherlands, and in the Ministry of Economic and Business Affairs in Denmark.

The integration of RIA with performance review does not always pursue such relevant purposes in controlling (punishing or rewarding) regulators. Following specific guidelines (Regulatory Affairs and Orders in Council Secretariat 2002; Treasury Board of Canada Secretariat 2003), Canadian departments report annually to parliament with the aim of demonstrating 'the links between policies and programs (including regulatory initiatives) and their actual outcomes' (Argy and Johnson 2003). For instance, a 'regulatory performance measurement' is integrated into the annual performance report of Environment Canada and takes the form of the rate of compliance with regulation.[15] Because the guidelines do not set stringent requirements in terms of measurement, the evaluation system is not systematic and among Canadian government departments the criteria used to assess the performance of regulation vary markedly.

7.5 Evaluation measures

Beyond institutions and networks, it is important to understand to what extent an adopting unit is able to evaluate an administrative innovation. A coherent evaluation process is based on a set of auditing and monitoring measures. According to their complexity, objective evaluation measures used by governments can be grouped into three types: single measures, sets of single measures and aggregate measures. Taking subjective measures into account also, the following subsections review the most significant international experiences with each group of measures.

7.5.1 Single measures

This category of evaluative measures is common in most countries. Governments tend to use simple measures. Usually, the most widely used measure is the yes/no format to assess the degree of compliance with regulation (as in the above mentioned case of Environment Canada), RIA guidance and simplification procedures. In the UK, the BRE had a target of full compliance with the RIA process by departments and agencies for every regulatory proposal that might affect businesses, charities or voluntary organisations (National Audit Office 2004).[16] Another quantitative target was to deliver over sixty drafts of regulatory reform orders by 2006 (House of Commons 2003). Similarly, in Australia, the OBPR is now in charge of monitoring and reviewing RISs, requiring departments and agencies to provide a list of regulations specifying whether preliminary assessment, business cost

---

15. Available Online: http://www.ec.gc.ca/dpr/index_e.htm (accessed 2 February 2010).

16. A Cabinet Office statement declares that in 2004 and 2005 the level of compliance was 100 per cent.

assessment and RISs were drafted. A further list is required to indicate whether departments and agencies performed a post-implementation review. In the US, the annual report on federal regulatory benefits and costs refers, among other things, to indicators of the impact on small business (micro-economic indicators) and on wages and economic growth (macro-economic indicators). The 25 per cent administrative burdens reduction target is also a single measure.

7.5.2 Sets of single measures

This category of measures is distinct from the previous one because of its more comprehensive presentation. Indicators, scorecards, process standards or checklists are usually employed for assessing whether appropriate guidance or generally accepted practices were followed. Their purpose is to identify possible improvements in the conduct and methodology of *ex ante* economic analysis.

In Australia, departments and agencies are required to compile a set of 'regulatory performance indicators' every year. The OBPR has the duty of reporting annually on performance measurement according to a set of five indicators associated with the following five objectives of regulatory policy:

- there has been adequate analysis of significant regulatory proposals

  Indicator: proportion of regulations requiring an RIS for which an adequate RIS was prepared

- compliance costs have been assessed as required

  Indicator: proportion of regulations requiring a stand-alone assessment of compliance costs (as a business cost calculator report or equivalent) for which an assessment was provided and certified by the OBPR

- the agency's procedures for identifying proposals that might require regulatory impact analysis worked effectively

  Indicator: proportion of regulations requiring an RIS or stand-alone assessment of compliance costs which met the requirement to undertake a preliminary assessment and consultation with the OBPR before a decision was made

- the agency has consulted appropriately on significant regulatory issues

  Indicator: proportion of regulations requiring an RIS for which the consultation process, as described in the RIS, was adequate

- the agency used its regulatory plan to inform stakeholders about regulatory proposals

  Indicator: proportion of regulatory agencies that have published a regulatory plan for the introduction and review of regulation

This is a small set of indicators that have four desirable properties: they are rich in information; they are easy to understand; they are monitored by an important government department; and they are clearly linked to the principles of regulatory governance. Nevertheless, this model of a direct and coherent relationship between principles of regulatory quality and performance measures is unique and has not been 'learned' by any other government.

Another experience with a collection of single measures can be found in Canada, where the Treasury Board of Canada Secretariat (TBS) has responsibility for reviewing regulatory proposals and is also in charge of assuring compliance with federal management standards for the regulatory process. These standards provide checklists for each stage of the regulatory process. In particular, the quality assurance process terminates with regular internal self-assessments of performance and policy compliance (Treasury Board of Canada Secretariat 1996). In this case, though, this mode of evaluating regulatory policy has not been a point of reference for any other government.

7.5.3 Aggregate measures

Sets of indicators have also been used to score departments and governments. In assessments of the quality of RIA programmes in the USA, the UK and at the European level, scorecards have been widely used by academics (Hahn *et al.* 2000; Hahn *et al.* 2004; Opoku and Jordan 2004; Lee and Kirkpatrick 2004) and think-tanks (Vibert 2005; Vibert 2004; Institute for European Environmental Policy 2004). Such scorecards are composed of a series of yes/no questions that generate simple measures, weighted and aggregated in an overall composite indicator.

The US provides an interesting example of the use of scorecards. The PART questions on regulatory programmes 'require the user to provide a brief narrative explanation of the answer, including any relevant evidence to substantiate the answer. Responses should be evidence based and not rely on impressions or generalities' (Office for Management and Budget 2003). As a result, these performance indicators are categorical and designed to be objective, providing a consistent approach to benchmarking, rating and scoring federal regulatory and spending programmes (General Accounting Office 2004a). Indeed, the principle guiding this rating exercise is that regulatory programmes are appropriate and deserve funding when they show clear evidence of effectiveness and are capable of maximising the benefits to society.[17]

Besides PART, the OIRA quantifies the total net benefit of the federal regulatory programmes enacted in a given year. Because an aggregate indicator such as this is a compilation of RIAs, there is the problem of drawing inferences from different methodologies used in economic analyses (Government Accountability Office 2005). Moreover, given the high probability of *ex ante* errors in the economic analysis of regulatory impact, scholars are aware of the methodological flaw of treating estimations as measures of the actual impact of regulations (Parker 2003; McGarity and Ruttenberg 2002). Overall, the US quality assurance system combines simple indicators of real-world outcomes, such as the total net benefits,

---

17. Yet such an evaluation system has been criticised for the degree of discretion that the questionnaire's formulation contains (General Accounting Office 2004b). Also, the yes/no format has been judged too restrictive for the assessment of complex programmes with multiple purposes and goals (General Accounting Office 2004a).

with measures of regulatory process quality.

Instead of an aggregate measure of net benefit, several European countries rely on a simpler aggregate measure of administrative burdens. Although there is no specific evaluation system composed of regulatory quality indicators, the total administrative burden per sector, in transport regulation and across the economy, is known. As a result, in terms of communicability, the Dutch experience provides an interesting approach to the measurement of total administrative burden and this measure has been easily linked to reduction targets. Thanks to its characteristics, the SCM has now become a term of reference in the better regulation policies of European countries such as Belgium, Denmark, Sweden,[18] Norway and, most recently, the UK, the EU itself, as well as in many of the laggard countries, such as Portugal, Romania, Slovenia, Spain and Turkey. Nineteen countries are now involved in the SCM networks promoted by the Dutch government.[19]

Belgium has an even simpler, qualitative, approach to the measurement of administrative burdens. In 2004, the *Agence pour la Simplification Administrative* (ASA) launched the 'Kafka test', an appraisal tool, structured in phases, that supports the decision-making process in the Council of Ministers by showing whether (and how) a new proposal is worsening the regulatory environment (*Agence pour la Simplification Administrative* 2004). First, regulators are called to identify the target group and to estimate the number of citizens, businesses and non-profit organisations affected by a regulatory proposal. Second, the type of information obligation is selected and described, referring to an inventory of the most common administrative duties. Third, regulators are called to establish who triggers the information obligation – in some cases it is the public administration that sends forms and requests data, while in others it is the target group that contacts the administration requesting a subsidy or product licence and so on. Successive steps determine the frequency of the proposed obligation and the type of data and certificates required. Finally, regulators describe how citizens, businesses and non-profit organisations would be able to send the information required to the public administration. Essentially, the Kafka test is a tool for gathering qualitative information on administrative burdens.

By way of contrast, a more comprehensive and economically sound method for estimating compliance costs has been formulated in Australia. The Business Cost Calculator is a web-based[20] procedure for developing compliance cost estimations for each proposed regulatory option. The procedure accounts for levels (low, medium and high) of the analyst's uncertainty concerning the accuracy of information on the number of businesses that will be affected by regulation. This function overcame one of the major criticisms of the SCM, namely, that it involves the unrealistic assumption of total compliance with regulation (Radaelli and De

---

18. In cooperation with Denmark and the Netherlands, Sweden has developed an administrative reduction methodology starting from the SCM.

19. Source: http://www.administrative-burdens.com (accessed 26 June 2012).

20. Available online: https://bcc.obpr.gov.au/ (accessed 21 June 2010).

Francesco 2007). The Australian method of calculating administrative burdens has been recently compared with the SCM by the New Zealand Government. The comparative findings suggest that the Government should adopt the Australian model 'because of its potential broader coverage and more simple application' (Pricewaterhouse Coopers 2006). But besides the findings and recommendations, what is important to remark on here is that a comprehensive comparative assessment has been conducted by a government on specific models for cutting administrative burdens.

There are few other comprehensive reviews of international experience with regulatory management. In 2003, the Danish Commerce and Companies Agency (Danish Commerce and Companies Agency 2003) produced the first comprehensive review of strategies for simplifying and reducing administrative burdens, covering dimensions such as institutional design, regulatory process, methodology and best practice. Argy and Johnson (2003) summarised for the Australian government the different approaches to measurement of regulatory quality adopted around the world. In a similar vein, in Canada, the Government commissioned a comprehensive review of 'RIA trends' in order to achieve a common understanding of performance measurement that could identify potential indicators. The initiative identified existing work done by pertinent domestic or international institutions, including the identification of common best practices and performance indicators and areas of marked differences (Regulatory Affairs and Orders in Council Secretariat 2002). Scott Jacobs, a leading consultant, produced a lesson-drawing report highlighting current trends in the process and methods of RIA by Canada's peers and competitors in global markets. He concluded by pointing out that:

> [w]hereas countries such as the United States, Australia, Ireland, New Zealand, and the European Commission are actively improving the rigour and quality of RIA as an integrated framework to deal with the complexity of modern public policy, the vision in Canada is much less clear about how RIA can improve public policy. (Jacobs 2006)

This was also reflected in the 'weakness in the incentives and quality controls for good RIA in the [Canadian] federal government' (Jacobs 2006). This initiative was inserted in the broader activity of the 'Smart Regulation' advisory board that was the main driver behind the 2007 change in the Canadian regulatory analysis procedure. Taking a different approach from the previous reviews of the experience, the Italian Government funded a comparative research project after the adoption of RIA (Radaelli 2001). Because the Italian RIA system was still in its embryonic phase, such a comparative exercise did not fully assess the differences in setting, e.g. the dissimilarity in administrative and political structures and application, and the actual use of knowledge gathered in the decision-making process (Mossberger and Wolman 2003).

7.5.4 Subjective measures

Governments have acknowledged the impossibility of measuring – through synthetic and objective methods – the achievement of their key objective of regulatory policy. Accordingly, they turned their attention to anecdotal evidence of the quality of regulatory decisions. To illustrate, in Canada an evaluation was undertaken to ascertain whether departments had internalised the new innovation. This was done through structured interviews in order to capture the change in regulators' perceptions of the usefulness of RIA (Regulatory Consulting Group and Delphi Group 2000). The interviews showed that all regulatory departments accepted the principle that the economic impact of proposed regulations should be examined before the formulation of rules (Regulatory Consulting Group and Delphi Group 2000). The Canadian experience shows a possible approach to the measurement of cultural change. Structured interviews can be usefully employed to analyse the extent of institutionalisation. Items in interview schedules can be inserted into the more comprehensive and systematic surveys of regulators and external evaluations. This evaluation approach was followed by the Evaluation Partnership in a recent assessment of the EU Commission's IA system (The Evaluation Partnership 2007).

Several countries conduct surveys of businesses and (occasionally) citizens. Before the complete endorsement of the SCM, the leading European country in the business survey field was Denmark. The so-called 'model companies' method, used as a template for the European Business Test Panel, is based on a random sample of 1,000 firms which are surveyed on the economic impact of given regulatory sectors. Relying on a representative sample of business sectors and firm sizes, it provides a quantification of the total administrative burden. Belgium is another country with a consolidated tradition of measuring the reduction in administrative burdens through business surveys (De Vil and Kegels 2001; Kegels 2008). In addition, in Belgium, e-government initiatives (for example, to reduce the formalities necessary for enterprise start-up) are also measured on the basis of World Bank benchmarks, such as the time necessary to set up a new firm.[21] Belgium represents a good example of a coherent set of regulatory measures. This gives the government greater control, since the different measurement exercises reinforce one another.

The US provides the only example of a business survey that measures the cumulative impact of environmental regulations, that is, the Pollution Abatement Costs and Expenditures Survey. The survey collects data on pollution abatement and prevention, capital expenditures and operating costs for air, water, solid waste and multimedia. The survey also collects data on disposal, recycling, site clean-

---

21. In a press note dated 22 October 2004, the ASA emphasised the success of the simplification action plan, with reference to the Doing Business World Bank indicator. The latter measures the number of days it takes to set up an enterprise. In one year, this indicator had decreased, from twenty-two to three, the time taken to set up a small or medium-sized enterprise, and from fifty-six to thirty-three to set up a large enterprise.

up, habitat protection, environmental monitoring and testing and administrative costs, as well as other payments, such as permits, fees, fines, penalties and tradable permits bought or sold. Overall, the experiences with subjective measures are limited and only marginally transferred to other contexts.

7.6 Conclusion

This chapter has illustrated how governments monitor and measure quality and the specific initiatives under way. Although the number of countries with measurement initiatives is increasing, the majority of EU and OECD member states have not put in place any monitoring and evaluation system for regulatory policy. This is an indication of incomplete rationality in the choices and design for RIA, and suggests that in several countries the adoption of RIA was driven by a desire to make only a symbolic gesture. The OECD reports that few late adopters have gone so far as to institutionalise RIA or to evaluate its effectiveness and impact.

Although networks composed of independent bodies and stakeholders are emerging, evaluation systems are generally centred on the central oversight units which annually report to parliaments. Further, there are few cases of RIA's deep institutionalisation in other policy areas, especially budget control. For instance, the SCM ceiling system, linked to budget policy, is also now well established among Continental European and Scandinavian governments. The review of the institutional design of evaluation also signals cases of policy transfer. For instance, the evaluation mode through independent advisory bodies originated in the UK and the Netherlands and has been copied by other European countries engaged in reducing administrative burdens. This institutional model has only recently captured the attention of the OECD, which then organised an international conference on RIA 'independent watchdogs'.[22] This is another instance of the OECD's capacity to scan and promote the most promising institutional and policy innovations.

Turning to measures and indicators of regulatory quality, quantitative targets are a more popular option than qualitative measures and anecdotal evidence. Some countries have gone further than that by introducing systematic reviews and monitoring tools based on quantifiable variables. The experience of evaluation, however, did not travel. Good performance measurement systems, like the Australian indicators of regulatory principles, the Canadian standards and the Belgian annual quantification of administrative burdens, have not been copied by any other country. Moreover, governments tend to rely on their direct experience of regulatory reform and RIA.

---

22. Held in Prague on 1 June 2012, the workshop was organised jointly with the Office of the Government of the Czech Republic and the Charles University in Prague. The aim of the workshop was to present recent developments in implementing RIA in the Czech Republic as well as to give exposure to different approaches in some leading OECD countries, with the goal of learning from their experience of independent regulatory oversight bodies and the implementation of EU legislation in national regulatory frameworks through regulatory appraisal systems.

Instead, scorecards and checklists are the commonest approach, not only of governments but also of academics and stakeholders. However, there is no general agreement on how regulatory quality should be observed and measured. This problem has been simplified by those governments which stripped down regulatory quality in a war on bureaucratic red tape. The SCM is without doubt a model which has been transferred to other European countries, as well as Australia and New Zealand. It is evident that the preference of governments is to use single measures but these can at least be potentially turned into systems of indicators. However, this potential has not yet been exploited, and governments are still not systematising the available single measures.

The OECD seeks to promote comparative knowledge and to share experience of regulatory reform among its member state governments. Accordingly, its communication strategy is more oriented towards its member states than the one used by the World Bank (De Francesco, forthcoming). Policy benchmarking is mainly for internal use and mainly focuses on the extent of regulation and the qualitative proxies of the national institutions governing at the national-level regulatory process. There is no attempt to prove any theory or to correlate reform efforts to economic growth and performance. Overall, the OECD has built up evaluation systems in order to compare the progress of governments in regulatory reform and governance but, as the previous sections showed, governments still seem not to be importing them completely into their evaluation practices.

Also at the European level, the European Commission is still in search of the most appropriate mode of evaluating its own regulatory process in a similar manner to the evaluation which takes place in individual EU member states. The Mandelkern Report and the Hellenic Presidency Review on the state-of-the-art of European better regulation were sporadic practices, as was the DG Enterprise project on measuring regulatory quality across Europe which has not been concretised. The more systematic comparison relies on the national reports of the implementation of the European Charter for Small Enterprises which now includes specific items on better regulation. The European Commission's evaluation system is the cumulative result of previous initiatives, such as the Better Lawmaking Report and the Charter for Small Enterprises, as well as the annual report of the Impact Assessment Board. The project for more comprehensive indicators has been abandoned. The European Commission performs an annual assessment of its effort to achieve 'better lawmaking' and since the establishment of the Impact Assessment Board a more transparent and sound impact assessment process is possible. This still emerging system of evaluation has not been a model for any of the member states.

Overall, the OECD has not proposed any recommendation on specific systems for evaluating RIA. Neither are transnational evaluative models applied in member states. National governments have looked to IOs to provide hints of how successful their policies were. Governments have not imported such models at their national level. Even the simplest indexes, comprising time and costs to comply with regulation of entry (Djankov et al. 2002), are not currently used. Considering that most EU member states are targeting red tape and that the literature has discussed several indexes, there is considerable potential for a closer dialogue between policy makers and social scientists.[23]

On the other hand, transfer is evident among the clusters of countries which adopted the SCM. Such a simplification strategy is easy to understand and to 'pack' across countries. The model has a simple formula to achieve a specific target, the same 25 per cent target for all countries, that can be easily developed in an evaluation system composed of independent advisory bodies, an annual report to be tabled to parliament, linkage to budgetary policy and also a well established network of experts. The Netherlands provides a strong pivotal centre for the promotion of this model through its activities on the European Council. By contrast, countries which rely on a more comprehensive approach to regulatory quality and CBA tend to benefit exclusively from their direct experience. This is confirmed by the variety of methodologies for reporting to parliament: sets of indicators, as in Australia; overall costs and benefits, as in the US; or compliance measures, as in the EU and the UK. Also, comparative analysis and scanning of international experience and solutions are rare and somewhat limited where they are used.

This review has covered five EU member states as well as Canada, Australia and the US. Following Radaelli and De Francesco (2007), these eight countries can be divided into two groups according to two dimensions: comprehensiveness of regulatory quality, and intensity of interdependence of evaluative practices. The researchers found that countries such as Australia, Canada, the UK and the US have a robust network of quality assurance actors and also look at RIA beyond the issue of red tape, whereas those targeting administrative burdens – Belgium, Denmark and the Netherlands – are characterised by a simpler system of monitoring (Table 7.1).

This diffusion analysis of evaluation experience added another aspect to the two classificatory dimensions by revealing that within the cluster of countries targeting administrative burden there are several instances of evidence of policy transfer founded on the SCM, an innovation characterised by higher levels of compatibility,[24] observability[25] and simplicity.[26] By contrast, an RIA system based on CBA is more complex and does not inherently develop a quantifiable target and an evaluation mode. As a result, governments tend to reflect on RIA through an accurate analysis of their own experiences.

23. For example, Djankov *et al.* (2002) developed an index for ranking all the costs of specific actions to be undertaken in order to set up a new firm (as a percentage of GDP). This index can provide policy makers with a shortlist of administrative burdens for which simplification is more cost-effective.

24. Defined as 'the degree to which an innovation is perceived as consistent with the existing values, past experiences, and needs of potential adopters' (Rogers 2003).

25. Defined as 'the degree to which the results of an innovation are visible to others' (Rogers 2003).

26. Defined as 'the degree to which as innovation is perceived as relatively simple to understand and use' (Rogers 2003).

Table 7.1: Quality assurance systems, approach to regulatory quality, and policy transfer

	Simple quality assurance	**Sophisticated quality assurance**
Administrative burdens and SCM	Denmark, the Netherlands, Sweden *Policy transfer*	
Net-benefit principle		Australia, Canada, the UK, the US *Direct experience*

Based on Radaelli and De Francesco (2007: 105).

chapter | conclusion
eight |

This book has provided the first analysis of the extent of interdependence among governments undertaking regulatory reform. To explore this issue, large-n comparative analyses assess how regulatory appraisal systems have been adopted and institutionalised in EU and OECD member states. RIA is a major innovation in modern public administration and deserves an analysis which takes context, time and interdependence seriously. By arguing that RIA is a transnational policy innovation, this book has linked the literature on global governance and the OECD to the methodology of policy diffusion and comparative politics. Indeed, whereas the standpoint of policy and technological innovation is essential for positing the theoretical foundation of an agency's decision-making and problem-solving capacity and for disentangling the concept of adoptability, the role of the OECD in global governance highlights the extent of interaction, influence, exchange of information and, ultimately, learning among governments.

The cumulative analysis of the sequence of adoption, implementation and *ex post* evaluation has overcome the major methodological flaws of previous policy diffusion studies, which isolated innovation from broader phenomena and theoretical concepts and focused on the event of adoption. The present research strategy has allowed not only an assessment of the extent of interdependence across the stages of institutionalisation of a policy innovation, but also emphasised the role of the OECD as an orchestrator capable of promoting an interpretation which is more attractive to a broader audience. Scanning and benchmarking international experience on regulatory reform, the OECD has also branded and provided an implementation model of RIA which has emerged as a global standard for modern and rational regulatory governance. In other words, through an arsenal of mechanisms the OECD has selected and transnationalised RIA as *the* innovation of regulatory governance, de-emphasising other innovations such as consultation and simplification, as well as the aim of political control. These two major methodological enhancements have been brought together in an analytical framework that also takes into account the country-to-country policy interdependence. This three-layered analytical framework has guided the systematic and comprehensive assessment of policy diffusion and interdependence, and provided three different settings of learning.

The main argument of the book is that an encompassing clarification of concepts and a cumulative exploration of adoption, implementation and evaluation provide a better assessment and explanation of the extent of interaction between governments associated with a transnationally framed policy innovation. Accordingly, this book has considered policy diffusion as a dynamic process. RIA and the resulting interdependence of policy makers have been analysed in five ways. Firstly, its concept has been clarified as an administrative requirement to control regulators while also deriving modes of regulatory oversight. The qualitative analysis of the process of institutionalisation among a sample of pioneer countries specified that RIA is a general administrative requirement, rather than a specific methodological model for assessing regulatory quality. Secondly, the OECD has encompassed many methodologies under the same policy label of RIA but has transnationally framed a normative template as a tool for enhancing evidence-based decision making based on economic welfare principles and CBA. Thirdly, empirical tests have evidenced the impact of this OECD editing activity on the adoption of RIA. Fourthly, the extent of implementation has been assessed according to categories of adopters and legal origin, and has been correlated with year of adoption, which has highlighted the limited role of the OECD in promoting the homogenisation of legal and economic rational dimensions through mediative and cognitive interactions. Finally, a qualitative survey has assessed the extent of learning from evaluative practices. In short, incorporating several aspects and elements of an administrative innovation and, consequently, relying on different dependent variables and research methods, this 'organization-centred' (Savage 1985)[1] research has underlined the proposition that only an integrated analysis of policy diffusion enables us to grasp the symbolic and rhetorical meanings associated with the decision to adopt a policy innovation. More importantly, empirical analysis of the innovation's prerequisites and actual utilisation reveals the main rationale and mechanism behind the choice to adopt an administrative reform that is affected by political rhetoric.

The central finding is that the OECD, which has influenced the decision of governments to adopt RIA, has nonetheless had only a marginal impact on its member states' choice to implement and evaluate RIA. Relying on their direct experience and acknowledging the institutional setting, domestic policy makers retained considerable autonomy. This argument is also supported by the rapidity of the diffusion of the SCM, notwithstanding the OECD's lack of enthusiasm for this model for measuring administrative burden.

A number of other important findings were observed throughout these studies. As also shown by the theoretical and empirical literature, the first important conclusion is that RIA is about political control. Conceptually, RIA is an ongoing and hierarchical control mechanism at the disposal of the head of the executive. Over time, its institutional design has been strengthened in order to control regulators. This occurred through the establishment of an oversight body, empowered to control the quality of economic analysis, and the establishment of quantifiable

---

1.   Savage provided a useful classification of research foci across the different disciplines that have analysed policy diffusion:

   Client-centered studies revolve about the individual adoption process and primarily utilize cross-sectional analyses of survey data. Geographic-centered studies focus on the spread of adoptions across given populations and more often resort to analyses of recorded data. Organ-ization-centered studies incorporate aspects of the other two traditions and, consequently, are typically more variable in research methods. (Savage 1985)

targets such as the reduction of 25 per cent of administrative burden on business. Specifically, the implementation score (in 2008 the OECD score was five) has confirmed that political control is relevant in the US, Canada, the Netherlands, Sweden and the UK among the pioneers, as well as Italy, Korea, Belgium and Poland among the majority of followers, and only Greece among the laggards. Accordingly, political control is not immediate and requires the institutionalisation of innovation. However, the complexity of regulatory governance – as evidenced by the size of government, which has proved to be statistically highly significant in the discrete EHA – requires a system based on hierarchical supervision and control through economic analysis and information.

The second remarkable item of evidence is the role of the OECD in facilitating the adoption of such an administrative innovation. Indeed, the OECD was effective in packaging and re-branding a set of diverse appraisal methodologies as a compelling instrument for enhancing the rationality and legitimacy of regulatory outcome, rather than political control of regulators. This provides a common knowledge and shared language for networks of experts and high-level civil servants, facilitating the diffusion of RIA. A given country's membership of OECD networks increased the probability of adoption consistently and significantly. Qualitative analyses have also shown that the OECD was effective in shifting the mode of policy transfer and constructing a social system composed of expert networks. On the other hand, the OECD is not a teacher of norms, given that the adoption of RIA is on average not concomitant with the publication of its regulatory reform reports and, with few exceptions, regulatory reform reviews have had a marginal effect on domestic policy. Further, the role of this IO has, up until now, been marginal in the successive stages of administrative institutionalisation. The OECD has not been active and effective in sharing knowledge within its networks about how to achieve effective and efficient implementation and evaluation. By situating RIA within the broader setting of administrative governance, the OECD has only recently opened the discussion on the implementation gap and the aim of political control.

Finally, this book has also found that administrative traditions matter. Although the influence of legal origin is marginal as a determinant of adoption, countries with an English legal origin have higher implementation scores and are generally involved in evaluating their RIA programmes. Institutional patterns are also derived from previous administrative innovations such as FOI laws, which are correlated with the adoption ranks of RIA and partially confirmed by the diffusion models.

The relationship between governments' interdependence and the policy process has been explored, with three aims: (i) understanding how RIA has diffused, by focusing on the policy innovation attributes and the role of the OECD; (ii) ascertaining whether and how knowledge about implementation and evaluation practices has been facilitated by the OECD; and (iii) assessing the overall patterns and the extent of policy change provoked by this diffused innovation. Each of these areas is discussed in more detail in the next sections, which also remark on the main contributions of this book to the literature on RIA, NPM, policy diffusion and public policy, as well as formulating normative claims for policy makers and stakeholders. Suggestions for further analyses of the diffusion of administrative innovations are also provided in order to tackle the limitations of this research.

8.1 Innovation adoptability and the influence of the OECD

This book started by showing RIA as a normally spread administrative principle which encompasses several policy appraisal methodologies. This finding has been the foundation for developing and structuring the central concepts and epistemological emphases of policy innovation which are peculiar to the politics of administrative reform and NPM. The first fundamental element drawn from the analytical framework concerned the definition of RIA, an ongoing control mechanism which does not assume the connotations of a well defined model. Rather, it is a general framework, an administrative requirement to appraise foreseeable impacts of new regulations. RIA is a policy label and a referential symbol for regulatory reform. The OECD has been effective in increasing the perception that RIA is compatible with different administrative settings by framing a common discourse on regulatory quality.

Beyond the definitional aspects, RIA has been inserted within the broader administrative context that is composed of principles and institutions as well as previous administrative innovations. The argument is that an adopting unit's institutional context shapes the definition and effects of this administrative innovation. In other words, the first (conceptual) part of this book has refined the understanding of the adoption environment in which attributes of innovation and of adopting unit interact, resulting in the concept of adoptability. Accordingly, P-A models have described the evolution of RIA within the US administrative state. Elman's methodological recommendations for deriving explanatory typologies were used in order to draw the intersection between two institutional dimensions, i.e. the institutionalisation of RIA as a control mechanism within the executive and the institution in charge of reviewing the regulatory process. Modes of regulatory review have provided expectations about the adoptability of RIA. Specifically, countries with legal systems based on English common law tend to adopt and institutionalise RIA earlier than countries with French or German legal origins.

The concept of adoptability requires a deep knowledge of the innovation context for discerning the analytical framework, which, given the lack of theorisation and large-n comparative studies of RIA, was found in the NPM literature. Furthermore, the 1995 OECD recommendation on regulatory reform and the 2002 European Commission guidelines on IA were the main events which signalled a likely change of diffusion patterns and delineated the categories of adopters. Indeed, the initial phase of the RIA diffusion process was characterised by transfer activities among the Anglo-Saxon countries whereas, in the later stages of diffusion, the interaction among and interdependence of governments increased through the formation of transnational networks. The analysis of the extent of variance in the process of emergence and institutionalisation concluded that RIA is not a global paradigm. In Continental Europe, the pattern of RIA emergence differed from the pattern seen in the common-law countries, and different patterns of institutionalisation still persist, with the emphasis in the SCM. Accordingly, the analytical framework is situated in the decision-centred concept of policy change, which assumes that the types and intensity of communication matter and excludes forms of collective rationality.

The role of the OECD was analysed through the content analysis of documents. The findings supported a sequence of ideational activities. In the case of regulatory reform, the OECD first scanned and categorised international experience in order to draw up a set of best practices. The organisation then selected RIA as the policy innovation for simplifying the policy discourse on regulatory reform. Recommendations for regulatory reform and a checklist for the implementation of RIA were then approved but were constantly based on the principle of the maximisation of socio-economic welfare. The administrative preconditions for and political ideologies of RIA were omitted. Such a steadiness in the OECD policy discourse has also allowed a normative template to be used for peer review and to rank government capacity to assure high-quality regulation. If they are effective, such OECD activities should lead to policy convergence and homogenisation. Contrarily, the studies on implementation and evaluation found evidence of variance in governmental decisions.

The analysis of the OECD's ideational role has also indicated how RIA was made more intelligible as a tool for enhancing the empirical basis of decision making. Economic rationality mirrored the aspiration of OECD member states to be modern. Therefore, the OECD has de-contextualised this policy innovation from a specific country's administrative setting and the attributes of a country's legal system. In other words, the OECD has overlooked the relationship between the attributes of the innovation and the attributes of the adopting country, i.e. the adoptability of innovations, by focusing instead on a partial representation of the function of RIA. The OECD itself has aimed to fill gaps in the implementation and institutionalisation of RIA among its members. The EU 15 Better Regulation project and the more recent publication and policy recommendation on regulatory governance attempted to coherently embed policy objectives, tools and institutions. Indeed, other good-governance principles, such as the rule of law and democratic accountability, are taken into account. Furthermore, the political dimension of RIA has emerged in several OECD publications. As an information-generating device, RIA shifts the relative advantage between departmental regulators and the head or core of the executive. In the 2012 version of the recommendation on regulatory policy and governance, the OECD also recognised the importance of other innovative regulatory institutions such as independent regulatory agencies and judicial review. Overall, the OECD is an ideational agency with an enormous capacity to frame policy innovations and establish good-governance principles and standards which are, broadly, well received by its member states. And in the last ten years or so, the OECD has also been flexible enough to update its organisational discourse by going beyond the simplistic translation of international experience in a one-size-fits-all approach.

8.2 Probability of adoption

The extent of interdependence on the decision to adopt RIA was tested according to three explanatory layers. Empirical evidence supported the formulation of the hypotheses. Contingent and complementary innovations were useful in indicating the sequence of adoption. Ranking correlations and the fact that only a few countries adopted RIA before EIA or a FOI law indicated that previous innovations were necessary conditions, especially among the laggards. Other internal determinants, such as the size of government and the extent of economic growth, were tested through correlations. Furthermore, the average proportions of adopters evidenced that fixed regional effects, considered as countries with the same legal origin, were constant across time. English legal origin countries constitute the majority of the pioneers, whereas French legal origin countries are the most numerous among the laggards. The pioneers are also the usual suspects among the most active NPM reformers. Looking at the sequence of adoption, the case of Hungary, the only former socialist country to have adopted RIA as a pioneer, is remarkable. Among the early majority it is possible to see the influence of the OECD on several countries, including France, Iceland, Italy and Switzerland. But it is also present in the form of spatially induced adoption for countries like Austria, Belgium and Norway.

The discrete EHA results of the first stripped-down model of only internal determinants showed the importance of open and transparent governments as well as legal origin. Adding the horizontal dimension of diffusion to the basic model, the results confirmed the hypothesis of a spatial explanation of diffusion. That is to say, FOI law and government expenditure still matter. In the final integrated models the importance of the OECD was remarkable and, among the internal determinants, government expenditure was significant.

The overall conclusion of the adoption analysis is that the institutionalised patterns of interaction among governments facilitated by the OECD have provided governments, which were already aware of the necessity to oversee regulators, with simplified cognitive frameworks and maps for taking the decision to adopt RIA. The role of the OECD in reframing and packaging such innovation as a tool to enhance the empirical evidence of decision making overcame the uncertainty faced by governments due to a lack of information about the benefits and costs of RIA.

8.3 Causal mechanisms in the diffusion process

Given that diffusion involves the decisional interdependence of governments, this study relies on the main argument that the measurement of its extent must not be limited to the probability of adoption. Large-n policy diffusion studies tend to oversimplify the policy process, assuming implicitly that governments adopt exactly the same innovation (Clark 1985). In addition, determinants of adoption are supposed constantly valid across the policy process (Brooks 2007). But adoption is a partial representation – generally the most evident and easy to observe – of policy change (Blomquist 2007).

The extent and modes of governments' interdependence across the policy process vary according to the type of decision that policy makers take. If communication within transnational policy networks facilitated adoption in the majority of countries, there was nonetheless only partial interaction and influence in the choices of how to implement and evaluate RIA. In particular, such interaction has occurred in the legal dimension and in the economic rationality of RIA implementation. Governments tend to reinvent and adjust RIA without exchanging information on every single organisational and strategic detail of the appraisal system. This is a striking finding, given the fact that the OECD has provided normative templates for peer reviewing governments' efforts in implementing RIA systems.

Even more marginal has been the interdependence of evaluative practices. Only a few governments learnt from the others how to review the performance of RIA programmes. Interestingly, this has taken place for the SCM, which relies on a precise and simple formula to compute administrative burdens for businesses. The qualitative analysis of evaluative practices has shown that the role of the OECD and its benchmarking system has been marginal, whereas SCM leading countries, such as the Netherlands, have been active in sharing knowledge throughout the institutionalisation of the innovation.

The analyses of the implementation and evaluation of RIA corroborate the scenario of partial policy interdependence and learning. Policy makers tended to reflect on their own experience. Specifically, the analysis of implementation concluded that it is plausible to exclude emulation and learning from collective experience and best practice. Moreover, the OECD did not act as an ideational authority, given that its effects were limited to the homogenisation of the legal and economic rationality dimensions of implementation and across and within categories of adopter countries and those with common legal traditions. If these explanations were valid, all implementation sub-indexes would have marginal variations but the lowest variation was found on the legalist dimension, implying a symbolic adoption.

The implementation scores were higher in the group of pioneers and the early majority of followers. The latter category of adopters had higher implementation scores than those of the laggards, meaning that the incrementalist explanation is the most plausible. In other words, the later followers and laggards did not tend to adopt the most comprehensive systems of RIA, for instance, those that developed in the US and the UK. Further evidence of marginal interdependence and learning is provided by the negative correlations between years of adoption and implementation indexes. Furthermore, there were significant correlations between the extent of implementation and effective performance of the innovation.

Pioneers are characterised by an even implementation of RIA across its functional uses. Indeed, political control that requires the institutionalisation of the administrative innovation has progressed mainly among the pioneers, while it is not yet consolidated among late followers. Similarly, high economic rationality scores are common among pioneers and early followers. Late followers and laggards have similar overall scores. However, laggards focused on the legalistic dimension by getting the highest score among the entire adopter group but still lagged considerably behind on the legitimacy dimension. Similarly, later followers had a low score for organisational, strategic and legitimacy dimensions of implementation.

Administrative legal tradition, captured by legal origin, has provided straightforward evidence of clustered but still dispersed implementation. English legal origin countries tended to have the highest implementation scores. Both in 2005 and 2008, French and German legal origin countries scored very similarly. In 2008, Scandinavian legal origin countries lagged behind even the post-socialist countries.

Overall, the implementation analyses have shown that there is still variation in the choices for RIA and there is a marked persistence of national features and legal traditions. Trends of convergence are mainly associated with the legalistic and economic rationality dimensions of implementation. There are manifestations of only symbolic adoption of overall principles of regulatory reform. Laggards have higher scores on the legal dimension and the legal dimension has the lowest variance among the implementation scores. Further findings suggest that values and institutions for democratic accountability, such as regulatory transparency, systematic stakeholder consultation and judicial review, have not yet become transnational standards, as the OECD took these concepts of regulatory governance into account only in its 2012 recommendation. Within these findings, the effect of the OECD is attested to by the convergence trend on the dimension of economic rationality. Moreover, the OECD has constantly promoted RIA as a decisional tool for enhancing evidence-based decision making, and the present qualitative findings have confirmed the impact of peer review on implementation.

The analysis of the evaluation practices has shown that the majority of adopters do not appraise the performance of RIA and this is yet another indication of symbolic adoption. Evaluation systems are generally unsophisticated annual reports drafted by the central oversight units and submitted to parliaments. Indeed, there are few cases of complete institutionalisation, that is, with the presence of effective oversight and reporting mechanisms as well as the involvement of a network of independent advisory bodies and stakeholder evaluators. Occurring essentially through government-to-government communication, transfers of evaluation practices were limited to institutional constraints, such as ministerial ceilings on the administrative burden, linked to budget policy. Experience with independent advisory bodies also proved to be transferable.

Quantitative measures of regulatory quality are preferred by governments because they are a tool which allows systematic evaluation based on quantifiable targets. Sound qualitative measures based on anecdotal evidence are rare. Despite running several regulatory quality indicators, the OECD has not been so effective in creating a transnational evaluation system. The OECD peer review is based on national policy makers' data collection and surveys. Through the participation of member states, the main aim is to share knowledge through lesson-drawing mechanisms among policy makers and practitioners. The information generated by indicators is directed at government, rather than the media and the general public. The OECD measures of regulatory quality are not systematically used by governments, notwithstanding that they are mainly based on approved policy recommendations.

For its simplicity, observability and compatibility, the SCM was a more easily transferable evaluative model. Governments that were engaged with more complex economic methodologies, such as CBA and risk analysis, tended to benefit from their own direct experience. In this cluster, transfer – if it occurred – was constrained by the complexity of the regulatory appraisal system and adjusted to the institutional actors and administrative context.

Overall, the implementation and evaluation analyses confirmed limited interdependence. The role of the OECD, a strong determinant of adoption, faded away in the successive stages of the institutionalisation of RIA. There was also limited evidence of a transfer of practices among countries, and the US has so far not been a model for implementing and evaluating regulatory reform. Other countries, such as the Netherlands, emerged as more successful change agents and promoters of a simpler version of regulatory policy appraisal. The cumulative evidence of the three decisional stages excludes emulation from the leaders, and quests for legitimacy, based on the OECD peer review mechanisms and indicator systems. Furthermore, there is no evidence of instrumental and comprehensive learning and, consequently, of convergence; the operation of a selective or clustered modality of learning generally founded on the adopters' direct experience and institutional features is more plausible. The overall diffusion process of RIA is characterised by administrative features and functionalist needs – to govern the regulatory state – that have been emphasised and channelled through institutionalised patterns of transnational networks set up and orchestrated by the OECD. The evidence of the role of the OECD as an effective editor of a transnational agenda around a selected innovative international policy experience and solution is uncontested. Such transnational networks, however, have so far focused mainly on the legalistic and economic rationality dimensions of implementation.

8.4 Contributions to the literature

Through a systematic review of different elements of a transnational policy innovation, this book makes an important contribution to the literature on RIA. Political control of bureaucracy is the central function of this administrative innovation and it therefore provides a useful theoretical framework for comparing regulatory processes across countries and legal traditions. Moreover, policy innovation as an analytical perspective allows us to conceive of reform through a dynamic process of institutionalisation, which includes the administrative preconditions for adoptability, such as previous innovations for enhancing the transparency and openness of regulatory process.

Several normative claims can be drawn from the acknowledgement of the conditions and time necessary to institutionalise RIA. First, effective implementation can be achieved by taking the several dimensions of an RIA system, such as access to information and reasoned decisions, into account.

Second, the empirical evidence shows us that policy makers do not tend to exploit all the experience available around the globe. With the exclusion of the SCM (a simple, neat and intelligible model), neither is there extensive interdependence and communication among governments about how to go about RIA. In addition, the OECD has only recently embedded RIA in the issue of regulatory governance, addressing its member states' implementation gaps, and there have been only a few projects on the *ex post* evaluation of RIA programmes. Finally, governments should be aware that the returns from the necessary long-term investments for implementing and evaluating RIA and other necessary and complementary innovations are slow and uncertain. Thus, there is a risk of becoming frustrated with the innovation before it yields its benefits.

The contribution of this study to the literature on public administration and NPM, in which diffusion studies are sparse, is also evident. Previous diffusion studies of administrative innovation tended to test only the spatial pattern, through the insertion of an additional diffusion variable into a set of internal determinants. This research, however, through a multi-layered analytical framework, tested diverse hypotheses regarding governmental interactions. The role of the OECD has been assessed jointly with horizontal communications channels. In order to avoid the risk of RIA being considered merely as a nuisance by administrators, the three functions: political control, economic rationality and legitimacy, have to be incorporated across the process of institutionalisation. This understanding has allowed us to understand the role of the OECD as a change agency, editor and translator of the attributes of RIA. The framework should be further tested by analysing other administrative innovations and NPM tools promoted by the OECD. Overall, administrative reform can be conceived of as an innovation which has to be analysed in order to derive an understanding of adoptability and sustainability.

Acknowledging the multiple dimensions of policy change caused by policy interdependence, this book has assisted the development of a deep understanding of what has spread. It has disentangled different elements of policy innovation, such as the normally distributed rate of adoption, adoptability, the translation and editing process, diffusion patterns and causal mechanisms, and the extent of learning. The task has been to devise effective measures for appreciating the actual impact of policy interdependence on public administrations, by relying on multiple methods and datasets on adoption and implementation, as well as a qualitative recognition of the most relevant evaluation practices.

The contribution to the overall literature on public policy is four-fold. Firstly, it has been argued that implementation and evaluation studies should take account of governments' interdependence, obtaining the same methodological improvements as those obtained by policy adoption scholars. Analysing the implementation and evaluation of an administrative innovation that has spread around the globe and has been experienced in many other countries is rather different from the analysis of a novel and emergent policy idea. The amount of information available is huge, impacting on the theoretical assumptions and normative claims. Secondly, through the categories of adopters and years of adoption, implementation has been linked to the main expectations of policy diffusion. This was the first step towards taking the dynamic of the policy process into proper consideration, through an analysis of the necessary steps of institutionalisation which ranged from the extent of legal implementation to the strategic use of the innovation. Overall, by not going beyond the interaction between national bureaucrats and politicians, implementation studies have so far failed to take full account of the role of external actors. Through governance mechanisms such as policy labels, documents and reports, peer review and indicators, the OECD and transnational networks may have a huge impact on the extent and process of institutionalisation. Thirdly, evaluation has been linked to policy diffusion, providing causal paths leading to different contexts in which learning may occur. With this in mind, policy interdependence is a perspective for better explaining the causal mechanisms of learning, and provides a framework that can be utilised in further research on administrative reform. The final contribution is in comparative analysis, in showing that political control, an institution-centred model, is most effective because institutions guaranteeing the constitutional checks and balances are stable and common in all democracies. Alternative administrative doctrines, such as pluralistic and deliberative doctrine models, are not well developed beyond the US.

8.5 Further research

Due to the scope and aims of the analysis as well as the levels of the theoretical explanations, there are several limitations in this organisation-centred analysis of policy diffusion. Firstly, the agenda-setting phases have been overlooked. For instance, the role of policy entrepreneurs and stakeholders and their interaction with the OECD may be relevant determinants of the adoption of administrative reforms. This would have demanded a micro-analysis of the decision making through either, process tracing (Mossberger 2000; Weyland 2006) or a survey of policy makers (Garrett 2002). Qualitative case studies of agenda setting and policy transfer could be conducted on countries which – according to their derived adoptability – adopted RIA unexpectedly. For instance, among the pioneers an interesting case is Hungary, which adopted RIA well before the collapse of its communist regime and, consequently, had no previous interaction with the other pioneers. Because of its peculiar tradition of open and transparent administrative governance, as well as independent regulatory agencies, Sweden is another pioneer – with a still ongoing institutionalisation of RIA – which deserves an in-depth analysis.

Bearing in mind the second aim of this research, i.e. the investigation of interdependence across the policy process, the other limitation of this study refers to the post-adoption phases, namely, implementation and evaluation. Although a thorough analysis of empirical findings has been done, this research relies on explanations from the policy diffusion literature which do not provide for precise measurements of the extent of interdependence of actual practices. Furthermore, a better understanding of the administrative capacity to appraise direct and indirect experiences as well as prerequisites for and constraints on institutionalisation is essential. This would enable us to include specific determinants. Moreover, the analysis should be made broader by focusing on the demand and supply sides of institutional change. In other words, implementation and evaluation could be assessed in a similar way to policy adoption, using the EHA for measuring the probability of having an effective implementation, on the one hand, and policy evaluation and learning on the other hand, and, consequently, discerning and distinguishing administrative capacity and diffusion explanations.

The third aim of this research, the overall extent of policy change given the diffusion of an administrative innovation, is the most challenging. This research has provided an accurate overview of the overall patterns of implementation and modes of evaluation across thirty-eight countries. However, a comprehensive measure of policy change is still lacking. Future research should address the question of policy interdependence, elucidating how profound the impact of a diffused innovation can be on national policy and institutions. Theories of policy process and decision making must be further developed in order to take into account external influences and information exchange. Reforms are induced not only by poor institutional performance, but also by the perceived potential of feasible policy alternatives (Weyland 2006). In addition, this research has shown how the OECD has been effective in emphasising the potential of RIA as a tool to improve the rationality of decision making. However, recommending RIA mainly for its potential to achieve economic rationality is biased, leading to incomplete institutionalisation.

Another limitation of this research, and of policy diffusion study more generally, is the neglect of the counterfactual scenario. Would regulators achieve the same regulatory outcome without control mechanisms? Obviously, this question is applicable only to those countries which went beyond the legal adoption of RIA and for which the conduct of regulatory appraisals has become routine. To answer this question, a micro-level analysis of knowledge production is required, assessing the extent of the behavioural changes, on the part of the regulators, which occurred as a result of the innovation. Observations should be collected on the impact of previous innovations with similar goals and scopes. The necessary multi-innovation perspective for this goes well beyond the scope of the present research.

appendix a | selection of the year of adoption: a methodological clarification

Constructing a database on the adoption years of a policy innovation may seem a simple task. For each country the researcher has 'only' to look at the first legislative source that has enacted the RIA programme in a given country.[1] However, the adoption of RIA does not always stem from a legal source, as in the case of the UK. Often the legislative basis is embedded in a much wider legislation, as in the case of the Italian government that adopted RIA via the annual simplification law. In other cases, a government's rule on the lawmaking process is the legal framework containing RIA. This is the case with Canada, the Czech Republic, the Netherlands, Denmark and several other countries. In Korea, RIA has been adopted within the context of the Administrative Procedure Act (Baum 2007; OECD 2000). Due to this variation, identifying the year of enactment of the administrative requirement to perform an RIA is a complex process. To avoid such an impasse, priority has been given to the OECD reviews on regulatory reform, even when other primary and secondary sources report different information. Two elements justify this choice. Firstly, the OECD has defined functions and purposes of RIA (OECD 1997a, OECD 1997b). Its definition has also been broadly accepted by scholars (Kirkpatrick and Parker 2004; Radaelli 2004; Radaelli *et al.* 2006). Secondly, the OECD's reviews on regulatory reform constitute the only systematic running count of the adoption of RIA, since a member state's efforts in reforming regulatory governance are peer reviewed on the basis of a set of recommendations composing the evaluation benchmark (OECD 1997a; OECD1997b, APEC-OECD Co-operative Initiative on Regulatory Reform 2005; OECD 2012).

Unfortunately, the OECD has still not reviewed all of its member states. Moreover, not all the EU member states are part of the OECD. Consequently, on several occasions alternative sources, such as the annual reports prepared by the EU member states for the DG Enterprises charter for small enterprises and the Lisbon strategy for growth and jobs have been used. Both of these examples involve a report on RIA produced via a self-assessed questionnaire. In a few other cases, sources from governments and the United Nations Development Programme (UNDP) have been employed.[2] Table A.1 shows the year of adoption for each of the thirty-five out of thirty-eight countries in the sample (Cyprus, Luxembourg,

---

1. Also, in this case, the task can be complex: two academic papers on the diffusion of FOI legislation, for which data are more consolidated than RIA (an online database also exists at http://www.freedominfo.org), have reported different years of adoption for a few cases (cfr. Bennett 1997: 218; Ackerman and Sandoval-Ballesteros 2006, 97–8).

2. http://europeandcis.undp.org/pia (accessed 13 June 2007).

and Malta did not adopt RIA within the time frame of the analysis 1968–2006). It also points out the differences with the OECD dataset (Jacobzone *et al.* 2007a).

Before turning to each difference in the two datasets, it is essential to clarify that the focus here is on the innovation, the new idea (Rogers 2003; Mossberger 2000:1) that regulators have to systematically assess (through the drafting of a dedicated report) the economic effects of their proposals. As mentioned in Section 1.1, RIA can rely on several appraisal methods, other than cost-benefit analysis applied to the regulatory process. It can also be a simple checklist demanding that regulators balance advantages and disadvantages of new regulatory provisions using whatever economic methodology they prefer.

Sections 1.1 and 4.3 show that the innovation under analysis is a principle, labelling a general lesson transferred from other countries' experience (Mossberger 1999:35), rather than a precise methodological model of regulatory governance. Further, the year of adoption is taken here to mean the year when the law, regulation, or policy concerning RIA was approved and not the year when the provision was effectively enacted.

Bearing in mind these specifications, Austria, Denmark, Greece, Finland, and Spain are considered to occur too early in the OECD dataset. In 1979, Austria adopted a Fiscal Impact Analysis which focuses on the direct consequences of new regulations on the public budget. The adoption of the Danish RIA in the mid-1960s is implausible, given that the idea was conceived in the US in 1971.[3] What the OECD considers here are general instructions for drafting regulations.

The same consideration is valid for Finland where the *Instructions on the Drafting of Government Proposals* date back to the mid-1970s. The adoption of the *Instructions for Assessing the Economic Impacts of Legislation* and of the checklist based on the OECD's recommendations on regulatory reform and RIA occurred in 1998.[4] Whereas the cases of Denmark and Finland highlight a situation where adoption of RIA is confused by the previous adoption of the administrative requirements of the rulemaking process, in the case of Greece and Spain the differences between the two datasets is related to the OECD's consideration of earlier steps toward a formal RIA adoption. Indeed, the governments reported a later adoption of RIA in their reports on the Lisbon strategy on growth and jobs and in the European SME charter. There are also cases in which the OECD considered the late adoption of RIA. In several cases (France, Korea, Switzerland and Turkey) this is due to the fact that the OECD reports the year when the law was enacted. The differences are indeed marginal, being only of one year. In other cases, such as with New Zealand, Sweden and the US, the differences are relevant. In the case of New Zealand, the so-called Compliance Cost Statement, adopted since 1995, is similar to the British CCA which has been reckoned to be RIA by the OECD. Similarly, 1971 was the year of adoption of RIA in the US. Indeed,

---

3. In the same paper Jacobzone *et al.* (2007) confirm that the first country to adopt RIA was the US.

4. This interpretation is also confirmed by the first Finnish report on the European Charter for Small Enterprises (Finnish Ministry of Trade and Industry 2001).

in 1974 there was a strengthening of the Nixon administration's 'Quality of Life' review which was already established RIA in 1971. Finally, it is the OECD itself that reports, in Sweden, '[i]n 1987, the first Government Agencies and Institutes Ordinance was adopted, under which agencies are obliged to investigate and analyse the consequences of new regulations and compile this investigation into an impact assessment.' (OECD 2007c) Having specified these differences in the consideration of years of adoption, the next section turns to the analysis of the trend of diffusion, highlighting the major events which occurred during more than three decades and remarking on the major clusters of adopting units.

Table A.1: Years of adoption of RIA in EU and OECD member states

Country	Adoption years	Source	Difference with the OECD database
Australia	1985	OECD report	
Austria	1999	National report on European Charter for SME	1979
Belgium	1998	OECD report	Missing data
Bulgaria	2003	OECD Sigma	Not available
Canada	1978	OECD report	
Cyprus	No adoption	OECD Sigma	Not available
Czech Republic	1998	UNDP	
Denmark	1993	OECD report	1966
Estonia	1996	OECD Sigma	Not available
Finland	1998	OECD report	Mid-1970s
France	1995	OECD report and National report on European Charter for SME	1996
Germany	1984	OECD report	
Greece	2006	National report on Lisbon strategy for growth and jobs	Developed since 2001
Hungary	1987	OECD report	
Iceland	1999	OECD indicators of product market	
Ireland	1999	OECD report	
Italy	1999	OECD report	
Japan	2004	OECD report	
Korea	1997	OECD report	
Latvia	1998	OECD Sigma, National report on European Charter for SME and UNDP	Not available
Lithuania	2003	National report on Lisbon strategy on growth and jobs	Not available

(Cont'd.)

Table A.1: (Cont'd.)

Country	Adoption years	Source	Difference with the OECD database
Luxembourg	No adoption	National report on Lisbon strategy on growth and jobs	Missing data
Malta	No adoption	National report on Lisbon strategy on growth and jobs	Not available
Mexico	1996	OECD report	
Netherlands	1985	OECD report	
New Zealand	1995	Government guidelines	1998
Norway	1995	OECD report	
Poland	2001	Government guidelines	Not available
Portugal	2006	National report on Lisbon strategy on growth and jobs	Missing data
Romania	2005	UNDP	Not available
Slovak Republic	2001	Republic National report on European Charter for SME and UNDP	Missing data
Slovenia	2004	National report on European Charter for SME and OECD Sigma	Not available
Spain	2004	National report on European Charter for SME	1997
Sweden	1987	OECD report	1998
Switzerland	1999	OECD report	2000
Turkey	2006	Government website	To be introduced in 2007
UK	1985	OECD report	
US	1971	Government primary sources	1974

appendix b | OECD recommendations and best practice

This appendix lists the OECD policy recommendations and best practices on regulatory quality reform and RIA.

B.1 The 1995 Recommendation of the Council of the OECD on improving the quality of government regulation

- Is the problem correctly defined? The problem to be solved should be precisely stated, giving clear evidence of its nature and magnitude, and explaining why it has arisen (identifying the incentives of affected entities).

- Is government action justified? Government intervention should be based on clear evidence that government action is justified, given the nature of the problem, the likely benefits and costs of action (based on a realistic assessment of government effectiveness), and alternative mechanisms for addressing the problem.

- Is regulation the best form of government action? Regulators should carry out, early in the regulatory process, an informed comparison of a variety of regulatory and non-regulatory policy instruments, considering relevant issues such as costs, benefits, distributional effects, and administrative requirements.

- Is there a legal basis for regulation? Regulatory processes should be structured so that all regulatory decisions rigorously respect the rule of law; that is, responsibility should be explicit for ensuring that all regulations are authorised by higher-level regulations and consistent with treaty obligations, and comply with relevant legal principles such as certainty, proportionality, and applicable procedural requirements.

- What is the appropriate level (or levels) of government for this action? Regulators should choose the most appropriate level of government to take action, or, if multiple levels are involved, should design effective systems of coordination between levels of government.

- Do the benefits of regulation justify the costs? Regulators should estimate the total expected costs and benefits of each regulatory proposal and of feasible alternatives, and should make the estimates available in accessible format to decision-makers. The costs of government action should be justified by its benefits before action is taken.

- Is the distribution of effects across society transparent? To the extent that distributive and equity values are affected by government intervention, regulators should make transparent the distribution of regulatory costs and benefits across social groups.

- Is the regulation clear, consistent, comprehensible, and accessible to users? Regulators should assess whether rules will be understood by likely users, and to that end should take steps to ensure that the text and structure of rules are as clear as possible.
- Have all interested parties had the opportunity to present their views? Regulations should be developed in an open and transparent fashion, with appropriate procedures for effective and timely input from interested parties such as affected businesses and trade unions, other interest groups, or other levels of government.
- How will compliance be achieved? Regulators should assess the incentives and institutions through which the regulation will take effect, and should design responsive implementation strategies that make the best use of them.

B.2 The 1997 regulatory reform best practice

1. Adopt at the political level broad programmes of regulatory reform that establish clear objectives and frameworks for implementation.
   - Establish principles of "good regulation" to guide reform, drawing on the 1995 OECD Recommendation on Improving the Quality of Government Regulation. Good regulation should: (i) be needed to serve clearly identified policy goals, and be effective in achieving those goals; (ii) have a sound legal basis; (iii) produce benefits that justify costs, considering the distribution of effects across society; (iv) minimise costs and market distortions; (v) promote innovation through market incentives and goal-based approaches; (vi) be clear, simple, and practical for users; (vii) be consistent with other regulations and policies; and (viii) be compatible as far as possible with competition, trade and investment-facilitating principles at domestic and international levels.
   - Create effective and credible mechanisms inside the government for managing and coordinating regulation and its reform; avoid overlapping or duplicative responsibilities among regulatory authorities and levels of government.
   - Encourage reform at all levels of government and in private bodies such as standard-setting organisations.
2. Review regulations systematically to ensure that they continue to meet their intended objectives efficiently and effectively.
   - Review regulations (economic, social, and administrative) against the principles of good regulation and from the point of view of the user rather than the regulator.

- Target reviews at regulations where change will yield the highest and most visible benefits, particularly regulations restricting competition and trade, and affecting enterprises, including SMEs.
- Review proposals for new regulations as well as existing regulations. Integrate regulatory impact analysis into the development, review, and reform of regulations. Update regulations through automatic review methods, such as sunsetting.

3. Ensure that regulations and regulatory processes are transparent, non-discriminatory and efficiently applied.

- Ensure that reform goals and strategies are articulated clearly to the public. Consult with affected parties, whether domestic or foreign, while developing or reviewing regulations, ensuring that the consultation itself is transparent.
- Create and update on a continuing basis public registries of regulations and business formalities, or use other means of ensuring that domestic and foreign businesses can easily identify all requirements applicable to them.
- Ensure that procedures for applying regulations are transparent, non-discriminatory, contain an appeals process, and do not unduly delay business decisions.

4. Review and strengthen where necessary the scope, effectiveness and enforcement of competition policy.

- Eliminate sectoral gaps in coverage of competition law unless evidence suggests that compelling public interests cannot be served in better ways.
- Enforce competition law vigorously where collusive behaviour, abuse of dominant position, or anticompetitive mergers risk frustrating reform.
- Provide competition authorities with the authority and capacity to advocate reform.

5. Reform economic regulations in all sectors to stimulate competition, and eliminate them except where clear evidence demonstrates that they are the best way to serve broad public interests.

- Review as a high priority those aspects of economic regulations that restrict entry, exit, pricing, output, normal commercial practices, and forms of business organisation.
- Promote efficiency and the transition to effective competition where economic regulations continue to be needed because of the potential for abuse of market power. In particular: (i) separate potentially competitive activities from regulated utility networks, and otherwise restructure as needed to reduce the market power of incumbents; (ii) guarantee access to essential network facilities to all market

entrants on a transparent and non-discriminatory basis; (iii) use price caps and other mechanisms to encourage efficiency gains when price controls are needed during the transition to competition.

6. Eliminate unnecessary regulatory barriers to trade and investment by enhancing implementation of international agreements and strengthening international principles.

- Implement, and work with other countries to strengthen, international rules and principles to liberalise trade and investment (such as transparency, non-discrimination, avoidance of unnecessary trade restrictiveness, and attention to competition principles), as contained in WTO agreements, OECD recommendations and policy guidelines, and other agreements.

- Reduce as a priority matter those regulatory barriers to trade and investment arising from divergent and duplicative requirements by countries.

- Develop and use whenever possible internationally harmonised standards as a basis for domestic regulations, while collaborating with other countries to review and improve international standards to assure they continue to achieve the intended policy goals efficiently and effectively.

- Expand recognition of other countries' conformity assessment procedures and results through, for example, mutual recognition agreements (MRAs) or other means.

7. Identify important linkages with other policy objectives and develop policies to achieve those objectives in ways that support reform.

- Adapt as necessary prudential and other public policies in areas such as safety, health, consumer protection, and energy security so that they remain effective, and as efficient as possible within competitive market environments.

- Review non-regulatory policies, including subsidies, taxes, procurement policies, trade instruments such as tariffs, and other support policies, and reform them where they unnecessarily distort competition.

- Ensure that programmes designed to ease the potential costs of regulatory reform are focused, transitional, and facilitate, rather than delay, reform.

- Implement the full range of recommendations of the OECD Jobs Study to improve the capacity of workers and enterprises to adjust and take advantage of new job and business opportunities.

B.3 Good practices for improving the capacities of national administrations to assure high quality regulation

The OECD Report on Regulatory Reform, which was welcomed by ministers in May 1997, includes a coordinated set of strategies for improving regulatory quality, many of which were based on the 1995 Recommendation of the OECD Council on Improving the Quality of Government Regulation.

These form the basis of the analysis undertaken in this report and are reproduced below:

A. *Building a regulatory management system*
1. Adopt regulatory reform policy at the highest political levels.
2. Establish explicit standards for regulatory quality and principles of regulatory decision-making.
3. Build regulatory management capacities.

B. *Improving the quality of new regulations*
1. Assess regulatory impacts.
2. Consult systematically with affected interests.
3. Use alternatives to regulation.
4. Improve regulatory coordination.

C. *Upgrading the quality of existing regulations* (In addition to the strategies listed above)
1. Review and update existing regulations.
2. Reduce red tape and government formalities.

B.4 The 1997 best practices for achieving maximum benefit from RIA

1. Maximise political commitment to RIA. Reform principles and the use of RIA should be endorsed at the highest levels of government. RIA should be supported by clear ministerial accountability for compliance.
2. Allocate responsibilities for RIA programme elements carefully. Locating responsibility for RIA with regulators improves 'ownership' and integration into decision-making. A central body is needed to oversee the RIA process and ensure consistency, credibility and quality. It needs adequate authority and skills to perform this function.
3. Train the regulators. Ensure that formal, properly designed programmes exist to give regulators the skills required to do high quality RIA.
4. Use a consistent but flexible analytical method. The benefit/cost principle should be adopted for all regulations but analytical methods can vary as long as RIA identifies and weighs all significant positive and negative effects and integrates qualitative and quantitative analyses. Mandatory guidelines should be issued to maximise consistency.

5. Develop and implement data collection strategies. Data quality is essential to useful analysis. An explicit policy should clarify quality standards for acceptable data and suggest strategies for collecting high quality data at minimum cost within time constraints.

6. Target RIA efforts. Resources should be applied to those regulations where impacts are most significant and where the prospects are best for altering regulatory outcomes. RIA should be applied to all significant policy proposals, whether implemented by law, lower level rules or ministerial actions.

7. Integrate RIA with the policy-making process, beginning as early as possible. Regulators should see RIA insights as integral to policy decisions, rather than as an add-on requirement for external consumption.

8. Communicate the results. Policy makers are rarely analysts. Results of RIA must be communicated clearly with concrete implications and options explicitly identified. The use of a common format aids effective communication.

9. Involve the public extensively. Interest groups should be consulted widely and in a timely fashion. This is likely to mean a consultation process with a number of steps.

10. Apply RIA to existing as well as new regulation. RIA disciplines should also be applied to reviews of existing regulation.

B.5 The 2012 recommendation of the Council on Regulatory Policy and Governance

1. Commit at the highest political level to an explicit whole-of-government policy for regulatory quality. The policy should have clear objectives and frameworks for implementation to ensure that, if regulation is used, the economic, social and environmental benefits justify the costs, the distributional effects are considered and the net benefits are maximised.

2. Adhere to principles of open government, including transparency and participation in the regulatory process, to ensure that regulation serves the public interest and is informed by the legitimate needs of those interested in and affected by regulation. This includes providing meaningful opportunities (including online) for the public to contribute to the process of preparing draft regulatory proposals and to the quality of the supporting analysis. Governments should ensure that regulations are comprehensible and clear and that parties can easily understand their rights and obligations.

3. Establish mechanisms and institutions to actively provide oversight of regulatory policy procedures and goals, support and implement regulatory policy, and thereby foster regulatory quality.

4. Integrate Regulatory Impact Assessment (RIA) into the early stages of the policy process for the formulation of new regulatory proposals. Clearly identify policy goals, and evaluate if regulation is necessary and how it can be most effective and efficient in achieving those goals. Consider means other than regulation and identify the tradeoffs of the different approaches analysed in order to identify the best approach.

5. Conduct systematic programme reviews of the stock of significant regulation against clearly defined policy goals, including consideration of costs and benefits, to ensure that regulations remain up to date, cost justified, cost effective and consistent, and deliver the intended policy objectives.

6. Regularly publish reports on the performance of regulatory policy and reform programmes and the public authorities applying the regulations. Such reports should also include information on how regulatory tools such as RIA, public consultation practices and reviews of existing regulations are functioning in practice.

7. Develop a consistent policy covering the role and functions of regulatory agencies in order to provide greater confidence that regulatory decisions are made on an objective, impartial and consistent basis, without conflicts of interest, bias or improper influence.

8. Ensure the effectiveness of systems for the review of the legality and procedural fairness of regulations and of decisions made by bodies empowered to issue regulatory sanctions. Ensure that citizens and businesses have access to these systems of review at a reasonable cost and receive decisions in a timely manner.

9. As appropriate apply risk assessment, risk management, and risk communication strategies to the design and implementation of regulations to ensure that regulation is targeted and effective. Regulators should assess how regulations will be given effect and should design responsive implementation and enforcement strategies.

10. Where appropriate promote regulatory coherence through coordination mechanisms between the supranational, national and sub-national levels of government. Identify cross-cutting regulatory issues at all levels of government to promote coherence between regulatory approaches and avoid duplication or conflict of regulations.

11. Foster the development of regulatory management capacity and performance at sub-national levels of government.

12. In developing regulatory measures, give consideration to all relevant international standards and frameworks for cooperation in the same field and, where appropriate, their likely effects on parties outside the jurisdiction.

appendix | data sources of the
c | implementation score

This appendix provides details on the data sources, highlighting the problems in integrating them into the implementation index.

C.1 OECD database on government capacity to produce high-quality regulations

This database on regulatory reform and RIA relies on the pioneering and pivotal surveys conducted by the OECD. The database originated from the 1995 OECD recommendations signed by the Ministers for Public Administration on Regulatory Reform (OECD 1995) and the 1997 OECD benchmarks for implementing RIA (OECD 1997a). Through a set of recommendations,[1] its main purpose is to benchmark OECD countries' initiatives for producing high-quality regulations. The detailed 2005 self-assessed questionnaire (sent to the formal group of directors and experts for better regulation and RIA programmes) is composed of eighty items, grouped in five sections:

- Content of regulatory policies
- Regulatory quality tools
- Institutional arrangements to promote regulatory quality
- Dynamic aspects of regulatory quality
- Performance/outcome indicators

The last two sections clearly derive from the recent evolution of the OECD in its benchmarking exercise.

C.2 ENBR and DIADEM database

This database was developed by a project coordinated by CEPS, a Brussels based think tank. The main aim of this project was to disseminate knowledge on RIA and to systematise in a database all information available both at the macro and micro levels. In particular, the 'country fact sheets' are composed of three parts: constitutional structure, horizontal regulatory policy, the impact assessment system, and other better regulation tools (consultation, simplification and access to regulation). The constitutional structure contains information on the regulators, the role of the judiciary in the regulatory process and the integration of IA provisions with administrative law. The second level of analysis focuses on the

---

1.   They concern the institutional design of regulatory reform and RIA and were recently updated in 2012 (OECD 2012).

principles, design, targets and measures of better regulation. Finally, the last part of the fact sheet focuses on the extent of provisions required for the four tools of better regulation. The variables are generally expressed in a Yes/No format.

C.3 EVIA's country microfiches

The EVIA project was led by the Environmental Policy Research Centre at Frei University in Berlin. The main goal of this project was to disentangle the concept of quality in regulatory appraisal. A theoretical framework was drawn for evaluating RIA and, ultimately, formulating policy recommendations. The project was mainly comparative, and brief countries reports were drafted for the twenty-seven EU member states and the European Commission. Information gathering methodologies varied, i.e. face-to-face interview, phone interview, informal communication with experts, evaluation reports, academic literature, review of guidelines and review of RIAs. The country reports are essentially composed of two parts: i) design of the impact assessment system, containing factual data on adoption, legal provisions, institutional design, and financial resources; and ii) overall RIA framework referring to both objective and subjective data on the quality of implementation. The advantage of this database is its comprehensiveness both in terms of variables and countries observed. The major flaw is related to the variability of methodologies used in data gathering and the lack of a more theoretically structured definition of the quality of implementation.

C.4 Problems in integrating the existing datasets

Notwithstanding the number of datasets available, the integration of their data is not straightforward. This is essentially due to the lack of a common data-gathering template. For instance, the OECD has conducted an additional government survey, the RIA Inventory,[2] that does not take into account the existence of the previous surveys, or specify how to integrate the different data. In the same vein, the two 6FP research projects have different survey designs and methodologies. ENBR relied on the knowledge of national experts present in the country under observation; the EVIA project, by contrast, involved data collection by a small number of researchers using different methods (primary and secondary sources, interviews and personal communication with experts). The datasets also have different purposes: ENBR was aimed at delivering an on-line database (composed of a series of factual sentences) and a series of papers on the politics and features

---

2. Drafted in 2004, the OECD RIA inventory is a compilation of ten items, such as scope of coverage, public disclosure, quality control mechanisms, CBA, risk assessment and discount rate, on the modes of and choices for RIA and rely on information provided by governments. Due to the limited range of items and the fact that this survey has been conducted only once, this database has been used only to complement information not available from the previous source of information. Available Online: http://www.oecd.org/gov/regulatory-policy/riainventory.htm (accessed 7 June 2013).

of RIA in each country; EVIA produced a series of streamlined country reports drafted by researchers, successively peer-reviewed by national high-level civil servants in charge of better regulation and RIA. In EVIA, the design used and the variables generated are innovative; however, sometimes the researchers' discretion was too broad. ENBR used instead an approach similar to the OECD survey but relying on national experts (from academia and think tanks) rather than government officials and peer-review mechanisms.

To summarise, the following are the main critical issues faced in constructing the RIA implementation index. Several EU member states are not OECD countries, thus the three waves of the OECD survey cannot be used for such countries. Although the OECD and the EU, with their joint SIGMA project on regulatory quality, funded reviews of the ten new EU member states (OECD 2007b), the data collection is not systematised according to the survey. It assumes instead the form of a peer review document relying on the 1997 OECD's benchmarks for implementing RIA. Furthermore, several items have been conducted among the OECD countries, without being replicated among EU member states. For instance, an essential question on the training of regulators for RIA and CBA was not asked by ENBR and EVIA, and a significant number of items refer to similar concepts whilst using different question formulations (see Tables 6.1, 6.2, 6.3 and 6.4). Finally, some databases rely on governments' surveys, others on experts' data gathering. This leads to the assignment of different scores to identical or similar items, particularly among ENBR and EVIA items, notwithstanding the exchange of information between the two projects. For all these reasons, in cases of contrasting data, the most recent OECD survey has been given precedence; the other data sources have been used only in cases of missing data.

| bibliography

Abrahamson, E. (1991) 'Managerial fads and fashions: The diffusion and rejection of innovations', *The Academy of Management Review*, 16(3): 586–612.

Access Economics Pty Limited (2010) 'Reviewing the effectiveness of the regulatory impact statement (RIS) process in Victoria', Report for Department of Treasury and Finance, Canberra.

Ackerman, B. A. (1981) *Social Justice in the Liberal State*, 4th edn, New Haven, Connecticut: Yale University Press.

Ackerman, J. M. and Sandoval-Ballesteros, I. E. (2006) 'The global explosion of freedom of information laws', *Administrative Law Review*, 58(1): 85–130.

ACTAL (2003) *Work Programme* 2004, The Hague: ACTAL.

Agence pour la Simplification (2004) *Fil conducteur pour le test Kafka*, Brussels: ACTAL.

— (2004) *Fil Conducteur pour le Test Kafka*, Brussels: Agence pour la Simplification.

Allio, L. (2008) *The Emergence of Better Regulation in the European Union*, unpublished thesis, King's College.

Allison, P. D. (2008) 'Convergence failures in logistic regression', *SAS Global Forum: Statistics and Data Analysis* (Paper 306–2008): 1–11.

Ambler, T., Chittenden, F. and Obodovski, M. (2003) *Are Regulators Raising their Game? UK regulatory impact assessment in 2002/3*, London: British Chamber of Commerce.

Andrews, R. N. (1984) 'Economics and environmental decisions, past and present', *Environmental Policy Under Reagan's Executive Order*, Chapel Hill, North Carolina: University of North Carolina Press, pp. 43–85

Ansell, C. and Gingrich, J. (2003) 'Reforming the administrative state', in B. E. Cain, R. J. Dalton and S. E. Scarrow (eds) *Democracy Transformed? Expanding political opportunities in advanced industrial democracies*, New York: Oxford University Press, pp. 164–91.

APEC-OECD Co-operative Initiative on Regulatory Reform (2005) The Integrated Checklist on Regulatory Reform: A policy instrument for regulatory quality, competition policy and market openness, APEC and OECD. Online. Available; http://www.oecd.org/regreform/34989455.pdf (accessed 22 November 2012).

Argy, S. and Johnson, M. (2003) *Mechanisms for Improving the Quality of Regulations: Australia in an international context*, Melbourne, Australia: Productivity Commission.

Armingeon, K. and Beyeler, M. (2004) *The OECD and European Welfare States*, Cheltenham: Edward Elgar.

Arndt, C. and Oman, C. (2006) *Uses and Abuses of Governance Indicators*, Paris: OECD Publishing.

Arnold, R. (1987) 'Political control of administrative officials', *Journal of Law, Economics and Organization*, 3(2): 279–86.

Arrow, K. J., Cropper, M. L., Eads, G. C., Hahn, R. W., Lave, L. B., Noll, R. G., *et al.* (1996a) 'Is there a role for benefit-cost analysis in environmental, health, and safety regulation?', *Science*, 272(5259): 221–2.

Arrow, K. J., Kenney, J., Cropper, M. L., Eads, G. C. and Hahn, R. W. (1996b) *Benefit-Cost Analysis in Environmental, Health, and Safety Regulation*. Washington DC: AEI Press.

Aubrey, H. G. (1967) *Atlantic Economic Cooperation: The case of the OECD*, New York: Preager for the Council on Foreign Relations.

Australian Government (2010) *Best Practice Regulation Handbook*. Canberra: Australian Government.

Ayers, I. and Braithwaite, J. (1992) *Responsive Regulation: Transcending the deregulation debate*, Oxford: Oxford University Press.

Baldwin, R., Cave, M. and Lodge, M. (eds) *The Oxford Handbook of Regulation*, Oxford: Oxford University Press, 2010 pp. 1 of Acknowledgement.

Bardhan, P. (1997) 'Corruption and development: A review of issues', *Journal of Economic Literature*, 35(3): 1320–46.

Bartlett, R. V. (1989) 'Impact assessment as a policy strategy', in R. V. Bartlett (ed.), *Policy Through Impact Assessment: Institutionalized analysis as a policy strategy*, Westport, Conn: Greenwood Press, pp. 1–4.

Baum, J. R. (2007) 'Presidents have problems too: The logic of intra-branch delegation in East Asian democracies', *British Journal of Political Science*, 37(4): 659–84.

Baum, J. R. and Bawn, K. (2005) 'Slowing at sunset: Administrative procedures and the pace of reform in Korea' paper presented at the annual meeting of American Political Science Association, Washington DC, September 2005.

Bawn, K. (1997) 'Choosing strategies to control the bureaucracy: Statutory constraints, oversight, and the committee system', *Journal of Law, Economics and Organization*, 13(1): 101–20.

Bearce, D. H. and Bondanella, S. (2007) 'Intergovernmental organizations, socialization, and member-state interest convergence', *International Organization*, 61(4): 703–33.

Beck, N., Katz, J. N. and Tucker, R. (1998) 'Taking time seriously: Time-series-cross-section analysis with a binary dependent variable', *American Journal of Political Science*, 42(2): 1260–88.

Benner, T., Reinicke, W. H. and Witte, J. M. (2004) 'Multisectoral networks in global governance: Towards a pluralistic system of accountability', *Government and Opposition*, 39(2): 191–210.

Bennett, C. J. (1997) 'Understanding the ripple effects: The cross-national adoption of policy instruments for bureaucratic accountability', *Governance*, 10(3) 213–33.

Berry, F. S. (1994) 'Innovation in public management: The adoption of strategic planning', *Public Administration Review*, 54(4): 322–30.

Berry, F. S. and Berry, W. D. (1990) 'State lottery adoptions as policy innovations: An event history analysis', *American Political Science Review*, 84(2): 395–415.

—— (2007) 'Innovation and diffusion models in policy research', in P. A. Sabatier (ed.) *Theories of Policy Process*, 2nd edn, Boulder, Colorado: Westview Press, pp. 223–60.

Better Regulation Task Force (2005) *Less is More: Reducing burdens, improving outcomes,* London: Better Regulation Task Force.

Better Regulation Unit (1998) *The Better Regulation Guide and Regulatory Impact Assessment,* London: Better Regulation Unit, Cabinet Office.

Beyeler, M. (2004) 'Introduction: A comparative study of the OECD and European welfare states', in K. Armingeon and M. Beyeler (eds) *The OECD and European Welfare State*, Cheltenham: Edward Elgar, pp. 1–12.

Bignami, F. (2001) 'The reformation of European administrative law', paper presented at the 2001 European Community Studies Association conference, 31 May–2 June 2001.

Bishop, W. (1990) 'A theory of administrative law', *Journal of Legal Studies*, 19 (2): 489–530.

Blomquist, W. (2007) 'The policy process and large-n comparative studies', in P. A. Sabatier (ed.) *Theories of the Policy Process*, 2nd edn, Boulder, Colorado: Westview Press, pp. 261–89.

Blumstein, J. F. (2001) 'Regulatory review by the executive office of the president: An overview and policy analysis of current issues', *Duke Law Journal*, 51(3): 851–99.

Board of Swedish Industry and Commerce for Better Regulation (2002) *How High is the Quality of the Swedish Central Government's Regulatory Impact Analysis (RIAS) in the Business Sector? The NNR regulation indicator for 2002*, Stockholm: NNR.

Boulton, E. (1989) *Administrative Law in EU,* Cambridge: Cambridge University Press.

Boyne, G. A., Gould-Williams, J. S., Law, J. and Walker, R. M. (2005) 'Explaining the adoption of innovation: An empirical analysis of public management reform', *Environment and Planning C: Government and Policy*, 23(3): 419–35.

Bradford, N. (2008) 'The OECD's local turn: "Innovative liberalism" for the cities?', in R. Mahon and S. McBride (eds) *The OECD and Transnational Governance*, Vancouver: UBC Press, pp. 134–51.

Brams, S. J. (1966) 'Transaction flows in the international system', *American Political Science Review*, 60(4): 880–98.

Breyer, S. (1993) *Breaking the Vicious Circle: Towards effective risk regulation,* Cambridge, Massachusetts: Harvard University Press.

Brickman, R., Jasanoff, S. and Ilgen, T. (1985) *Controlling Chemicals: The politics of regulation in Europe and the United States*, Ithaca, New York: Cornell University Press.

Brooks, S. M. (2005) 'Interdependent and domestic foundations of policy change: The diffusion of pension privatization around the world', *International Studies Quarterly*, 49(2): 273–94.

—   (2007). 'When does diffusion matter? Explaining the spread of structural pension reforms across nations', *Journal of Politics*, 69(3): 701–15.

Broome, A. and Seabrooke, L. (2012) 'Seeing like an international organisation', *New Political Economy*, 17(1): 1–16.

Brunsson, N. (1989) *The Organisation of Hypocrisy: Talk, decisions and actions in organisations*, Chichester and New York: John Wiley and Sons.

Buckley, J. and Westerland, C. (2004) 'Duration standard errors: Improving EHA models of state policy diffusion', *State Politics and Policy Quarterly*, 4(1): 94–113.

Cabinet Office (2006). Online. Available. http://www.webarchive.nationalarchives. gov.uk and http://www.cabinetoffice.gov.uk/regulation/ria/overview/ start_ria.asp (accessed 1 March 2006)

Carley, M. (1980) *Rational Techniques in Policy Analysis*, London: Heinemann Educational Books.

Carroll, P. and Kellow, A. (2011) *The OECD: A study of organisational adaptation*, Cheltenham: Edward Elgar.

Carter, D. B. and Signorino, C. S. (2010) 'Back to the future: Modelling time dependence in binary data', *Political Analysis*, 18(3): 271–92.

Cassese, S. (2003) 'The age of administrative reforms', in J. Hayward and A. Menon (eds) *Governing Europe*, Oxford: Oxford University Press, pp. 128–39.

Cassese, S. and Savino, M. (2005) 'The global economy, accountable governance, and administrative reform', paper presented at the 6th Global Forum on Reinventing Government: toward participatory and transparent governance, Seoul: United Nations Public Administration Programme.

Castles, F. G. (1993) *Families of Nations: Patterns of public policy in Western democracies*, Aldershot: Dartmouth Publication Company.

—   (1998) *Comparative Public Policy: Patterns of post-war transformation*, Cheltenham: Edward Elgar Publishing.

Cecot, C., Hahn, R. W., Renda, A. and Schrefler, L. (2008) 'An evaluation of the quality of impact assessment in the European Union with lessons for the U.S. and the EU, *Regulation and Governance*, 2(4): 238–58.

Chiti, M. P. (2004) 'Forms of European administrative action', *Law and Contemporary Problems*, 28(1): 37–60.

Clark, J. (1985) 'Policy diffusion and program scope: Research directions', *Publius*, 15(4): 61–70.

Coglianese, C. (2002) 'Empirical analysis and administrative law', *University of Illinois Law Journal*, 2002(4), 1111–37.

Cohen, D. and Strauss, P. L. (1995) 'Congressional reviews of agency regulations', *Administrative Law Review*, 49(1), 95–110.

Collier, D. and Messick, R. E. (1975) 'Prerequisites versus diffusion: Testing alternative explanations of social security adoption', *American Political Science Review*, 69 (4): 1299–315.

Conway, P., Janod, V. and Nicoletti, G. (2005) 'Product market regulation in OECD countries: 1998 to 2003', *Economic Department Working Paper*, (419, ECO/WKP (2005)6).

Conzelmann, T. (2010) 'Beyond the carrot and the stick: The authority of peer reviews in the WTO and the OECD', paper presented at the 7th European conference of the ECPR Standing Group for International Relations, Stockholm, 9–11 September 2010.

Cordova-Novion, C. and Jacobzone, S. (2011) 'Strengthening the institutional setting for regulatory reform: The experience from OECD Countries', *OECD working papers on public governance*, Paris: OECD.

Council of the OECD (2009) 'In-depth evaluation of the group on regulatory policy', C(2009)39, 12 June 2009.

Cowen, T. (2005) 'Using cost-benefit analysis to review regulation', paper presented at the New Zealand business roundtable, 2005. Online. Available; http://www.gmu.edu/centers/publicchoice/faculty%20pages/ Tyler/Cowen%20on%20cost%20benefit.pdf (accessed 7 July 2013).

Croley, S. P. (1996) 'The administrative procedure act and regulatory reform: A reconciliation', *Administrative Law Journal*, 10(1): 35–49.

—   (1998) 'Theories of regulation: Incorporating the administrative process', *Columbia Law Review*, 98(1): 1–168.

Danish Commerce and Companies Agency (2003) *International Study: Efforts to reduce administrative burdens and improve business regulation*. Copenhagen: Danish Commerce and Companies Agency.

De Francesco, F. (2012) 'Diffusion of Regulatory Impact Analysis Among OECD and EU Member States', Comparative Political Studies 45 (10): 1277-305. Available online http://cps.sagepub.com/content/45/10/1277.short.

—   (forthcoming) 'Change agencies, regulatory quality indices, and the media: Comparing the World Bank and the OECD', *Journal of Comparative Policy Analysis: Research and practice*.

De Francesco, F., Radaelli, C. M. and Troeger, V. E. (2012) 'Implementing regulatory innovations in Europe: the case of impact assessment', *Journal of European Public Policy*, 19(4): 491–511.

Deighton-Smith, R. (1997) 'Regulatory impact analysis: Best practice in OECD countries', in *Regulatory Impact Analysis: Best practice in OECD*, Paris: OECD Publishing, pp. 211–41.

Delacroix, J., and Ragin, C. (1981) 'Structural blockage: A cross-national study of economic dependency, state efficiency, and underdevelopment', *American Journal of Sociology*, 86(6): 1311–47.

DeLisle, J. (1999) 'Lex Americana? United States legal assistance, American legal models, and legal change in the post-communist world and beyond', *University of Pennsylvania Journal of International Economic Law*, 20(2): 179–308.

Dellepiane-Avellaneda, S. (2009) 'Good governance, institutions and economic development: Beyond the conventional wisdom', *British Journal of Political Science*, 40(1): 195–224.

De Vil, G. and Kegels, C. (2001) *Les charges administratives en belgique pour l'annee 2000*, Brussels: Bureau Federal du Plan. Online. Available; http://www.plan.fgov.be/admin/uploaded/200605091448070.PP092fr.pdf (accessed 3 February 2013).

DiMaggio, P. J. and Powell, W. W. (1983) 'The iron cage revisited: Institutional isomorphism and collective rationality in organizational fields' *American Sociological Review*, 48(2): 147–60.

Djankov, S., La Porta, R., de Silanes, F. L. and Shleifer, A. (2002) 'The regulation of entry', *Quarterly Journal of Economics*, 117(1): 1–37.

Dobbin, F. R., Edelman, L., Meyer, J. W., Scott, W. R. and Swidler, A. (1988) 'The expansion of due process in organizations', in L. G. Zucker (ed.) *Institutional Patterns and Organizations: Culture and environment*, Cambridge, Mass: Ballinger, pp. 71–98.

Dobbin, F., Simmons, B. A. and Garrett, G. (2007) 'The global diffusion of public policies: Social construction, coercion, competition, or learning?', *Annual Review of Sociology*, 33(2): 449–72.

Dolowitz, D. P. (2009) 'Learning by observing: Surveying the international arena', *Policy and Politics*, 37(3): 317–34.

Dolowitz, D. P. and Marsh, D. (2000) 'Learning from abroad: The role of policy transfer in contemporary policy-making', *Governance*, 13(1): 5—23.

Downs, G. (1976) *Bureaucracy, Innovation, and Public Policy,* Lexington, Massachusetts: Lexington Books.

Downs, G. and Mohr, L. B. (1976) 'Conceptual issues in study innovation', *Administrative Science Quarterly*, 21(4): 700–14.

Drori, G. S., Jang, Y. S. and Meyer, J. W. (2006a) Sources of rationalized governance: Cross-national longitudinal analyses, 1985–2002, *Administrative Science Quarterly*, 51(2): 205–29.

Drori, G. S., Meyer, J. W. and Hwang, H. (2006b) *'Globalization and Organization: World society and organizational change*, New York: Oxford University Press.

Drouillard, L. and Gold, E. R. (2008) 'The OECD guidelines for the licensing of genetic inventions: Policy learning in response to the gene patenting controversy', in R. Mahon and S. McBride (eds) *The OECD and Transnational Governance*, Vancouver: UBC Press, pp. 205–25.

Elliott, E. D. (2003) *Administrative Law in Canada*, Toronto: Sage Publications.

Elman, C. (2005) 'Explanatory typologies in qualitative studies of international politics', *International Organization*, 59(2): 293–326.

Epstein, D. and O'Halloran, S. (1994) 'Administrative procedures, information, and agency discretion', *American Journal of Political Science*, 38(3): 697–722.

— (1999) *Delegating Powers: A transaction cost politics approach to policy making under separate powers*, Cambridge: Cambridge University Press.

Erkkilä, T. and Piironen, O. (2010) 'Debating numbers: Expertise, politics, and governance indicators', paper presented at the 7th European conference of the ECPR Standing Group for International Relations, Stockholm 9–11 September 2010.

Ervik, R. (2009) 'Policy actors, ideas and power: EU and OECD pension policy recommendations and national policies in Norway and the UK', in R. Ervik, N. Kildal and E. Nilssen (eds) *The Role of International Organizations in Social Policy: Ideas, actors and impact*, Cheltenham: Edward Elgar, pp. 138–65.

Ervik, R., Kildal, N. and Nilssen, E. (eds) (2009) *The Role of International Organizations in Social Policy: Ideas, actors and impact*, Cheltenham: Edward Elgar Publishing Limited.

European Commission (2001) *White Paper on Governance*, Brussels: European Commission.

—— (2005) 'Better regulation for growth and jobs in the European Union', European Commission Communication, COM (2005) 97 final, Brussels: European Commission.

European Commission and OECD (2008) *Better Regulation in Europe: An OECD assessment of regulatory capacity in the 15 original member states of the EU. Project policy baseline and scope*, Brussels and Paris. Online. Available; http://www.oecd.org/regref/eu15 (accessed 9 July 2012).

The Evaluation Partnership (2007) 'Evaluation of the Commission's impact assessment system', Report for the Secretariat General of the European Commission, Brussels.

Eyestone, R. (1977) 'Confusion, diffusion, and innovation' *The American Political Science Review*, 71(2): 441–47.

Finnemore, M. (1993) 'International organizations as teachers of norms: The United Nations educational, scientific, and cultural organization and science policy', *International Organization*, 47(4): 565–97.

Finnemore, M. and Sikkink, K. (1998) 'International norm dynamics and political change', *International Organization*, 52(4): 887–917.

Finnish Ministry of Trade and Industry (2001) Implementation report on the European charter for small enterprises, (Report No. 20/710/2001, Helsinki, 17 October).

Franzese, R. J. and Hays, J. C. (2007) 'Spatial econometric models of cross-sectional interdependence in political science panel and time-series-cross-section data', *Political Analysis*, 15(2): 1–25.

Freedman, J. O. (1978) *Crisis and Legitimacy: The administrative process and American Government*. Cambridge: Cambridge University Press.

Froud, J., Boden, R., Ogus, A. and Stubbs, P. (1998) *Controlling the Regulator*, Houndmills, Basingstoke: Palgrave Macmillan.

Frumkin, P. and Galaskiewicz, J. (2004) 'Institutional isomorphism and public sector organizations', *Journal of Public Administration Research and Theory*, 14(3): 283–307.

Garrett, B. (2002) *The role of policy entrepreneurs in policy diffusion*, unpublished thesis, University of Kentucky.

Garrett, G. (1995) 'Capital mobility, trade, and the domestic politics of economic policy', *International Organization*, 49(4): 657–87.

— (1998) 'Global markets and national politics: Collision course or virtuous circle?', *International Organization*, 52(4): 787-824.

Gehring, T. and Oberthür, S. (2009) 'The causal mechanisms of interaction between international institutions', *European Journal of International Relations*, 15(1): 125–56.

General Accounting Office (1998) *Regulatory Reform: Agencies could improve development, documentation and clarity of regulatory economic analyses*, Washington DC: General Accounting Office.

— (1999) *Regulatory Accounting: Analysis of OMB's reports on the costs and benefits of federal regulation.* Washington DC: General Accounting Office.

— (2000) *Regulatory Reform: Procedural and analytical requirements in federal rulemaking*, Washington DC: General Accounting Office.

— (2001) *Regulatory Management: Communication about technology-based innovations can be improved*, Washington DC: General Accounting Office.

— (2003) *Rulemaking: OMB's role in reviews of agencies' draft rules and the transparency of those reviews*, Washington DC: General Accounting Office.

— (2004a) *Performance Budgeting: Observation on the use of OMB's program assessment rating tool for the fiscal year 2004 budget*, Washington DC: General Accounting Office.

— (2004b) *Performance Budgeting: PMB's performance rating tool presents opportunity and challenges for evaluating program performance*, Washington DC: General Accounting Office.

Geroski, P. (2000) 'Models of technology diffusion', *Research Policy*, 29(4–5): 603–625.

Gerring, J. (2010) 'Causal mechanisms: Yes, but...', *Comparative Political Studies*, 43 (10), 1499–526.

Gilardi, F. (2004) *Delegation in the Regulatory State: Origins and diffusion of independent regulatory agencies in Western Europe*, unpublished thesis, University of Lausanne.

— (2005) 'The institutional foundations of regulatory capitalism: The diffusion of independent regulatory agencies in Western Europe', *Annals of the American Academy of Political and Social Science*, 5898(1): 84–101.

— (2008) *Delegation in the Regulatory State: Independent regulatory agencies in Western Europe*, Cheltenham, UK: Edward Elgar.

— (2010) 'Who learns from what in policy diffusion processes?', *American Journal of Political Science*, 54 (3): 650–66.

— (2012) 'Transnational diffusion: Norms, ideas, and policies', in W. Carlsnaes, T. Risse and B. Simmons (eds) *Handbook of International Relations*, London: Sage Publications.

Gilardi, F., Füglister, K. and Luyet, S. (2009) 'Learning from others: the diffusion of hospital financing reforms in OECD countries', *Comparative Political Studies*, 42(2): 549–73.

Ginsburg, T. (2002) 'Comparative administrative procedure: Evidence from Northeast Asia', *Constitutional Political Economy*, 13(3): 247–64.

Gleditsch, K. S. and Ward, M. D. (2001) 'Measuring space: A minimum-distance database and applications to international studies', *Journal of Peace Research*, 38 (6): 739–58.

Glick, H. R., and Hays, S. P. (1991) 'Innovation and reinvention in state policymaking: Theory and the evolution of living will laws', *The Journal of Politics*, 53(3): 835–50.

Goldsmith, A. A. (1999) 'Africa's overgrown state reconsidered: Bureaucracy and economic growth', *World Politics*, 51(4): 520–46.

Goodman, R. M. and Steckler, A. (1989) 'A framework for assessing program institutionalization', *Knowledge in Society: The International Journal of Knowledge Transfer*, 2(1): 57–71.

Government Accountability Office (2005) *Economic Performance: Highlights of a workshop on economic performance measures*, Washington DC: Government Accountability Office.

Government of Canada (2007) *Cabinet Directive on Streamlining Regulation*, Ottawa: Government of Canada.

Gow, J. I. and Dufour, C. (2000) 'Is the new public management a paradigm? Does it matter?', *International Review of Administrative Sciences*, 66(4): 573–97.

Graham, E. R., Shipan C.R. and Volden, C. (2013) 'The diffusion of policy diffusion research', *British Journal of Political Science*, 43(3): 673-701.

Gray, V. (1973) 'Innovation in the States: A diffusion study', *American Political Science Review*, 67(4): 1174–85.

Grigorescu, A. (2003) 'International organizations and government transparency: Linking the international and domestic realms', *International Studies Quarterly*, 47 (4): 643–67.

Grinvalds, H. (2008) 'Lost in translation? OECD ideas and Danish labour market policy', in R. Mahon and S. McBride (eds), *The OECD and Transnational Governance*, Vancouver: UBC Press.

— (2011) *The Power of Ideas: The OECD and labour market policy in Canada, Denmark and Sweden*, unpublished thesis, Queen's University, Kingston, Ontario, Canada, pp. 118–202.

Groenendijk, N. (2011) 'EU and OECD benchmarking and peer review compared', in F. Laursen, *The EU and Federalism: Polities and policies compared*, Ashgate Publishing Company, pp. 181-202.

Guseh, J. S. (2003) 'The theory of decision making in administrative organizations', in J. Rabin (ed.) *Encyclopedia of Public Administration and Public Policy*, New York: Marcel Dekker, pp. 317–22.

Haas, P. M. (1992) 'Introduction: Epistemic communities and international policy coordination', *International Organization*, 46(1): 1–35.

Hahn, R. W. (1999) 'Regulatory reform: Assessing the government's number', Working Paper No. 99–06, AEI-Brookings Joint Center, Washington DC.

Hahn, R. W., Burnett, J. K., Chan, Y., Mader, E. and Moyle, P. (2000) 'Assessing the quality of regulatory impact analyses', Working Paper No. 00–01, AEI-Brookings Joint Center, Washington DC.

Hahn, R. W., Malik, R. P. and Dudley, M. (2004) 'Reviewing the government's number on regulation', Working Paper No. 04–03, AEI-Brooking Joint Center, Washington DC.

Hammond, T. and Knott, J. (1999) 'Political institutions, public management, and policy choice', *Journal of Public Administration Research and Theory*, 9(1): 33–86.

Harter, P. J. (1987) 'Executive oversight of rulemaking: The president is no stranger', *American University Law Review*, 36(2): 557–71.

Hays, S. P. (1996a) 'Influences on reinvention during the diffusion of innovations', *Political Research Quarterly*, 49(3): 631–50.

—   (1996b) 'Patterns of reinvention: The nature of evolution during policy diffusion', *Policy Studies Journal*, 24(4): 551–66.

—   (1996c) 'The states and policy innovation research' *Policy Studies Journal*, 24(2) 321–326.

Hays, S. P. and Glick, H. R. (1997) 'The role of agenda setting in policy innovation: An event history analysis of Living-Will laws', *American Politics Research*, 25(4): 497–516.

Heichel, S., Pape, J. and Sommerer, T. (2005) 'Is there convergence in convergence research? An overview of empirical studies on policy convergence', *Journal of European Public Policy*, 12(5): 817–40.

Hellenic Presidency of the Council of the European Union (2003) 'Report to the ministers responsible for public administration in the EU member states on the progress of the implementation of the Mandelkern report's action plan on better regulation', Hellenic Presidency of the Council of the European Union.

Heydebrand, W. (2003) 'Process rationality as legal governance: A comparative perspective' *International Sociology*, 22(2): 325–49.

Hironaka, A. (2002) 'The globalization of environmental protection: The case of environmental impact assessment', *International Journal of Comparative Sociology*, 43(1): 65–78.

HM Treasury (2005) *Reducing Administrative Burdens: Effective inspections and enforcement*, London: HM Treasury.

Holmberg, S., Rothstein, B. and Nasiritousi, N. (2009) 'Quality of government: What you get', *Annual Review of Political Science*, 12: 135–61.

Hood, C. (1995) 'Contemporary public management: A new global paradigm?', *Public Policy and Administration*, 10(2): 104–17.

—   (1996) 'Beyond "progressivism": A new "global paradigm" in public management?', *International Journal of Public Administration*, 19(2): 151–77.

Hood, C. and Dunsire, A. (1981) *Bureaumetrics: The quantitative comparison of British central government agencies*, Farnborough: Gower.

House of Common (2003) 'The operation of the regulatory reform act 2001: A progress report', First special report of session 2002–03 (Nos. HC 908, Session 2002–03), London: The Stationery Office.

Howlett, M. and Ramesh, M (2003) *Studying Public Policy: Policy cycles and policy subsystems*, 2nd edn, Toronto: Oxford University Press.

Huber, J. D. (2002) 'Delegation to civil servants in parliamentary democracies', *European Journal of Political Research*, 37(3): 18–33.

Hugill, P. J. (2003) 'Technology, its innovation and diffusion as the motor of capitalism', *Comparative Technology Transfer and Society*, 1(1): 89–113.

Institute for European Environmental Policy (2004) Sustainable development in the European Commission's integrated impact assessment for 2003, London: Institute for European Environmental Policy.

Italian Presidency of the Council of Ministries (2011) 'Relazione sullo stato di applicazione dell'analisi di impatto della regolamentazione (AIR)', Report to the Lower Chamber of Parliament, Rome.

Jacob, K., Hertin, J., Hjerp, P., Radaelli, C. M., Meuwese, A. C., Wolf, O., *et al.* (2008) 'Improving the practice of impact assessment', Final Report for DG Research, European Commission, Frei University, Berlin, February 2008.

Jacobs, S. H. (1997) 'An overview of regulatory impact analysis in OECD countries', in *Regulatory Impact Analysis: Best practice in OECD*, Paris: OECD pp. 13-32.

— (2006) 'Regulatory impact analysis in regulatory process, method, and cooperation', Ottawa. Online. Available; http://www.bibliotheque.assnat. qc.ca/01/mono/2007/04/933268.pdf (accessed 3 February 2013)

Jacobs, S. H., and Renda, A. (2007) *RIA and better regulation: International experiences*, Brussels: Centre for European Policy Studies.

Jacobzone, S., Bounds, G., Choi, C.W. and Miguet, C. (2007) 'Regulatory management systems across OECD countries: Indicators of recent achievements and challenges', in OECD working papers on public governance (Vol. 2007/7), Paris: OECD Publishing.

Jacobzone, S., Choi, C.W. and Miguet, C. (2007) 'Indicators of regulatory management systems', in OECD Working Papers on Public Governance (Vol. 2007/4), Paris: OECD Publishing.

Jacobzone, S., Steiner, F., Lopez Ponton, E., Job, E. (2010), 'Assessing the Impact of Regulatory Management Systems: Preliminary Statistical and Econometric Estimates', in OECD Working Papers on Public Governance, No. 17, OECD Publishing.

Jahn, D. (2006) 'Globalization as "Galton's problem": The missing link in the analysis of diffusion patterns in welfare state development', *International Organization*, 60(2): 401–31.

Jakobi, A. P. and Martens, K. (2010) 'Conclusion: Findings, implications and outlook of OECD governance', in *Mechanisms of OECD Governance: International Incentives for National Policy Making*, Oxford and New York: Oxford University Press, pp. 260–79.

James, O. and Manning, N. (1996) 'Public management reform: A global perspective', *Politics*, 16(3): 143–9.

Jann, W. and Wegrich, K. (2007) 'Theories of the policy cycle', in F. Fischer, G. Miller and M. S. Sidney (eds) *Handbook of Public Policy Analysis*, Boca Raton, FL: CRC Press, pp. 43–62.

Jensen, C. B. and McGrath, R. J. (2010) 'Making rules about rulemaking: A comparison of presidential and parliamentary systems', *Political Research Quarterly*, 20 (10): 1–10.

Jensen, J. L. (2003) 'Policy diffusion through institutional legitimation: State lotteries', *Journal of Public Administration Research and Theory*, 13(4): 521–41.

Johnston, J. S. (2002) 'A game theoretic analysis of alternative institutions for regulatory cost-benefit analysis', *University of Pennsylvania Law Review*, 150(5): 1343–429.

Jordana, J. and Levi-Faur, D. (2005) 'The diffusion of regulatory capitalism in Latin America', *Annals of the American Academy of Political and Social Science*, 598(1): 102–24.

Kagan, R. A. (1991) 'Adversarial legalism and American government', *Journal of Policy Analysis and Management*, 10(3): 369–406.

— (2001) *Adversarial Legalism: The American way of law*, Cambridge, Mass: Harvard University Press.

Karmack, E. (2004) 'Government innovations around the world', John F. Kennedy School of Government Faculty Research Working Papers Series, Washington DC.

Kegels, C. (2008) *Les charges administratives en Belgique pour l'année 2006*, Brussels: Bureau fédéral du Plan.

Kelemen, R. D. (1998) *Regulatory federalism: The European Union in comparative perspective*, unpublished thesis, Stanford University.

— (2006) 'Suing for Europe: Adversarial legalism and European governance' *Comparative Political Studies*, 39(1): 101–27.

— (2011) *Eurolegalism: The transformation of law and regulation in the European Union*, Cambridge, MA: Harvard University Press.

Kelemen, R. D. and Sibbitt, E. C. (2004) 'The globalization of American law', *International Organization*, 58(1): 103–36.

Kelly, R. M. (1996) 'An inclusive democratic polity, representative bureaucracies, and the new public management', *Public Administration Review*, 58(3): 201–8.

Kerwin, C. M. (2003) *Rulemaking: How government agencies write law and make policy*, Washington DC: CQ Press.

Kim, J. and Gerber, B. (2005) 'Bureaucratic leverage over policy choice: Explaining the dynamics of state-level reforms in telecommunications regulation', *Policy Studies Journal*, 33(4): 613–33.

King, G. and Zeng, L. (2001) 'Logistic regression in rare events data', *Political Analysis*, 9(2): 137–63.

Kirkpatrick, C. and Parker, D. (2004) 'Regulatory impact assessment and regulatory governance in developing countries', *Public Administration and Development*, 24(4): 333–44.

Kirkpatrick, C., Parker, D. and Zhang, Y-F. (2004) 'Regulatory impact assessment in developing and transition economies: A survey of current practice', *Public Money and Management*, 24(5): 291–6.

Knoke, D. (1982) 'The spread of municipal reform: Temporal, spatial, and social dynamics', *American Journal of Sociology*, 87(6): 1314–39.

Koch, C. H. (1997) *Administrative Law and Practice*, 2nd ed, St. Paul, Minnesota: West Publishing Company.

Kopstein, J. S. and Reilly, D. A. (2000) 'Geographic diffusion and the transformation of the postcommunist world', *World Politics*, 53(1): 1–37.

La Porta, R., de Silanes, F. L., Shleifer, A. and Vishny, R. (1999) 'The quality of government', *Journal of Law, Economics, and Organization*, 15(1): 222–79.

Ladegaard, P. 'Improving business environments through regulatory impact analysis. Opportunities and challenges for developing countries', paper presented at the international conférence on reforming the business environment, Cairo, Egypt, 29 November–1 December 2005.

Lamothe, S. (2004) 'Across and within state reinvention of workplace drug testing legislation', *Politics and Policy*, 32(4): 684–707.

— (2005) 'State policy adoption and content: A study of drug testing in the workplace legislation', *State and Local Government Review*, 37(1): 25–39.

Landis, J. M. (1938) *The Administrative Process*, New Haven, Connecticut: Yale University Press.

Landy, M. K., Roberts, M. J. and Thomas, S. R. (1994) *The Environmental Protection Agency: Asking the wrong questions, from Nixon to Clinton*, New York: Oxford University Press USA.

Langner, I., Bender, R., Lenz-Tönjes, R., Küchenhoff, H. and Blettner, M. (2003) 'Bias of maximum-likelihood estimates in logistic and Cox regression models: A comparative simulation study', Collaborative Research Center 386, Discussion Paper No. 362, Munich. Online. Available http://www.econstor.eu/dspace/bitstream/10419/31093/1/481668578. PDF (accessed 3 February 2013).

Lawrence, T. B., Winn, M. I. and Jennings, P. D. (2001) 'The temporal dynamics of institutionalization', *The Academy of Management Review*, 26(4): 624–44.

Lee, N. and Kirkpatrick, C. (2004) 'A pilot study on the quality of European Commission extended impact assessment', Institute for Development Policy and Management, Manchester: University of Manchester.

Legislative Burden Department (2003) *Focus on Burden!*, The Hague: Ministry of Finance.

Leichter, H. M. (1983) 'The patterns and origins of policy diffusion: The case of the Commonwealth', *Comparative Politics*, 15(2): 223–33.

Levitt, B. and March, J. G. (1988) 'Organizational learning', *American Review of Sociology*, 14: 319–40.

Lodge, M. (2005) 'The importance of being modern: International benchmarking and national regulatory innovation', *Journal of European Public Policy*, 12(4): 649–67.

Lubbers, J. S. (1998) *A Guide to Federal Agency Rulemaking*, 3rd edn., Chicago: American Bar Association.

Lupia, A. and McCubbins, M. D. (1994) 'Learning from oversight: Fire alarms and police patrols reconstructed', *Journal of Law, Economics, and Organization*, 10(1): 96–125.

Lynn, L. E. J. (2001) 'Globalization and administrative reform: What is happening in theory?', *Public Management Review*, 3(2): 191–208.

McBride, S., McNutt, K. and Williams, R. A. (2008) 'Policy learning? The OECD and its jobs strategy', in R. Mahon and S. McBride (eds) *The OECD and Transnational Governance*, Vancouver: UBC Press, pp. 125–69.

McBride, S. and Williams, R. A. (2001) 'Globalization, the restructuring of labour markets and policy convergence: The OECD's jobs strategy', *Global Social Policy*, 1(3): 281–309.

McCubbins, M. D., Noll, R. G. and Weingast, B. R. (1987) 'Administrative procedures as instruments of political control', *Journal of Law, Economics and Organization*, 3(2): 243–77.

— (1989) 'Structure and process, politics and policy: Administrative arrangements and the political control of agencies', *Virginia Law Review*, 75(2): 431–82.

McDonald, F. (1994) *The American Presidency: An intellectual history*, Kansas: University Press of Kansas.

McGarity, T. O. (1991) *Reinventing Rationality: The role of regulatory analysis in the federal bureaucracy*, Cambridge and New York: Cambridge University Press.

McGarity, T. O. and Ruttenberg, R. (2002) 'Counting the cost of health, safety, and environmental regulation', *Texas Law Review*, 80(7): 1997–2058.

McGuinn, P. (2004) 'Path dependency, punctuated equilibria, and the politics of policy change', paper presented at the annual meeting of the American Political Science Association, Chicago, 2 September 2004.

McNollgast (1999) 'The political origins of the administrative procedure act', Journal of Law, Economics, and Organization, 15(1): 180–217.

Mahajan, V., Muller, E. and Bass, F. M. (1995) 'Diffusion of new products: Empirical generalizations and managerial uses', *Marketing Science*, 14(3): G79–G88.

Mahajan, V. and Peterson, R. A. (1985) *Models for Innovation Diffusion*, Beverly Hills, California: Sage Publications.

Mahon, R. (2008) 'Babies and bosses: Gendering the OECD's social policy discourse', in R. Mahon and S. McBride (eds) *The OECD and Transnational Governance*, UBC Press, pp. 260–75.

Mahon, R. and McBride, S. (eds) (2008) *The OECD and Transnational Governance*, Vancouver: UBC Press.
—   (2009) 'Standardizing and disseminating knowledge: The role of the OECD in global governance', *European Political Science Review*, 1(1): 83–101.
Majone, G. (1989) *Evidence, Argument and Persuasion in the Policy Process*, New Haven and London: Yale University Press.
—   (1996) *Regulating Europe*, London: Routledge.
March, J. G. and Olson, J. P. (1983) 'Organizing political life: What administrative reorganization tells us about government', *American Political Science Review*, 77(2): 281–96.
Marcussen, M. (2004a) 'Multilateral suveillance and the OECD: Playing the idea game', in K. Armingeon and M. Beyler (eds) *The OECD and European Welfare States*, Cheltenham: Edward Elgar, pp. 13–31.
—   (2004b) 'OECD governance through soft law', in U. Mörth (ed.) *Soft Law in Governance and Regulation: An interdisciplinary analysis*, Cheltenham: Edward Elgar, pp. 103–28.
Markoff, J. and Montecinos, V. (1993) 'The ubiquitous rise of economists', *Journal of Public Policy*, 13(1): 37–68.
Martens, K. and Jakobi, A. P. (eds) (2010) *Mechanisms of OECD Governance: International incentives for national policy making*, Oxford and New York: Oxford University Press.
May, P. J. (1992) 'Policy learning and failure', *Journal of Public Policy*, 12(4): 331–54.
Meir, A. (1982) 'A spatial-humanistic perspective of innovation diffusion processes', *Geoforum*, 13(1): 57–68.
Melo, M. A. (2004) 'Institutional choice and the diffusion of policy paradigms: Brazil and the second wave of pension reform', *International Political Science Review/Revue internationale de science politique*, 25(3): 320–41.
Menzel, D. C. and Feller, I. (1977) 'Leadership and interaction patterns in the diffusion of innovations among the American states', *Western Political Quarterly*, 30(4): 528-36.
Meseguer, C. (2006) 'Rational learning and bounded learning in the diffusion of policy innovations', *Rationality and Society*, 18(1): 35–66.
—   (2009) *Learning, Policy Making, and Market Reform*, New York: Cambridge University Press.
Meseguer, C. and Gilardi, F. (2009) 'What is new in the study of policy diffusion?', *Review of International Political Economy*, 16(3): 527–43.
Meyer, J. and Rowan, B. (1977) 'Institutionalized organizations: Formal structure as myth and ceremony', *American Journal of Sociology*, 83(2): 363–40.
Meyer, J. W., Boli, J., Thomas, G. M. and Ramirez, F. O. (1997) 'World society and the nation-state', *American Journal of Sociology*, 103(1): 144–81.
Mintrom, M. (2000) *Policy Entrepreneurs and School Choice*, Washington DC: Georgetown University Press.

Moon, S. and Deleon, P. (2005) 'The patterns of institutional interaction and ISO 14001 adoption', *Comparative Technology Transfer and Society*, 3(1): 35–59.

Mooney, C. Z. (2001) 'Modeling regional effects on state policy diffusion'. *Political Research Quarterly*, 54(1): 103–24.

Moral Soriano, L. (2002) 'A theoretical approach to the tension between form and substance in English judicial reasoning', in K. H. Ladeur, *The Europeanisation of Administrative Law: Transforming national decision-making procedures*, Aldershot: Ashgate, pp. 122–34.

Mossberger, K. (1999) 'State-federal diffusion and policy learning: From enterprise zones to empowerment zones', *Publius*, 29(3): 31–50.

— (2000) *The Politics of Ideas and the Spread of Enterprise Zones*, Washington DC: Georgetown University Press.

Mossberger, K. and Wolman, H. (2003) 'Policy transfer as a form of prospective policy evaluation: Challenges and recommendations', *Public Administration Review*, 63 (4): 428–440.

Moynihan, D. P. (2005) 'Why and how do state governments adopt and implement "managing for results" reforms?', *Journal of Public Administration Research and Theory*, 15(2): 219–43.

Natalini, A and Stolfi, F, (2012) 'Mechanisms and public administration reform: Italian cases of better regulation and digitalization', *Public Administration*, 90(2): 529-43.

National Audit Office (2001) *Evaluation of Regulatory Impact Assessment 2006–07*, No. HM 329 Session 2001–04, London: The Stationery Office.

— (2004) *Evaluation of Regulatory Impact Assessments Compendium Report 2003–04*, No. HC 358 Session 2003–04, London: The Stationery Office.

— (2005) *Evaluation of Regulatory Impact Assessment 2004–05*, No. HC 341 Session 2004–05, London: The Stationery Office.

Newmark, A. J. (2002) 'An integrated approach to policy transfer and diffusion' *Review of Policy Research*, 19(2): 151–78.

Noordegraaf, M. and Abma, T. (2003) 'Management by measurement? Public management practices amidst ambiguity', *Public Administration*, 81(4): 853–71.

OECD (1960) Convention on the organisation for economic co-operation and development. Online. Available; http://www.oecd.org/general/conventionontheorganisationforeconomicco-operationanddevelopment.htm (accessed 22 August 2012).

— (1987) *Structural Adjustment and Economic Performance*, Paris: OECD Publishing.

— (1994) *Improving the Quality of Laws and Regulations: Economic, legal and managerial techniques*, Paris: OECD.

— (1995) Recommendation of the Council of the OECD on Improving the Quality of Government Regulation, Paris: OECD Publishing. Online. Available; http://www.oecd.org/gov/regulatorypolicy/recommendation-ofthecounciloftheoecdonimprovingthequalityofgovernmentregulation.htm (accessed 22 November 2012).

— (1997a) *Regulatory Impact Analysis: Best practices in OECD countries*, Paris: OECD publishing.

— (1997b) *The OECD Report on Regulatory Reform: Thematic Studies*, Paris: OECD Publishing.

— (1997c) *The OECD Report on Regulatory Reform: Synthesis*, Paris: OECD Publishing.

— (1997d) 'Administrative procedures and the supervision of administration in Hungary, Poland, Bulgaria, Estonia and Albania', SIGMA Working Paper No. 17. Online. Available; http://dx.doi.org/10.1787/5kml6198lvkf-en (accessed 9 July 2012).

— (1999) *Regulatory Reform in the Netherlands*, Paris: OECD Publishing.

— (2000) *Regulatory Reform in Korea*, Paris: OECD Publishing.

— (2001) *Regulatory Reform in the Czech Republic*, Paris: OECD Publishing.

— (2002a) *Regulatory Policies in OECD Countries: From interventionism to regulatory Governance*, Paris: OECD Publishing.

— (2002b) *Regulatory Reform in Canada*, Paris: OECD Publishing.

— (2003) 'Ex post evaluation of regulatory policy', proceeding of from the OECD expert meeting on regulatory performance, Paris, 22 September 2003, Online. Available; http://www.oecd.org/dataoecd/34/30/30401951.pdf (accessed on 22 November 2012).

— (2004a) *France: Charting a clearer way forward*, Paris: OECD Publishing.

— (2004b) *Germany: Consolidating economic and social renewal*, Paris: OECD Publishing.

— (2005) *OECD Guiding Principles for Regulatory Quality and Performance*, Paris: OECD Publishing.

— (2006a) 'OECD reviews of regulatory reform: Background document on regulatory reform in OECD countries', Paris: OECD.

— (2006b) 'Determinants of quality in regulatory impact analysis', Paris: OECD. Online. Available; http://www.oecd.org/gov/regulatorypolicy/42047618.pdf (accessed 22 November 2012).

— (2006c) *Regulatory Reform in Switzerland: Seizing the opportunities for growth*, Paris: OECD Publishing.

— (2006c) *Regulatory Reform in Switzerland: Seizing the opportunities for growth*, Paris: OECD Publishing.

— (2007a) *OECD Reviews of Regulatory Reform. Korea: Progress in implementing regulatory reform*, Paris: OECD Publishing.

— (2007b) 'Regulatory management capacities of member states of the European Union that joined the Union on 1 May 2004: Sustaining regulatory management improvements through a better regulation policy', SIGMA Working Paper No. 42, Paris: OECD. Online. Available; http://dx.doi.org/10.1787/5kml60q573g6-en (accessed 22 November 2012).

— (2007c) 'Government capacity to assure high quality regulation in Sweden', Paris: OECD. Online. Available http://www.oecd.org/gov/regulatorypolicy/ 38286959.pdf (accessed 22 November 2012).

— (2008a) 'Building an institutional framework for regulatory impact analysis (RIA): Guidance for policy makers', Paris: OECD. Online. Available; http://www.oecd.org/dataoecd/44/15/40984990.pdf (accessed 22 November 2012).

— (2008b) 'Introductory handbook for undertaking regulatory impact analysis (RIA)', Paris: OECD. Online. Available; http://www.oecd.org/gov/regulatorypolicy/44789472.pdf (accessed 22 November 2012).

— (2009a) *Regulatory Impact Analysis: A tool for policy coherence*, Paris: OECD Publishing.

— (2009b) Evaluation Study

— (2010a) 'Regulatory Policy: Towards a new agenda. Pathways to the Future', key messages of the OECD regulatory policy conference, Paris, 28–29 October 2010. Online. Available; http://www.oecd.org/gov/regulatorypolicy/47298590.pdf (accessed 22 November 2012).

— (2010b) *Better Regulation in Europe: France*, Paris: OECD Publishing.

— (2010c) *Better Regulation in Europe: Denmark*, Paris: OECD Publishing.

— (2010d) *Better Regulation in Europe: Germany*, Paris: OECD Publishing.

— (2010e) *Better Regulation in Europe: Sweden*, Paris: OECD Publishing.

— (2010f) *Better regulation in Europe: The Netherlands*, Paris: OECD Publishing.

— (2011) *Regulatory Policy and Governance: Supporting economic growth and serving the public interest*, Paris: OECD Publishing.

— (2012) Recommendation of the Council of the OECD on Regulatory Policy and Governance, Paris: OECD Publishing. Online. Available; http://www.oecd.org/gov/regulatorypolicy/49990817.pdf (accessed 22 November 2012).

OECD Public Management (1992) 'Regulatory management and reform: Current concerns in OECD countries', working paper OCDE/GD(92)58, Paris: OECD.

— Public Management (1993) 'The design and use of regulatory checklists in OECD countries', working paper No. OEDE/GD(93)181, Paris: OECD.

OECD Regulatory Policy Committee (2009) *Indicators of Regulatory Management Systems*, Paris: OECD Publishing.

OECD SIGMA (1997a) 'Assessing the impact of proposed laws and regulations' SIGMA Paper No. 13, Paris: OECD.

— (1997b) 'Checklist on law drafting and regulatory management in central and eastern Europe', SIGMA Paper No. 15, Paris: OECD.

— (1997c) 'Law drafting and regulatory management in central and eastern Europe', SIGMA Paper No. 18, Paris: OECD.

Office for Management and Budget (2003) *Program assessment rating tool. instructions for part worksheets, fiscal year 2004*. Washington DC: Office for Management and Budget.

Oliver, C. (1991) 'Strategic responses to institutional processes', *The Academy of Management Review*, 16 (1): 145–179.

Opoku, C. and Jordan, A. (2004) 'Impact assessment in the EU: A global sustainable development perspective', paper presented at the conference on the human dimension of global environmental change, Berlin, 3–4 December 2004.

Orenstein, M. A. (2008) *Privatizing Pensions: The transnational campaign for social security reform*, Princeton, New Jersey: Princeton University Press.

Osborne, D. and Gaebler, T. (1993) *Reinventing Government: How the entrepreneurial spirit is transforming the public sector*, New York: Plume.

Ostrom, E. (2007) 'Institutional rational choice. An assessment of the institutional analysis and development framework', in P. A. Sabatier (ed.) *Theories of the Policy Process*, 2nd edn, Boulder, Colorado: Westview Press, pp. 21–64.

Pagani, F. (2002) 'Peer review: A tool for co-operation and change. An analysis of an OECD working method', working paper No. SG/LEG(2002)1, Paris: OECD.

Page, E. C. (2001) *Governing by Numbers: Delegated legislation and everyday policy-making*, Oxford: Hart.

— (2003) 'Europeanization and the persistence of administrative systems', in J. Hayward and A. Menon (eds) *Governing Europe*, Oxford: Oxford University Press, pp. 162–77.

— (2010) 'Accountability as a bureaucratic minefield: Lessons from a comparative study', *West European Politics*, 33(5): 1010—29.

Pal, L. A. 'The OECD and global public management reform', paper presented at the NISPAcee 17th annual conference, Budva, *Montenegro*, 14–16 May 2009.

— (2012) *Frontiers of Governance: The OECD and global public management reform*, Houndmills, Basingstoke: Palgrave Macmillan.

Parker, R. W. (2003) 'Grading the government', *University of Chicago Law Review*, 70: 1345–486.

Peters, B. G. (1992) 'Government reorganization: A theoretical analysis', *International Political Science Review/Revue internationale de science politique*, 13(2): 199–217.

— (1997) 'Policy transfers between governments: The case of administrative reforms', *West European Politics*, 20(4): 71–88.

— (1998) *Comparing Public Bureaucracies: Problems of theory and method*, Tuscaloosa, Alabama: University of Alabama Press.

— (2008) 'The Napoleonic tradition', *International Journal of Public Sector Management*, 21(2): 118–32.

Pierce, R. J., Shapiro, S. A. and Verkuil, P. R. (2004) *Administrative Law and Process*, 4th edn, New York: Foundation Press.

Pildes, R. H. and Sunstein, C. R. (1995) 'Reinventing the regulatory state', *University of Chicago Law Review*, 62(1): 1–129.

Pollitt, C. (2001) 'Convergence: The useful myth?', *Public Administration*, 79(4): 933–47.

— (2002) 'Clarifying convergence. Striking similarities and durable differences in public management reform', *Public Management Review*, 4(1): 471–92.

Pollitt, C. and Bouckaert, G. (2004) *Public Management Reform: A comparative analysis*, Oxford; New York: Oxford University Press.

Porter, T. (2009) 'Making serious measures: Numerical national indices, peer review and global governance', paper presented at the International Studies Association annual meeting, New York, 17 February 2009.

Porter, T. and Webb, M. (2008) 'Role of the OECD in the orchestration of global knowledge networks' in R. Mahon and S. McBride (eds) *The OECD and Transnational Governance*, Vancouver: UBC Press, pp. 43–59.

Posner, E. A. (2001) 'Controlling agencies with cost-benefit analysis: a positive political theory perspective', *University of Chicago Law Review*, 68(4): 1137–99.

Power, M. (1997) *The Audit Society: Rituals of verification*, Oxford: Oxford University Press.

PricewaterhouseCoopers (2006) 'Measuring compliance costs evaluation of the Dutch standard cost model and the Australian cost model (incorporating a trial measurement of the costs arising from the schedules to the securities regulations 1983), Report for the New Zealand Ministry of Economic Development.

Prince, E. (1999) *Canada and Administrative Law*, Cambridge: Cambridge University Press.

Productivity Commission (2012) 'Regulatory Impact Analysis: Benchmarking', Productivity Commission issues paper, Canberra: Productivity Commission.

Radaelli, C. M. (ed.) (2001) *L'Analisi di Impatto della Regolazione in Prospettiva Comparata*, Soveria Mannelli, Catanzaro, Italy: Rubbettino.

— (2004) 'The diffusion of regulatory impact analysis in OECD countries: Best practices or lesson-drawing', *Journal of Public Policy*, 43(5): 725–49.

— (2005a) 'Diffusion without convergence: How political context shapes the adoption of regulatory impact assessment', *Journal of European Public Policy*, 12(5): 924–43.

— (2005b) 'What does regulatory impact assessment mean in Europe?', Working Paper AEI-Brookings Joint Center 05–02, Washington DC.

— (2007) 'Whither better regulation for the Lisbon agenda?', *Journal of European Public Policy*, 14 (2): 190–207.

— (2009). Measuring policy learning: Regulatory impact assessment in Europe, *Journal of European Public Policy*, 16 (8): 1145–64.

Radaelli, C. M. and De Francesco, F. (2007) *Regulatory Quality in Europe. Concepts, measures and policy processes*, Manchester: Manchester University Press.

— (2010) 'Regulatory impact assessment', in R. Baldwin, M. Cave and M. Lodge (eds) *The Oxford Handbook of Regulation*, Oxford: Oxford University Press, pp. 279–301.

Radaelli, C. M., Dente, B., Jacobs, S. H., Kirkpatrick, C., Meuwese, A. C. and Renda, A. (2006) *How to perform the DIAMDEM data collection*, unpublished working paper.

Radaelli, C. M. and Meuwese, A. C. (2009) 'Better regulation in Europe: Between management and regulation', *Public Administration*, 87(3): 639–54.

Regulatory Affairs and Orders in Council Secretariat (2002) 'The government of Canada action plan', Ottawa.

Regulatory Consulting Group and Delphi Group (2000) 'Assessing the contribution of regulatory impact analysis on decision making and the development of regulation', Ottawa: Regulatory Consulting Group and Delphi Group.

Reynolds, T H. and Flores, A. A. (2000) *Foreign Law Guide: Current sources of codes and basic Legislation in Jurisdictions of the World*, Berkley, California: University of California Press.

Ripley, R. B. (1985) *Policy Analysis in Political Science*, Chicago: Nelson-Hall.

Robertson, D. B. (1991) 'Political conflict and lesson-drawing', *Journal of Public Policy*, 11 (1): 55–78.

Rogers, E. M. (2003) *Diffusion of innovations*, 5th edn, New York: Free Press.

Rose, N. and Miller, P. (1992) 'Political power beyond the state: Problematics of government', *British Journal of Sociology*, 43(2): 173–205.

Rose, R. (1993) *Lesson-Drawing in Public Policy: A guide to learning across time and space*, London: Chatham House Publishers.

Rose-Ackerman, S. 'Introduction', *Economics of Administrative Law*, Cheltenham: Edward Elgar.

— (2007b) 'Public choice, public law and public policy', paper presented at the first world meeting of the Public Choice Society, Amsterdam.

Rosenbloom, D. H. (2000) 'Retrofitting the administrative state to the constitution: Congress and the judiciary's twentieth-century progress', *Public Administration Review*, 60(1): 39–46.

— (2002) 'Building a legislative-centered public administration: Congress and the administrative state, 1946–1999', Tuscaloosa, Alabama: University of Alabama Press.

Rowat, D. (1973) *The Ombudsman Plan: Essays on the worldwide spread of an idea*, Toronto: McLelland and Stewart.

Rusch, W. (2009) 'Administrative procedures in EU member states', proceeding from a SIGMA conference on public administration reform and European integration, Paris: SIGMA OECD. Online. Available; http://www.oecd.org/site/sigma/publicationsdocuments/42754772.pdf (accessed 22 November 2012).

Russell, M. (1990) 'The making of cruel choice', in P. B. Hammond and R. Coppock (eds) *Valuing Health Risks, Costs, and Benefits for Environmental Decision Making. Report of a conference,* National Academic Press, pp. 15–22).

Sabatier, P. A. (ed.) (1999) *Theories of the policy process: Theoretical lenses on public policy,* 1st edn, Boulder, Colorado: Westview Press.

— (ed.) (2007) *Theories of policy process,* 2nd edn, Boulder, Colorado: Westview Press.

Sadler, B. (1996) *Environmental Assessment in a Changing World: Evaluating practice to improve performance,* Ottawa: Canadian Environmental Assessment Agency and International Association for Impact Assessment.

Sahlin, K. and Wedlin, L. (2010) 'Circulating ideas: imitation, translation and editing', in R. Greenwood, C. Oliver, R. Suddaby and K. Sahlin (eds) *The SAGE Handbook of Organizational Institutionalism,* London: SAGE Publications Limited, pp. 218–42.

Sahlin-Andersson, K. (2001) 'National, international and transnational constructions of new public management', in T. Christensen, and P. Lægreid (eds) *New public management: The transformation of ideas and practice,* Aldershot, England: Ashgate, pp. 43–72.

Sahlin-Andersson, K. and Engwall, L. (eds) (2002) *The Expansion of Management Knowledge: Carriers, flows, and sources,* Stanford, California: Stanford University Press.

Savage, R. L. (1985) 'Diffusion research traditions and the spread of policy innovations in a federal system', *Publius,* 15(4): 1–27.

Schmidt-Assmann, E. (1998) *Das allgemeine verwaltungsrecht als ordnungsidee: Grundlagen und aufgaben der verwaltungsrechtlichen systembildung,* Berlin: Springer.

Schrefler, L. (2010) 'The usage of scientific knowledge by independent regulatory agencies', *Governance,* 23(2): 309–30.

Schwartz, B. (2006) *French Administrative Law and the Common-Law World,* Clark, New Jersey: Lawbook Exchange.

Seerden, R. and Stroink, F. (eds) (2002) *Administrative Law of the European Union, Its Member States and the United States: A comparative analysis,* Antwerpen: Intersentia.

Shane, P. (1995) 'Political accountability in a system of checks and balances: The case of presidential review of rulemaking', *Arkansas Law Review,* 48(1): 161–214.

Shapiro, M. (2001) 'The institutionalization of the European administrative space', in A. Stone Sweet, W. Sandholtz and N. Fligstein (eds) *The Institutionalization of Europe,* New York: Oxford University Press, pp. 94-112.

Shapiro, S. (2005) 'Unequal partners: Cost-benefit analysis and executive review of Regulations', *Environmental Law Reporter,* 35 (7): 10433–44.

Sharman, J. C. (2012) 'Seeing like the OECD on tax', *New Political Economy,* 17 (1): 17–33.

Simmons, B. A., Dobbin, F. and Garrett, G. (2008) 'Introduction: The diffusion of Liberalization', in B. A. Simmons, F. Dobbin, and G. Garrett (eds) *The Global Diffusion of Markets and Democracy*, Cambridge and New York: Cambridge University Press, pp. 1–63.

Simmons, B. A. and Elkins, Z. (2004) 'The globalization of liberalization: Policy diffusion in the international political economy', *American Political Science Review*, 98 (1): 171–89.

Simmons, B. A., Garrett, G. and Dobbin, F. 'The international diffusion of democracy and markets', paper presented at the annual meeting of the American Political Science Association, Philadelphia, 27 August 2003.

Singh, M. P. (2001) *German Administrative Law in Common Law Perspective*, revised edn, Berlin: Springer.

Smith, T. (1996) 'Regulatory reform in the USA and Europe', *Journal of Environmental Law*, 8(2): 257–82.

Stanbury, W. T. and Thompson, F. (1982) *Regulatory Reform in Canada*, Montreal: The Institute for Research on Public Policy.

Steckler, A., Goodman, R. M., McLeroy, K. R., Davis, S. and Koch, G. (1992) 'Measuring the diffusion of innovative health promotion programs', *American Journal of Health Promotion*, 6(3): 214–25.

Stewart, R. B. (1975) 'The reformation of American administrative law', *Harvard Law Review*, 88(8): 1667–780.

— (1981) 'Regulation, innovation, and administrative law: A conceptual framework', *California Law Review*, 69(5): 1256–377.

— (2005) 'U.S. administrative law: A model for global administrative law?', *Law and Contemporary Problems*, 68(1): 63—108.

Stokey, E. and Zeckhauser, R. (1978) *A Primer for Policy Analysis*, New York: W.W. Norton and Company.

Stone, D. (1999) 'Learning lessons and transferring policy across time, space and disciplines', *Politics*, 19(1): 51–59.

— (2000a) 'Learning lessons, policy transfer and the international diffusion of policy ideas', working paper. Online. Available; http://poli.haifa. ac.il/~levi/res/stone-2000.pdf (accessed 20 May 2008).

— (2000b) 'Non-governmental policy transfer: The strategies of independent policy institutes', *Governance*, 13(1): 45–70.

Strang, D. and Meyer, J. W. (1993) 'Institutional conditions for diffusion', *Theory and Society*, 22(4): 487–511.

Strang, D. and Soule, S. A. (1998) 'Diffusion in organizations and social movements: From hybrid corn to poison pills', *Annual Review of Sociology*, 24, 265–90.

Suchman, M. C. (1995) 'Managing legitimacy: Strategic and institutional approaches', *The Academy of Management Review*, 20(3): 571–610.

Sullivan, S. (1997) *From War to Wealth: Fifty years of innovation*, Paris: OECD Publishing.

Sunstein, C. R. (1996) 'The cost-benefit state', Chicago Working Paper in Law and Economics.

Taylor, S. (1984) *Making Bureaucracies Think: The environmental impact statement*, Stanford, Stanford University Press.

Tolbert, P. S. (1985) 'Institutional environments and resource dependence: Sources of administrative structure in institutions of higher education', *Administrative Science Quarterly*, 30(1): 1–13.

Tolbert, P. S. and Zucker, L. G. (1983) 'Institutional sources of change in the formal structure of organizations: The diffusion of civil service reform, 1880–1935', *Administrative Science Quarterly*, 28(1): 22–39.

Treasury Board of Canada Secretariat (1996) *Federal Regulatory Process Management Standards. A self-assessment guide for departmental managers: Compliance guide*, Ottawa: Treasury Board of Canada Secretariat.

—— (2003) *Preparation Guide Departmental Performance Reports 2002–2003*, Ottawa: Treasury Board of Canada Secretariat.

True, J. and Mintrom, M. (2001) 'Transnational networks and policy diffusion: The case of gender mainstreaming', *International Studies Quarterly*, 45(1): 27–57.

Van den Bulte, C. and Lilien, G. L. (2001) 'Medical innovation revisited: Social contagion versus marketing effort', *American Journal of Sociology*, 106(5): 1409–35.

Vibert, F. (2004) *The EU's New System of Regulatory Impact Assessment: A scorecard*, London: European Policy Forum.

—— (2005) *The Itch to Regulate: Confirmation bias and the European Commission's new system of Impact Assessment*, London: European Policy Forum.

—— (2007) *The Rise of the Unelected: Democracy and the new separation of powers*, Cambridge: Cambridge University Press.

Vining, A. R. and Weimer, D. L. (1990) 'Government supply and government production failure: A framework based on contestability', *Journal of Public Policy*, 10(1), 1–22.

Viscusi, W. K. (1997) 'Improving the analytical basis for regulatory decision-making', in OECD *Regulatory impact analysis: Best practice in OECD* Paris: OECD Publishing, pp. 175–208.

Voermans, W. (2003) *Computer Assisted Legislative Drafting in the Netherlands: The leda-system*, unpublished report, University of Leiden. Online. Available; http://www.wimvoermans.nl/Leda/ledaarticle.pdf (accessed 22 November 2012).

Vogel, D. (1986) *National Styles of Regulation: Environmental policy in Great Britain and the United States*, Ithaca, New York: Cornell University Press.

Volden, C., Ting, M. M. and Carpenter, D. P. (2008) 'A formal model of learning and policy diffusion', *American Political Science Review*, 102(3): 319–32.

Walker, J. L. (1969) 'The diffusion of innovations among the American states', *American Political Science Review*, 63(3): 880–99.

Waterman, R. and Meier, K. (1998) 'Principal-agent models: An expansion?', *Journal of Public Administration Research and Theory*, 8(2): 173–202.

Weeks, D. (1937) 'Legislative power versus delegated legislative power', *Georgetown Law Journal*, 25(1): 314.

Weir, E. (1997) 'Delegated legislation: The weak link of parliamentary accountability?', *Canadian Parliamentary Review*, 20(3), unpaginated online version, (accessed 27 September 2007).

Wejnert, B. (2002) 'Integrating models of diffusion of innovations: A conceptual framework', *Annual Review of Sociology*, 28: 297–326.

West, W. F. (1988) 'The growth of internal conflict in administrative regulation', *Public Administration Review*, 48(4): 773–82.

— (2004) 'The institutionalisation of regulatory review: Organisational stability and responsive competence at OIRA', *Presidential Studies Quarterly*, 35(1): 76–93.

— (2005) 'Administrative rulemaking: An old and emerging literature', *Public Administration Review*, 48(4): 773–82.

Weyland, K. (2006) *Bounded Rationality and Policy Diffusion: Social sector reform in Latin America*, Princeton, New Jersey: Princeton University Press.

Williams, M. E. (2002) 'Market reforms, technocrats, and institutional innovation', *World Development*, 30(3): 395–412.

Williams, R. A. (2008) 'The OECD and foreign investment rules: The global promotion of liberalization', in R. Mahon and S. McBride (eds) *The OECD and Transnational Governance*, Vancouver: UBC Press, pp. 117–33.

Woodward, R. (2009) *The Organisation for Economic Co-operation and Development*, Oxon and New York: Routledge.

World Bank (2002) *World Development Report 2002: Building institutions for markets*, Washington DC: The World Bank.

Zito, A. R. and Schout, A. (2009) 'Learning theory reconsidered: EU integration theories and learning', *Journal of European Public Policy*, 16(8): 1103–23.

Zucker, L. G. (1987) 'Institutional theories of organization', *Annual Review of Sociology*, 13: 443–64.

| index

www.ingramcontent.com/pod-product-compliance
Lightning Source LLC
Chambersburg PA
CBHW072122020426

42334CB00018B/1678